AMERICAN ART IN THE BARBIZON MOOD

Peter Bermingham

Published for the National Collection of Fine Arts

by the Smithsonian Institution Press

City of Washington   1975

Published on the occasion of an exhibition at the
National Collection of Fine Arts
Smithsonian Institution
January 23—April 20, 1975

Cover: Elliott Daingerfield. *Return from the Farm,* cat. no. 26
Frontispiece: John Francis Murphy. *Path to the Village,* 1882, cat. no. 70

Library of Congress Cataloging in Publication Data
Bermingham, Peter.
American art in the Barbizon mood.
"Published on the occasion of an exhibition at the
National Collection of Fine Arts, Smithsonian Institu-
tion, January 23–April 20, 1975."
Bibliography: p.
Supt. of Docs. no.: SI 6.2:B23
1. Landscape painting, American—Exhibitions.
2. Barbizon school—Influence. I. Smithsonian
Institution. National Collection of Fine Arts.
II. Title.
ND1351.5.B47   758'.1'0973   74-26664

Smithsonian Institution Press Publication Number 5263

For sale by the Superintendent of Documents
United States Government Printing Office
Washington, D.C. 20402
Price: $7.70
Stock number: 4703-00029

The melancholy born of failure in fitting the issues of the world

to one's own desires turns naturally into contemplation of that over which

we have no control—that nature which continues undisturbed

by the vicissitudes of man.

JOHN LAFARGE

CONTENTS

ACKNOWLEDGMENTS

Whenever an author attempts to express his gratitude for aid and assistance on what is essentially a collaborative enterprise, it is axiomatic that time and space do not allow for a complete listing of those who have contributed along the way. I would like, however, to recognize at least those whose help comes most readily to mind.

Among many scholars who have been generous with advice and helpful hints, I wish to give special mention to Robert L. Herbert of Yale University, whose conversations with me as well as his studies on Millet and other members of the Barbizon school were always a fruitful source of information; David C. Huntington of the University of Michigan and Lois Fink of the National Collection of Fine Arts, who offered help and encouragement during my doctoral research on this subject; and John Minor Wisdom of the William Hays Ackland Art Center, William H. Gerdts of Brooklyn College, and Charles C. Eldredge of the University of Kansas Museum of Art, who assisted in locating some of the works displayed in this exhibition. A research fellowship from the National Collection of Fine Arts in 1971 allowed me to complete the dissertation on which most of the text is based.

Much of the basic research for the biographies in the catalog was prepared by Amelia Banister, formerly an intern in museum training in my office and now an assistant curator at the Dayton Art Institute. Her friendly reminders and countless other acts of assistance kept me on course during the more difficult months in the preparation of both this book and the exhibition.

Simply to list the lenders to the exhibition seems quite inadequate as an indication of our gratitude to those who have so generously allowed us to borrow from their collections. Many have gone well beyond the call of normal duty on our behalf, including Lucretia Giese of the Museum of Fine Arts, Boston; Robert C. Vose, Jr., and Morton Vose of Vose Galleries, Inc., Boston; J. David Selig of The Reading [Pennsylvania] Public Museum and Art Gallery; Fearn Thurlow of The Newark Museum; Dorothy Phillips of the Corcoran Gallery of Art; John Howat of The Metropolitan Museum of Art; and Ann Rogerson of the Montclair (New Jersey) Art Museum. A grant from the National Endowment for the Arts allowed The Newark Museum to restore a work for this show that otherwise would have remained in storage.

In addition, the efforts of several other scholars and critics cited in the footnotes and bibliography were, of course, an indispensable part of the preparation of this book. Errors of either omission or commission in the text and catalog, however, are solely the responsibility of the author.   P.B.

INTRODUCTION

Joshua C. Taylor, Director, National Collection of Fine Arts

"It is usual at a mature age," wrote Adolphe Thiers in 1822, "to regret the loss of childhood. We at the present, an old and civilized people, love to go back to those times when men cultivated their fields with their hands and were nourished by milk from their herds. . . . Among us one must have genius to be natural and simple like those who never dreamed of being so." Such were the thoughts about art and its culture in many countries of Europe in the 1820s and 1830s—Germany, Italy, France, and finally England—as if art to be art had always to be born again. This was not a point of view that could be sustained by an institutional concern for art—it was drastically opposed to the principles upon which all academies had been based—and yet it did encourage the formation of groups of artists, fraternities that could sustain the artist outside the accepted social structure. In the beginning, such artists looked to the past, to "primitive" times, for their inspiration and ideological support: early Greece, the imaginary world of Ossian, the Old Testament, or the Middle Ages. Eventually nature itself was looked upon as the key to the eternally primitive. It was not so much an attraction as an impulse that motivated the artists: a strong impulse to escape the weight of artistic tradition as well as the entanglements of an increasingly industrial and impersonal society. Such artists were not seeking a freedom for expressive license or caprice. They sought a ritual, a discipline that was rooted in the fundamental nature of man, in contrast to a practice that seemed to serve only the social expediencies of a modern political state.

For a growing number of French painters during the second quarter of the past century, the way was to be found not in a monasticism like that of their elder German confreres, but in a union with the changing aspects and rhythms of nature. There was nothing new about the direct depiction of nature; particularly outside of France it had become something of an artistic commonplace. But theirs was not primarily a concern for perception and technique. The artists were looking to nature for a way of life, for a new evaluation of existence in which progress, competition, or personal aggrandizement played no part. The artists, they felt, should draw from nature a vital daily sustenance much as the peasant who tills the fields. So instead of searching out sources of emotional excitement in magnificent panoramas of the Alps or vast reaches of the sea, they looked to the domesticated wilderness of the Forest of Fontainebleau and the peasant life of Barbizon. There they created a kind of poetry of acceptance that posed no questions and required no answers. In an intensely analytical age they wished only to be.

On the face of it, it is puzzling that artists from the United States, when they discovered the works of these painters at mid-century, considered them so appealing and so challenging. Throughout our brief history, many American artists, despite their protestations, had been busy trying to ally themselves with artistic tradition, not escape it. Furthermore, to rebel against the academy and official taste in the United States at that point meant nothing, because the academy had no stylistic preconceptions and there was no significant official patronage. As far as the direct study of nature was concerned, it had been formulated as a kind of American credo for many years. Possibly the explanation lies in the fact that American painters saw the artists of Barbizon within a context quite different from that in which the French painters saw themselves. To the Americans, the Barbizon painters provided a release from the depiction of specific nature, from that kind of literal truth supported by the ideas of Bryant, Emerson, and eventually Ruskin. Released from its function as a national and religious symbol, landscape took on through the model of Barbizon a persuasively mysterious sentiment that seemed at once humble and exotic. Its appeal was to the individual mind, to the imagination that looked for a new Forest of Arden without the trappings of Shakespeare. In other words, Barbizon painting provided the Americans with a state of mind, a mood in which creativity was possible. Ironically, considering the origins of the movement in France, the Barbizon mood in America did not mean a new earthiness, a rebellious concentration on nature rather than on art, but an individual poetic freedom uncommon in American painting until that time.

Although rural life had usually been looked on in the United States as morally superior to an urban existence, the Yankee farmer could hardly be equated with the French peasant. As a type, he was depicted as canny and aggressive, crude in his manners, but a model of industry and moral rectitude. In fact, it is usually the rural image that has been cited as typical of the restless, independent American. Significantly, those painters who discovered a special meaning and attraction in the French peasant showed no interest in depicting the American farmer. The American earth seemed not to yield the same magic, the sense of nostalgia born out of centuries of cyclical continuity. The American landscape was a symbol of progress, of opportunity; the Barbizon landscape, with its resigned peasants and domesticated livestock, provided in the American context a gentle decadence, a crepuscular tranquility remote from the grandeur of Yellowstone or the clatter of the McCormick reaper.

The Barbizon mood, then, as apprehended by the American artist and patron, was a state of mind through which nature could enter the realm of art without ceasing to be nature. And art, in this sense, no longer meant the perfection of order or the recording of fact but the provocation of the mind to ruminate and bask in a sensuous environment without thought of conclusion or consequence.

There was resistance to the Barbizon mood in America, but it was rarely based on the arguments, so common in France, that such nature was vulgar or that depicting agricultural workers constituted a political threat. No one seems to have equated the toiling French peasant with the immigrant worker in the urban slums. Rather, the newly imported French mode was criticized as too unspecific, too little pragmatic; it was too evidently characterized more by looking than artistic doing. Industry in execution as an aesthetic element obviously had been put aside by the licentious French in favor of sensitivity of response. Once poetry gained its evocative freedom, however, the goals of painting too were reassessed by the public, and the mood inspired by Barbizon became the touchstone by which pictorial poetry was known. So strong, in fact, was the attachment to the somber poetry Americans found in Barbizon that even when techniques changed and a new sunny range of colors was adopted by the painters, much of the reflective sentiment remained. Possibly the Barbizon mood, as they understood it, was a wishful creation of the American painters themselves.

AMERICAN ART IN THE BARBIZON MOOD

Peter Bermingham, Curator of Education, National Collection of Fine Arts

1. Barbizon Art—Background for America

Few methods used by historians of art have a more time-honored tradition behind them than the linking of isolable characteristics to specific locales. Yet, whether that locale be Siena, Pont Aven, Düsseldorf, or the more expansive reaches of the Hudson River, the place has invariably come to refer more to a style, a kind of subject matter, or a special frame of mind than to paintings actually executed at the site itself. Artists often gathered at common feeding grounds, moving by some inscrutable compulsion to the same current. The artists who comprise what came to be known by the mid-nineteenth century as the Barbizon school were no exception.[1] Even today, the region in and around the tiny hamlet of Barbizon serves as a reminder not just of an artistic habitat, but of certain fundamental concerns that all in the group seemed to share.

The Forest of Fontainebleau, within which Barbizon itself is little more than a brief incident, was in no true sense a primeval sector of untamed nature in the early nineteenth century, although James Fenimore Cooper (a visitor in 1827) was supposed to have found it "exceeding in savage variety anything he had ever seen in America."[2] Man had been at Fontainebleau since at least the tenth century, but wise forestry and planting—beginning with the reign of Louis XIV—had helped to preserve much of its rugged variety. Carefully tilled, undistinguished fields surrounded the thick undergrowth of the woods. There were no high mountains nearby, only small hills; instead of wild lakes and rivers, only shallow pools like the seductive Fairies' Pond

(*Mare aux Fees*) and a few ribbonlike streams. Numerous paths traversed the woods, sunlight easily penetrated all but the densest regions, and the forest was too small (about 42,000 acres) to inspire the excitement of exploration.

If the regions in and around Fontainebleau could not offer Alpine majesty or Hudson Valley sublimity, they were still filled with a multitude of picturesque effects. The variety and size of its trees constantly amazed visitors. Barbizon became especially famous for its giant oak trees, which seemed all the more massive next to the many elegant birches and elms. The gorges of Apremont and Franchard, made famous by the brush of Théodore Rousseau, were no less picturesque. Their fantastic piles of stone and solitary boulders even suggested to one American visitor Milton's description of the battle between the hosts of heaven and hell.[3] Rousseau, no doubt, would have agreed.

In addition to the Fontainebleau forest and its environs, and just as important for many of the artists who went there, were the people who for centuries had labored in the local fields and villages. Whether they were from Grez, Moret, Montigny, Lanchard, or Barbizon, their costumes, mores, and proverbial faith and persistence were probably little different from those of others of their class—and less remarkable than those of the Normandy peasants whom Jean-François Millet knew so well before he ever set foot in Barbizon.

The earliest "colonizing" of Barbizon by artists was—if the traditional stories about it can be de-

[11]

Figure 1. Ferdinand Chaigneau. *Barbizon in Snow*. Line etching.

Figure 2. Théodore Rousseau. *Lane in the Forest of Fontainebleau,
Storm Effect*, ca. 1860–1865. Collection: The Louvre, Paris.

pended upon—an accident of the early 1820s, a chance discovery by two lost painters trying to find their way through the Bas-Breau woods on the edge of town.[4] One of them, Caruelle d'Aligny, had been an advisor and companion of a young student from Paris named Jean-Baptiste Camille Corot. By 1825, either at the direct invitation of d'Aligny or mindful of rumors spread about the attraction of the area, the peripatetic Corot made his first of several appearances in Barbizon. Rousseau followed in the summer of 1827, visiting frequently after 1833 and finally making his permanent home at Barbizon in 1848. Of the other best known and influential members of the group—Charles-François Daubigny (1817–1878); Virgile Narcisse Diaz de la Peña (1808–1876); Jules Dupré (1811–1889); Charles-Émile Jacque (1813–1894); Constant Troyon (1810–1865); and Jean-François Millet (1814–1875)—only Millet, the last among them to make the Barbizon pilgrimage, would take up permanent residence there in 1849.[5]

Whether Barbizon was a mere way station or a *locus operandi* for its many artists, their ultimate test was still to be faced in the major urban centers of Europe, especially in Paris or, for the aspiring American, in New York, Philadelphia, or Boston. Although the purveyors of official art in Paris managed increasingly to recognize the validity of landscape painting as a pursuit worthy of an artist's undivided attention, Barbizon art in its early years was unacceptable because it seemed to evoke a peculiarly rural flavor, too Northern in feeling, with only the faintest echoes of the classical arrangements of Claude Lorraine and Nicolas Poussin. These seventeenth-century masters perfected their classical landscapes in Italy, and Fontainebleau was nothing like the Roman Campagna. An art that portrayed the provincial woodlands with more than a modicum of truth was doomed to risk the disapproval of the conservative establishment in France.

The active life of the Barbizon school in France, especially from the late 1830s to the mid-1850s, was inextricably bound up in the social history of the period and as such was subject to signal triumphs and major defeats depending on the course of shifting political and cultural currents. For example, after the short-lived victory of the naturalist artists in the jury-free salons of 1848 and 1849, the advent of the Second Empire served once again to widen the split between the acceptable and the progressive in French art. At times, painful compromises could be effected, but the suspicions of the French aristocratic and upper-middle class patrons toward the Barbizon artists were not easily overcome. The infamous Comte de Nieuwerkerke, the head of all official patronage for art during the Second Empire, summoned enough interest in Gustave Courbet to invite him to lunch in a vain attempt to curb that artist's realist proclivities. For the Barbizon painters, though, he had only contempt. "This is the painting of democrats," he exclaimed, "of those who don't change their linen and who want to put themselves above men of the world. This art displeases and disgusts me."[6]

In espousing the art of "men of the world," the count very nearly put his finger on the special attraction that Barbizon painting had for many artists of the mid-nineteenth century, as well as for a few enlightened patrons. As the large retrospective exhibition of Barbizon art held in America in 1962 and Robert Herbert's exemplary catalog for that show demonstrate, the *sine qua non* of most Barbizon landscapes was an evident opposition to the phenomena of industrialized society and a consequent release in nature and the rural past.[7] Millet spoke of this escape several times, perhaps most poignantly in this excerpt from a letter to Rousseau.

You are right. Life is a sad thing, and few spots in it are places of refuge. We come to understand those who sighed for a place of refreshment, of light, and of peace. One understands what Dante makes some of his people say, speaking of the time that they passed on earth— 'the time of my debt.'—Well, let us hold out as long as we can.[8]

Figure 3. Théodore Rousseau. *Landscape, Gathering Wood*. Collection: Museum of Fine Arts, Boston; bequest of Mrs. David P. Kimball.

Théodore Rousseau, the most intensely intellectual of the Barbizon group, fought a successful battle against deforestation of a part of Fontainebleau near Monts-Girard and, like his comrades, constantly compared the life and nature of the area (fig. 3) to that described in the poetry of Homer and Virgil. Nevertheless, Rousseau's attempts to wrest the very secrets from the substance of nature —to learn "the laws of growth" as he put it—is manifestly different from, say, the forest nymphs of Corot and Diaz, the wholly unpretentious melancholy of Daubigny, or the rustic permanence of the peasants and animals of Jacques, Troyon, and Millet.

In theory then, the Barbizon masters should have found themselves in concert with popular and official taste. That the opposite was often the case can best be explained in a pronouncement by Paul de Saint-Victor, the well-known conservative art critic, which was included in a book on the pleasures of Fontainebleau published in 1855.

We prefer the sacred grove where the fauns make their way, to the forest in which woodcutters are working: the Greek spring in which nymphs are bathing, to the Flemish pond in which ducks are paddling: and the half-naked shepherd who, with his Virgilian crook, drives his rams and she-goats along the Georgic paths of Poussin, to the peasant, pipe in mouth, who climbs Ruysdael's back road.[9]

The small but vocal group of critics, including Jules Castagnary and Théophile Thoré, who came to the Barbizon artists' defense usually chose to see in their work either symptoms or monuments to a much more personal confrontation between artist and nature, one that celebrated the painter's role as social worker and prophet, "regenerated," as Thoré exclaimed, "by the return to natural truth." The effort to memoralize essential verities of the natural world in the face of accelerating change could well be termed the conservative side of Barbizon art, and here the group made significant and fresh contributions to the narrower but no less important formal concerns of the landscape painter in the nineteenth century. Probably no landscape school before or since has drawn so effectively from the legacies of the past. With the exception of Rousseau, all were legitimate heirs to the rococo tradition of eighteenth-century French art. Indeed, Diaz, Dupré, and Troyon all began as decorators of porcelain. The example of Dutch baroque painting was crucial as well, especially for Troyon after his visit to Holland in 1847. The great stir caused by the English landscapes of Constable and Bonington at the Salon of 1824 no doubt spawned many an idea in the minds of the Barbizon painters, no less than in those of Delacroix and his followers.[10] The British contribution was augmented at this time by a few like-minded French landscapists, such as Paul Huet, Achille Michallon, and P. P. Valenciennes, whose plein-air paintings before 1800 helped set the precedent for the Barbizon artists' firsthand study of nature. Of the pre-Barbizon landscapists in France, only Paul Huet (1803–1869), a friend to Delacroix and Bonington, was an unabashed romantic. Valenciennes, along with Corot's early teachers,

Figure 4. Jean-Baptiste Camille Corot. *The Forest of Fontainebleau.* Collection: Museum of Fine Arts, Boston; gift of Mrs. Samuel Dennis Warren.

Figure 5. Narcisse V. Diaz de la Peña. *Gypsies Going to a Fair.* Collection: Museum of Fine Arts, Boston; bequest of Mrs. Samuel D. Warren.

Figure 6. Charles François Daubigny. *On the Oise.* Collection: Paine Art Center, Oshkosh, Wisconsin.

Figure 7. Charles-Émile Jacque. *Shepherdess with Her Sheep.*
Ville de Fontainebleau Collection.

Figure 8. Constant Troyon. *Watering Cattle.* Wallace Collection, London.

Figure 9. Jean-François Millet. *Young Shepherdess.*
Collection: Museum of Fine Arts, Boston; gift of
Samuel Dennis Warren.

Michallon, D'Aligny, and Victor Bertin, painted landscapes that were strongly set in the classical mold emanating from Poussin and Claude. (Where more established preferences lay is demonstrated in part by the fact that the revolutionary addition of a Prix de Rome for landscape in 1817 was largely the result of the good offices of the archclassicist Valenciennes.)

These and other tributaries that lead into and mix with the mainstream of Barbizon art will be illuminated in more detail later in this study. Suffice it to say for the moment that when American painters and patrons turned with favor to Barbizon painting in the late-nineteenth century, they were, in effect, legatees both of fairly specific attitudes toward the rendition of nature, and, at the same time, of a much broader tradition. For many an American painter, Barbizon and Barbizon-derived art was a first glimpse of poetic license, a privilege that led to both highly personalized studies of American nature and to crass imitations of the most tedious sort, the kind of dime-store "chestnuts" that prompted this observation by John Canaday in his *Mainstreams of Modern Art* (1959): "As a mine for imitators, the landscape tradition of the Barbizon painters has yielded some of the most inane paintings ever turned out by commercial hacks. Their work has been into countless pretty calendars, pasted on wastebaskets, and cut up for jigsaw puzzles."[11]

The increasing popularity of Barbizon painting in the post-Civil War era helped to color our art at several other levels in ways that were endemically American. For example, despite the implicit censure of the new technological age in much of Barbizon art, it still emerged by the late 1880s as the most consistently sought after item at galleries and auction blocks. Serious collectors, speculators, and dilettantes, healthy survivors in the race for success and prestige, all found emotional and financial compensation in the silvery glades of Corot, the contented cows and sheep of Jacques and Troyon, and a secular reaffirmation of the Puritan ethic in the stolid peasants of Millet.

The rolls of American artists in this new idiom were soon swollen with a plethora of painters now long neglected, many of them undeservedly so. After reexamining the work of the more important figures discussed in this essay, I based the criteria for emphasis on their roles in the overall scenario of events, even if their work fails today to completely engage our eye or quicken our pulse.

2. *Hunt, Inness, and a Few Friends: The Early Years*

William Hunt, all muscular spareness and brownness and absence of waste, all flagrant physiognomy, brave, bony arch of handsome nose, upwardness of strong eye-brow and glare, almost, of eyes that both recognized and wondered, strained eyes that played over questions as if they were objects and objects as if they were questions, might have stood, to the life, for Don Quixote.

—HENRY JAMES (from *A Small Boy and Others*)

Although the year 1881 was an otherwise uneventful one for the people of Boston, it was marked by at least two quite significant events in the cultural life of the city. The first was the publication by Ticknor and Company of the four-volume *Memorial History of Boston;* the other, a July retrospective exhibition of the work of the recently deceased painter William Morris Hunt (1824–1879). The two events had more in common than mere chronological coincidence. Hunt was himself a memorial to Boston, a man regarded by most of its citizens as the city's most influential painter and teacher; an artist—as the editor of the *Memorial* (IV, p. 399) put it—"whose genius gave him authority to speak, while his enthusiasm compelled all to listen." Hunt's charisma was all the more remarkable when one considers that, in his boundless respect for originality, he disliked telling anyone how to paint. In fact, when Hunt chose to elaborate on the proper exemplars for the aspiring artist, he rarely referred them to his own work, but most often to pictures by the best of the Barbizon painters. "The artist is an interpreter of nature," he wrote. "When I look at

Figure 10. William Morris Hunt. *Self-Portrait*, 1849. Collection: Museum of Fine Arts, Boston; gift of William P. Babcock.

nature, I think of Millet, Corot, Delacroix, and sometimes of Daubigny."[1]

Hunt's early training was a far more checkered affair than that of his students. On the whole it was the sort of search-and-reject mission that led Henry James to see him not only as a latter-day Quixote,

[18]

but as a victim of "the merciless manner in which a living and hurrying public educates itself."[2] The son of a jurist and congressman from Brattleboro, Vermont, Hunt was an undistinguished student at Harvard for a few years and a mildly interested student of a New Haven painter and a Boston sculptor. His early career was a fair beginning for a dilettante, but hardly for a serious professional.[3]

Hunt had a special advantage in his early years: a widowed mother with a passion for cosmopolitan life and education. In the fall of 1843, the entire Hunt family embarked on that obligatory ritual of the upper class, the European grand tour. Young William went first to Rome for lessons in drawing and modeling with Henry Kirke Brown, the American expatriot sculptor. The artistic milieu of Rome and Brown's instruction brought Hunt's latent talents more sharply into focus. Plans for a return to Harvard were scrapped and, after a tour of Greece, Turkey, and Switzerland, he decided in the winter of 1845 to study at the best known art school in Europe, the Düsseldorf Academy in Westphalia.

Hunt had always felt that pleasure and the pursuit of craft were inseparable, and the Teutonic discipline of the Düsseldorf curriculum was more than he could tolerate. Although he numbered among his friends at the academy its president, Richard Lessing, as well as the American-German painter Emanuel Leutze, he still could not reconcile himself to a school conducted "upon the principle that the education of art-genius, of a mechanic, and of a student of science were one and the same thing—a grinding methodical process for the accumulation of a required skill."[4]

In the fall of 1846, probably on the advice of his brother Richard (a future architect of great renown who longed to study at the École in Paris), the mercurial Hunt decided to study in Paris with a French sculptor, Jean-Jacques Pradier; however, he never arrived at Pradier's studio. While waiting for the first class to begin, he was struck by the verve and dash of a painting called *The Falconer* in the window of DeForge's art store in Paris. The painter was Thomas Couture and Hunt is said to have exclaimed on the spot, "If that is a painting, I am a painter."[5]

Surely *The Falconer*, a rather insipid piece of decorative genre, was not the sort of work that held strong possibilities for Hunt's subsequent contributions to art and taste in America. Couture was, however, an academic liberal and a clever, facile technician on the threshold of great acclaim in France.[6] As a teacher and painter, Couture's methods were very much a Salon variation of the Barbizon attitude towards landscape painting. His noble and quasi-exotic subject matter was conventional enough, but the painterly methods he taught were cast in a far different mold than the constipated handling of paint practiced by Düsseldorf and much of the Paris École.

After shedding the intensely analytical approach taught by his masters Gros and Delaroche, Couture developed an *en frottée* method based on a combination of simple light and dark patterns developed first through thin sepia washes. To these were added slightly thicker glazes in the half tones and darks with heavier (often exaggerated) impastos in the light areas (fig. 11). With practice the Couture method was accessible to any moderately talented pupil, and Hunt was certainly that.

Although Couture cared little for Barbizon landscapes and was greatly disappointed when Hunt went to Barbizon with Millet in 1852, he and such painters as Rousseau, Dupré, and Corot were leaders in the effort to overcome what might be termed the "finish fetish" of academic art. Retention of the spontaneous effect of the first impression or study (*ébauche*) is implicit in the Couture method. It is true that the *ébauche* and, indeed, landscape painting were very much a fixture at the École during the mid-nineteenth century as Albert Boime's recent examination of the Academy thoroughly demonstrates.[7] Studies, however, were considered just that, preparation without realization. Rousseau and Corot were repeatedly chided by Salon reviewers for what the critics considered to be an undue emphasis on *effet* and flimsy execution (not for their attention to landscape as such). In 1855,

Figure 11. Thomas Couture. *Study of a Head.*
Collection: Cincinnati Art Museum; gift of
Frank Duveneck, 1915.

Edmond About—by no means a die-hard reactionary— attributed this shortcoming to fear rather than to a lack of finesse: "Anyone who has any experience of ateliers knows that, somewhere about the second or third session, there is always a moment at which the *ébauche* looks just right. The difficulty then is to turn it into a picture without spoiling it. M. Rousseau and his school were so afraid of spoiling their landscapes that they often left off at the *ébauche* stage."[8]

About's remarks were close to the truth with regard to Couture, even if they did not apply to the Barbizon artists' conception of a "finished painting." Couture, in fact, would often suggest to his students that they start anew if a particular sketch would be endangered by further work, and Hunt later related that he would not even offer a comment on a student's work if it appeared retouched.[9] Both

Couture and Hunt, and the artists from Barbizon as well, realized then that whatever the demands placed upon the artist by a particular subject, the painter should still be free to show the viewer the excited traces of inspired execution rather than the tightly controlled residue of hard labor only.

Notwithstanding his lack of "finish" and the bitter opposition of many critics, Couture was still a widely applauded member of the so-called *juste-milieu* painters in Paris who were engaged in the painful compromise of "striving to conciliate avant-garde and conservative tendencies."[10] However close the parallels between his technique and that of the Barbizon painters may seem, Couture's penchant for narrative entertainment and his use of method as an end in itself demonstrate the fundamental differences between him and the men from Fontainebleau. Too often, Couture conceived of technique as the surface treatment of inspiration; for the best of the Barbizon group, it was the process of formation itself.[11]

As the brief observations above might suggest, it was no accident that the years of Couture's greatest popularity (the late 1840s) coincide with the first widespread acceptance of the Barbizon painters. With the Revolution of 1848 and the establishment of the Second Republic, the free-jury concept was introduced to the Salon of that year after the combined pleas of a liberal coalition that included Diaz, Barye, and Couture. Millet, Diaz, Daubigny, Corot, and Troyon exhibited, with Corot and Daubigny winning second-class medals. Government commissions were offered to Millet, Rousseau, Dupré, and Daubigny; in the Salon of the following year, Rousseau, after an exhibition drought of twelve years, won a first-class medal and Corot was even emboldened to show a plein-air painting for the first time, *The Colisseum at Rome,* now in the Louvre.[12]

While Hunt was busily perfecting the Couture method in his master's studio, he probably took little notice of the work of the Barbizon artists. In fact, it was a fellow Bostonian who had accompanied Hunt on his trip to Paris, Winkworth Allan Gay

Figure 12. Winckworth Allan Gay. *Mountain Landscape*. Collection: The Brooklyn Museum, New York.

(1821–1910), who was the first to take any lessons directly from a Barbizon painter. Gay studied briefly with Troyon in 1847 and thus may have been the earliest American to come in contact with Barbizon ideas, but he did little to publicize them. Returning to America in 1851, he set himself no higher task than the occasional exhibition of his small, tender treatments of the New England coastline (fig. 12), although he later achieved some measure of renown as one of the first American artists to visit Japan.[13] Worthington Whittredge (1820–1910), an unknown young landscapist from Cincinnati on his way to Düsseldorf, was attracted to Barbizon in the fall of 1849 by reports about a group of Frenchmen who "were represented as being very poor, but genuine 'Kickers' against all pre-existing art." Whittredge "liked the spirit of these men but did not think much of their pictures." After ten years in Europe, he returned to the United States to become one of the later stalwarts of the Hudson River school in New York.[14]

A far more puzzling figure than Gay or Whittredge at mid-century was yet another young man from Boston, William Babcock (1826–1899). A friend to both Hunt and Gay in Paris, Babcock followed Hunt's lead by entering Couture's studio in 1847, but apparently stayed for only a short time. He was probably the first American to befriend Millet, making his acquaintance in Paris at about the time he (Babcock) began his lessons with Couture.

The year 1847 was especially important for Millet, marked by the first important Salon notices of his career[15] as well as by his small but fairly profitable reputation as a painter of nudes—an aspect of his early career that his family and early biographers would later try to overlook. When Millet and Charles Jacques moved to Barbizon in 1849, Babcock soon followed and managed to stay there for some forty-three years, leaving finally in 1892.[16] A recluse with an unfortunate inability to complete much work, Babcock's struggles remind one of those of Albert Pinkham Ryder, but unlike Ryder, his tastes in art often bordered on outright hero worship—of Millet and Rousseau especially, as well as of Delacroix and Chassériau. Yet, Babcock's painting (fig. 13)—from what we know of his extant work—reflects only peripheral Barbizon concerns, particularly the opulent colorism of Diaz and Adolphe Monticelli, the Marseilles painter of woodland fetes. Babcock will be the subject of further discussion in a later chapter; at this point, it is important to note that in many ways Babcock was an ideal American representative at Barbizon, especially during his earliest days there. An avid collector of small paintings and prints by the Barbizon

Figure 13. William P. Babcock. *Landscape with Figures*. Collection: Museum of Fine Arts, Boston; gift of John Richardson Hall.

group despite his very limited means, he was always passionately curious and "filled to over-flowing with the tradition of the colony at Barbizon," even if his own equipment as an artist was curiously incomplete.[17] It should also be noted vis à vis later visits to Barbizon that Babcock, like the oaks in the Fontainebleau woods, was always there.

Babcock did not venture to exhibit at the Paris Salon until 1868, but the more ambitious Hunt was emboldened to show there as early as the Salon of 1852. One of his two exhibited paintings, *La Marguerite* (see fig. 14, a replica of this painting dating from 1853), featured a young woman in white blouse with gray skirt standing under a cloudy sky and holding a white marguerite delicately in her hand.[18] Its naive sentiment with vaguely allegorical

Figure 14. William Morris Hunt. *La Marguerite*, 1853. Collection: Museum of Fine Arts, Boston.

overtones demonstrates the most that Hunt was likely to derive from Couture at this point in his career. The values have a cold correctness about them, and the drawing shows the fruits of hard labor in the studio, but Hunt wanted something more.

Toward the end of his tenure in Couture's atelier (about 1851), Hunt first became aware of the work of the painter soon to be his next and most lasting idol, Jean-François Millet. First came exposure to Millet's works in the Salon and later an introduction to the French artist brought about through the worthy offices of Babcock and Antoine Barye, the sculptor of animals.[19] Ever impressionable, Hunt's conversion from the sociable surroundings of Couture's crowded studio to the intense, almost ascetic seclusion of Millet's Barbizon was performed with a resolution of purpose that indicates that the student from Boston had found the ingredient formerly lacking in his painting: a sincerity based on genuinely humanistic ideals. Nevertheless, the break in matters of technique was none too significant. Although Millet was more consistent and "sincere" than Couture, both were staunch supporters of a direct, painterly method (although Couture was more attracted to the intricacies of glazing). In this regard, the real key to Hunt's trek to Barbizon in 1853 may well be found in a short trip he took to Amsterdam in 1850 or 1851.[20] Here, he was immediately smitten with the work of Rembrandt, especially the famous *Night Watch*. Hunt's studies of Rembrandt's work were executed on the spot and convinced him that Couture's prescribed palette was too limited. Equally important, he probably learned more through Rembrandt about the Italian masters than he had ever been able to discern in Italy.

It may well have been the strong sense of monumentality and permanence that marks the work of Masaccio and Michelangelo that convinced Hunt to buy (probably in 1851) an early version of Millet's *The Sower* (fig. 15), for the paltry sum of 300 francs.[21] In this work, later acknowledged to be one of Millet's masterpieces but rejected by an art

Figure 15. Jean-François Millet. *The Sower*, 1850, cat. no. 8.

dealer at the Salon of 1850–1851 as "too sad a subject," a dark, foreboding figure dressed in a broadbrimmed hat, peasant's blouse, and boots is captured in the act of rhythmically spreading his seeds on a barren hillside. Silhouetted against a twilight sky, he fills the space around him with his gesture and his presence. Devoid of individual features, more symbol than fact, Millet's *Sower* was, as the critic Castagnary described the artist's peasants, "at one bound, the typical character of the race."[22] The search for the "typical," so dear to Millet, was a notion quickly grasped by Hunt, even though his training with Couture might have led him to add a dash of glamour to the final product. With Millet, Hunt "felt the infinitude of art . . . with Couture, there was a limit."[23]

The Sower was the first important painting bought from a Barbizon artist by any American; shortly, Hunt, Martin Brimmer (a Harvard graduate from Boston studying in Paris), and others of their colleagues in Paris would buy many more. Their patronage was especially timely, for Millet was then in difficult financial straits and the help of the Americans did much to pay his bills.[24] In return, Hunt's studies with Millet provided him less with practical recipes than with concepts that illuminated the "why" more than the "how" of painting. Despite several accounts to the contrary, Millet was no intellectual primitive. His cultural awareness was narrowly proscribed to be sure, but keynoted at all times by an aptness of selection that had a direct bearing on his feelings about art and nature. Millet's special literary favorites included the pastoral poetry of Homer, Virgil, and Milton, and, though an agnostic himself, he would gladly quote chapter and verse from the Bible. Only on rare occasions a depictor of scenes from mythical or religious sources, Millet, nevertheless, left little doubt in his art and studies that he thought himself an heir to the classical tradition.[25] His *Sower*, in fact, is far more than an anonymous peasant lost in his work and nature; it seems, even today, closer in spirit to antique personifications of fertility and agriculture.

Delighted that his new companion and different

locale camouflaged his blue-blooded background, Hunt donned peasant garb and followed Millet into the fields for demonstrations and advice. The transformation for Hunt was exciting and, because Millet was a far more determined worker than he, a bit puzzling. "I thought that I was working hard, 'he later reported,' but he considered me a loafer."[26] Millet took him to the Louvre to study Mantegna and Dürer, two artists whose reverence for line was echoed in Millet's own art (although this quality is easy to overlook in view of critical concentration on his more obvious interest in large, softly lit forms).[27]

Millet had been a practicing professional artist for nearly twenty years when Hunt first came to Barbizon, and undoubtedly there was much about his patient search for the internal logic of form and gesture that Hunt could not fully grasp. Millet's prelatical role as philosopher-artist, finding nobility in the homeliest of subjects, was perhaps the most compelling aspect of his art for the young New Englander. "When I came to know Millet I took broader views of humanity, of the world, of life. His subjects were real people who had work to do. If he painted a hay-stack it suggested life, animal as well as vegetable, and the life of man. . . . He was the greatest man in Europe."[28] Hunt's advice to his many students in Newport and Boston, from the late 1850s on, was filled with aphorisms, which emphasized the worthiness of humble subject matter.[29] Yet, several of Hunt's initial efforts at Barbizon, for example, his rather tame and awkward *French Peasant Woman with Pig* (fig. 16), demonstrate how difficult it was for him to translate the commonplace into a monumental art of dignity and presence (fig. 17).

Unlike Van Gogh or Seurat, both of whom would later derive great benefit from their study of Millet's work, Hunt was temperamentally unsuited and technically ill-equipped at this time to bring new powers of invention to his own study of Millet. Impatient and easily distracted from an appointed course, the erratic Hunt admired Millet in the way that opposites attract one another. When Hunt's

Figure 16. William Morris Hunt. *French Peasant Woman with Pig*, 1850–1855, cat. no. 48.

Figure 17. William Morris Hunt. *Sheep Shearing At Barbizon* (AFTER MILLET), ca. 1852, cat. no. 49.

friend, Edward Wheelwright, sought out Millet in Barbizon in 1855, his impression of the master's personality provides a clue to understanding the stabilizing influence of Millet on Hunt. "Force well ordered, well directed, calm, without bustle or excitement, not to be diverted from its aim; that was what Millet loved, and it was what he was."[30]

This seriousness of purpose, embodied in a language of strong, durable forms, was Millet's greatest gift to Hunt. Although the latter found it difficult to incorporate into his own work, he was gradually able to dispense with Couture's involved glazing methods, and to turn instead to a more direct ordering of strongly felt sensations. Hunt was certain that he had discovered the futility of wasted effort and the rewards wrought from simple truths (a lesson analogous, as Wheelwright indicates, to the labors of the *bêcheurs* that Hunt and Millet so often studied). Communicating this discovery to his countrymen back home was Hunt's next challenge, and one that he accepted with enthusiasm and high hopes.

At about the same time that Hunt decided to take up his faithful discipleship with Millet in Barbizon, George Inness (1825–1894) was making his way among the hundreds of works displayed at the Salon of 1852. Inness, as usual, had little to say about what he saw and thought on this occasion, though later he did comment that he could not understand the "small noise" made over a Rousseau landscape that to him seemed "rather metallic."[31] Although Inness's paintings were to undergo a profound transformation within a few years, in part because of the example of Rousseau and his compatriots, his work through the early 1850s was so thoroughly rooted in old-master tonalities and composition (fig. 18) that even the relatively fresh intimacy of Rousseau seemed too hard for his eyes.

Figure 18. George Inness. *Landscape,* 1849.
Collection: The California Palace of the Legion of
Honor, Lincoln Park, San Francisco;
Mildred Anna Williams Collection.

From all that he must have known about the
general tenor of American criticism at this stage in
his career, Inness may have been surprised that his
imitation of acknowledged masters would have been
held against him. His early critics, however, were
consistently fearful that in side-stepping the "modern" school of American landscape in favor of
Dutch and French masters, Inness was imitating art
history instead of natural history. In the same year
as his visit to the Salon, his ambitious *View of Berkshire* was shown at the American Art-Union. A
critic for the *Tribune* deemed it "as good as Gasper
[sic] Poussin," but added in the same breath,
"What then?" Inness had been "mastered by the
masters"; his brushwork was "wooly, scumby . . .
and dirty."[32]

Through this and similar assaults on his creative
powers,[33] Inness's course remained steady and his
admiration for the old masters undiminished. His
resolve in this regard owed a great deal to the
heterogeneous nature of his training: lessons from
an itinerant who advertised himself as "a pupil of
Sully"; a brief association with an engraving firm
in New York; and a limited tenure as a pupil of

Regis Gignoux (1816–1882), a Frenchman who had
studied with Millet's teacher, Paul Delaroche, and
from whose studio in New York a popular brand
of rococo landscape poured out in great profusion.
Gignoux was a collector of prints of Dutch, French,
and English paintings which Inness found especially
attractive for their "power of motive and bigness of
grasp." Here he found nature was "rendered grand
instead of being belittled by trifling detail and
puny execution."[34]

Like many of his colleagues Inness advertised his
talents as a painter of "views," but often the results
were something much more—or less, depending on
the patron's point of view. When he insisted on
altering a canvas for Samuel Ward, in 1852, he
wrote to reassure his patron, "You will find it con-
siderably lower in tone than when you saw it last
but I hope with increased colour and transparency
as well and also the dreamy obscurity of a lowering
day better represented."[35] There is no mention here
of descriptive fidelity or of changing the lay of the
land to fit the artist's or his patron's concept of a
chosen site. Indeed, Inness's earliest efforts were
usually painted with passable competence in this
regard, albeit with notable lapses in the drawing of
figures and animals. The "dreamy obscurity" he
sought, however, evoked a melancholy that his
critics found unresponsive to the "joys of nature."
When Inness's landscapes were displayed at the
American Art-Union in 1849, a reporter for the
Knickerbocker Magazine lamented that "a sad and
heavy tone pervades, and wounds the eye."[36] Inness
had violated a fundamental precept of American
transcendentalism in regard to the depiction of
native landscape; namely, that nature was good,
ordered, and somehow a reflection of God's promise
for man's immortality. Phrases like "sad and heavy
tone" or the "morbid French manner" (of Hunt)
were the critics' epithets for paintings thought to
disregard the elevating optimism of most American
landscapes of that time. Of course, paintings reviewed in most mid-century periodicals were rarely
dismissed on purely subjective grounds. The
Knickerbocker critic, for example, observed that as

a result of this "heavy tone," the trees in the foreground of Inness's paintings were "the same color with his distant hills." He further warned Inness to "study the colors of Nature and not so much the mere forms" (somewhat the reverse of later critical advice offered to Inness).

Inness's struggle to avoid niggling detail in favor of basic forms and strong design was closely allied to his keen interest in coordinating hand, brush, and paint in a way that could give new life to natural forms instead of merely rendering the appearance of their surface. If his emulation of the old-master format was an honest form of hero worship, his handling of paint was more an extension of an independent spirit already developed before the artist saw his first Barbizon landscape—although the critical reaction to his broad technique was symptomatic of the reception accorded French landscapes at the same time (see next chapter). Even before 1850, Inness's subject matter and selection of mood were akin to that of the Barbizon painters: pastoral scenes bisected by winding country roads with cattle or sheep and figures in the middle distance; dense forest interiors sometimes combined with solitary trees silhouetted against flat plains and sky. As Inness's biographer, Nicolai Cikovsky, Jr., explained in a discussion about his later, more "frenchified" landscapes, "many things about his paintings in the Barbizon vein are not so much additions to his art as modifications of qualities that had previously existed in it."[37] Examples for future reference, in fact, were more readily available to him in Dutch landscapes and prints than in anything of French origin. (Throughout his life, Inness was especially fond of the moody landscapes of Ruysdael and Hobbema.)[38]

How much Inness saw of European art either at home or abroad before the Civil War is difficult to assess, particularly since there is some dispute as to whether the trip to the Continent that included his visit to the Salon of 1852 was his first or second journey abroad.[39] At any rate, his stay in 1852 was spent almost entirely in Italy, with his visit to the Salon squeezed in during a brief stopover at Paris

on his return to America. His next journey abroad in 1854–1855 was apparently spent entirely in France, although regrettably little is known about it.

When Inness returned to his New York City studio in 1855 he received a commission from the president of the Delaware, Lackawanna, and Wyoming Railroad to paint a view in the Lackawanna Valley of the company's roundhouse and four of their nineteen engines.[40] The result was Inness's best known work from the 1850s, *The Lackawanna Valley,* now in the National Gallery of Art in Washington, D.C. (fig. 19). For all its ingratiating propaganda this canvas exhibits several hints of the painter's recent French interlude. Its informality of subject and subtlety of aerial perspective was rarely matched in the traditional format and heavy atmosphere of his earlier efforts. Asher Durand's definition of a "fine picture" in his "Letters on Landscape Painting" published in *The Crayon* in 1855, the same date as that of the Lackawanna painting, seems to describe Inness's view perfectly. "A fine picture . . . takes possession of you—draws you into it—you traverse it—breathe its atmosphere—feel its sunshine, and you repose in its shade."[41]

In retrospect, there is also an inescapable antiindustrial tone in Lackawanna Valley, an aspect of the work probably overlooked by its purchasers and possibly by Inness himself. In the foreground is a standard Hudson River school device, a lounging boy in the shade of a slender elm contemplating divine nature. Yet, what he must contemplate in addition to the natural environment is a different matter entirely. On both sides of the hillside, which provides him with shelter and rest, is a curving railroad track; once-virgin forests are transformed into tidy, gardenlike enclosures with wooden fences; and the green slope is covered with the stumps of severed trees. The forest in turn screens off the smoky edges of the busy factory town of Scranton, Pennsylvania. In the eyes of Inness's patrons, nature was here modeled to serve civilized progress. For an artist like Inness who viewed nature's domain as a spiritual world, perfect and beautiful, such a message must have been a bitter pill indeed. The

Figure 19. George Inness. *The Lackawanna Valley,* 1855. Collection: The National Gallery of Art, Washington, D.C.; gift of Mrs. Huddleston Rogers, 1945.

new symbolism of progress—the "machine in the garden," as Leo Marx described it—would never again play a major role in any of his canvases, although artists more thoroughly rooted in the picturesque tradition would continue to find compromise and accommodation in similar confrontations.[42]

Subsequent productions of the late 1850s did not fulfill the promise of *Lackawanna Valley.* One exception here, though its success is only partial, is Inness's *St. Peter's Rome* of 1857 (fig. 20), his most ambitious landscape from the fifties. In this large panorama, Inness seems to have tried to bring some of the suavity of his French experience to bear on one of the most hackneyed of famous "views."

Combining a taste for grandeur that is more reminiscent of Cole than of Barbizon, with the discretion in the handling of distance that was such an executive characteristic of Corot's and Rousseau's, Inness united two basically different pictorial styles. The contradiction was probably unavoidable since Inness had yet to acquire a consistent style. Later in his life, he articulated his awareness of the problem (though not its solution): "I could not sustain it [detail] everywhere and produce the sense of space and distances and with them that subjective mystery of Nature with which wherever I went was filled."[43]

Although the steady transition undergone by Inness in the late fifties was very much a stop-and-

Figure 20. George Inness. *St. Peter's Rome,* 1857.
Collection: The New Britain Museum of American Art,
Connecticut.

start operation, there is little reason to suspect that it is attributable solely to an inner need to completely transform his art. As indicated previously, the range of his subject matter, and his affinity for painting in the broad manner had already been established. Since his theoretical interests lay in the realm of religion rather than that of art, it can be concluded—albeit with some danger of overstatement—that the work of the men from Fontainebleau accommodated his frenetic idealism not simply because their attitudes toward composition and style were similar, but because the path charted by the Barbizon painters seemed more meaningful, more likely to express "that subjective mystery of Nature." In the main, his Hudson River school comrades found the Creator's hand in the finer points of nature, whereas Inness discovered it in her moods: a particular season or a special effect related to the time of day; the foreboding calm before a storm or the sparkling resonance of damp grass and trees in the sunny aftermath of a shower. He preferred to use long-forgotten sketches (even the studies of friends) as the basis of his studio work, thereby eliminating the distracting details that he termed "the impossible." In this respect he joins

Hunt and Rousseau, both of whom felt that studies were worthless until one's memory of the scene had faded.[44]

Given the thoroughly anti-institutional, mystical bent of Inness' religious leanings,[45] it is not too surprising to find that during the early 1860s, when patrons were difficult to come by even for recognized professionals, Inness found steady support in the person of the great evangelist Henry Ward Beecher, who thought Inness "the first of American painters." Beecher not only began to buy his work, but also rendered theological confirmation of Inness's metaphysical outlook on nature. In "Dream Culture" published in 1855 and "Hours of Exaltation" in 1857, Beecher implied that like Cole and the poet Bryant in Durand's famous painting, *Kindred Spirits,* he was as one with Inness before nature. In "Dream Culture," Beecher, in terms faintly premonitory of Proust, tells how the land was valuable to him for the "harvest of associations, fancies and dreamy broodings which it begets. . . . The very smell of fresh-turned earth brings up as many dreams and visions of the country as sandalwood does of oriental scenes."[46] As a further rationale for Inness's sense of poetry in nature, Beecher proclaimed in his "Hours" that "he will see the most without who has the most within . . . he who only sees with his bodily organs sees but surfaces."[47]

The enthusiastic support of Beecher helped convince Inness that such time-honored goals in art as Reason and Truth were not solely the property of the Hudson River school. Additional support came about 1859 with the sponsorship of the artist by George Nichols, a former pupil of Couture and owner of the newly opened Crayon Art Gallery on Eighth Street and Broadway in New York City. Lately arrived from Paris, the ruthless and unremitting Francophile Nichols sympathized with the nature of Inness's style. He quickly maneuvered himself into the position of art editor for the *New York Evening Post* and also wrote occasional anonymous articles for the *New York World.* With his glowing reviews of Inness's paintings, the critical pendulum slowly turned in the artist's favor.[48]

Figure 21. George Inness. *Hackensack Meadows, Sunset*, 1859.
Collection: The New-York Historical Society, New York.

Nichols was among the first New York dealers to carry the work of Rousseau and Corot. Inness's paintings were hung along with those of his Barbizon elders and, for the perceptive viewer, established his kinship before nature with the more sophisticated landscapes of the Frenchmen. The manner in which Nichols manipulated this combination to the best advantage of both the French artists and his American protégé can be appreciated in the following excerpt from a review in the *New York World* of September 26, 1860, written after a "visit" to the Crayon Art Gallery. Ostensibly a plea for support of Inness, it also contains uncommonly enthusiastic praise for Rousseau and French art:

"After the Shower" is a landscape by George Inness to be seen at the Crayon Art Gallery.... It is a matter of supreme wonder to us why this artist had not been given his place in the first rank of our landscape painters. Here is a picture of extraordinary power; a

Rysdael-like [*sic*] effect in the composition and comparable to Rousseau only in subtlety of color. It would place its author at the head of his profession in Paris but here he is absolutely suffering for the necessities of life.

At the same time that limited financial support and favorable criticism provided Inness with tangible encouragement, his landscapes began to lose the haphazard, indecisive look of his earlier transitional works. *Hackensack Meadows, Sunset* of 1859 (fig. 21) is one of his finest accomplishments from that year—a very productive one for Inness. Broad and free in touch and subtly balanced in its early autumn color, it is a work that reminds one of the finest landscapes of Jules Dupré, another Frenchman in the Nichols stable.[49] The painting, however, still lacks that persuasive illusion of texture that only the most astute use of the brush can give to the object it describes. In comparison with the

Figure 22. George Inness. *The Clearing Up*, 1860. Collection: The George Walter Vincent Smith Art Museum, Springfield, Massachusetts.

Hackensack landscape, Inness's *The Clearing Up* of the following year (fig. 22) is a remarkable demonstration of structural firmness, clear, natural light, and, in the damp fields a verdant sparkle that he would equal in the future but never surpass. Textural interest, though abundant, is a quality not forced for its own sake (as it so often was with Dupré), but rather a logical result of that peculiar clarity wrought by nature's mixture of sun and water.

The patchwork quality of Inness's topographical studies of the Delaware Valley in 1858–1860 demonstrates that the painter's stylistic evolution was far from complete when he entered the 1860s. As he incorporated a host of insights into his new and imaginative dialectic with nature—not the least of which was the Barbizon spirit—he was sure that his path would be the right one. His son wrote of him many years later, "I honestly believed that my father

thought he could surpass any artist that ever lived."[50] Possessed of such lofty aspirations, neither the lessons of the old masters nor those of the men from Barbizon were ever allowed to become more than steps in the slow legato of Inness's unhurried development.

In the fall of 1855, shortly after Inness had completed his *Lackawanna Valley*, William Morris Hunt had the good fortune—quite literally—to win the hand in marriage of Louisa Perkins of Boston, the daughter of Thomas Handasyd Perkins, a wealthy and highly respected Back Bay merchant. Entrée was gained immediately into the select circles of Boston society, and if Hunt had chosen to do so, he could have claimed a comfortable niche for himself in Boston's social register. Perhaps feeling that the change from the rough life in the fields of Barbizon to the gentility and brilliant conversation of the affluent Bostonians was too abrupt a break even for a mind as adaptable as his, he chose instead to set up residence in Newport, Rhode Island, an ocean-side town recently "discovered" by wealthy East-erners. After a European honeymoon he settled there in 1856, and, by 1858 had completed an ample, two-story studio building in the rear garden of "Hill-top," his mansion home.[51]

Hunt's mansion was no peasant hut and Newport had no woodlands of Bas-Breau or gorge of Apre-mont, but surely here Hunt must have rediscovered Barbizon on his own terms. Henry James, the novel-ist who later went on to painting pictures with words, was one of Hunt's pupils at the resort, which he described in terms that vividly recall its Bar-bizon-like attraction.

Newport imposed itself at that period to so remarkable a degree as the one right residence, in all our great country, for those tainted under whatever attenuations with the quality and effect of detachment.... The atmospheric tone, the careful selection of ingredients, your pleasant sense of a certain climatic ripeness—these are the real charms of Newport.... You are affected by the admirable art of the landscape—with so narrow a range of color and form.... It is in the combined lowness of tone, as painters call it ... in mingled shades of yellow and gray.[52]

James was one of several young men who went to Newport to gather informally and paint in the carefree atmosphere of Hunt's studio. The first to come, in 1859, was Edward Wheelwright, a wealthy amateur painter who had studied with Millet four years earlier, as well as with Couture. Wheelwright was already acquiring a sizable collection of Bar-bizon paintings, a few of which would later grace the walls of the Boston Museum of Fine Arts. He was followed in the spring of 1859 by John La-Farge, a New Yorker who had also studied briefly with Couture while fleeing from the study of law preferred by his parents. This small but eager group was soon completed with the arrival of the James brothers, William and Henry, then only nine-teen and seventeen years old, and John Bancroft, son of an eminent Harvard historian and himself a

student of optics and color theory. The James brothers had come to Hunt not from their native Boston, but from Paris—an extraordinary reversal of the route for most American students and ample testimony to the attraction that Hunt's personality and art had in this locale.

Given the fact that none of Hunt's circle in New-port went on to produce what could be termed substantial contributions to painting in the Barbizon mode, their experience there may seem irrelevant to this study. The eclectic LaFarge proceeded to a solid reputation as a muralist and stained-glass designer; Wheelwright's enthusiasm was never matched by the spark of real talent; and the James brothers found their calling in the study of the mind and the written word. Still, the Newport period was important for Hunt. The respect he later won in Boston as a fashionable portraitist in the Couture manner was largely a result of several widely acclaimed pictures produced in his New-port studio, the best known of which was a standing figure of the redoubtable Judge Lemuel Shaw executed in 1859 for the Salem courthouse.

Hunt's approach to teaching was formed in New-port, as well. Combined in his methods were the lessons he had learned from Couture and Millet, but, although his instruction would soon enthrall dozens of Boston ladies, it was apparently not so well received in Newport. LaFarge was especially puzzled by Hunt's free-wheeling commentaries, lacking as they did the sort of recipe he expected from a long-time pupil of Couture's.[53] Even more than Hunt, LaFarge was thoroughly a product of French training. As a child, he spoke French fluently and studied French literature in the original. His art teacher in college was a Frenchman and his earliest purchases as a student were prints by Diaz, Barye, and Troyon.[54] Unlike Hunt, who constantly warned against the "onslaught of details" in open-air painting, LaFarge had an early, intense distrust of studio light. Nevertheless, the remarkable series of landscapes that resulted from his stay with Hunt still reflect his mentor's strong preference for flat, simple arrangements of masses, values, and low key color. LaFarge's *Evening Sky, Newport* of 1859, (fig. 23) for example, is a simple mass of grey and brown rocks silhouetted against a pale sky flushed with pink. A sense of place, subject matter, and even scale (it was once called *Mountain Landscape*) is minimized in favor of a direct concern with light and atmosphere and their effect on nature's colors. An anomalous informality presides over this simple work making it appear, in LaFarge's words, "as if it had done itself, and had not been done by an artist."[55]

Both LaFarge and John Bancroft were busily engaged in a study of Chevreul's treatise on the simultaneous contrast of colors,[56] and LaFarge was intrigued as well by the compositional alternatives presented by Japanese prints (which, in a less decorative way, were already a part of Hunt's instructions).

In their humble realism, cyclical study of nature, and scientific study of color, LaFarge's landscapes anticipate by three or four years the early impressionist experiments of Monet and Jongkind in France. In retrospect, he seems almost to have accelerated the Barbizon-to-impressionism sequence soon to evolve in France and later in America. A major hindrance to LaFarge in this regard was undoubtedly Hunt's reticence about painstaking color analysis—a factor that, in its broader implications, would later help to delay the arrival of full-blown impressionism on American shores. An early reaction to the Couture-brown palette of Hunt is provided by LaFarge in his analysis of Hunt's aversion to applied science in art:

[He] thought it useless to carry the refinement of tone and color to the extent which I aimed at in my studies, telling me that there would not be one in five hundred artists capable of appreciating such differences in accuracy—their eyes and training would not be sufficient. . . . This objection seemed to me, as I told him, exactly the reason why I should, for certain aim at these variations from *recipe*.[57]

Hunt fervently believed that harmony of effect had priority over all other technical considerations

Figure 23. John LaFarge. *Evening Sky, Newport,* 1859. Courtesy of Kennedy Galleries, Inc., New York.

in painting. Color was "vulgar" because it was "in the direction of imitation." That Bancroft and LaFarge were already charting a far more challenging course seemed to hold little fascination for their mentor.

As a later eulogist for the Barbizon painters and as a civilizing influence on the progress of the arts in America, LaFarge would eventually become an influential arbiter in the acceptance of Barbizon art in America.[58] Regrettably, whatever contributions he may have made in this area with his own painting were soon deflected by other interests hither and yon, drawing his ever-inquiring mind on toward new and different challenges.

When William Morris Hunt moved out of his Newport retreat in 1862 to take up quarters in the Roxbury section of Boston, he went to surroundings already quite familiar to him.[59] He must have had misgivings then about the future of art in the city for—the contributions of Copley, Stuart, and Allston notwithstanding—the principal arts of Boston had always been literature and bright conversation, with Boston's sturdy, fastidious architecture running a distant third. When the erstwhile landscapist Ben-

[33]

jamin Champney returned to Boston from Paris in 1846, he found things "dull and prosaic. . . . No one seemed to care much for pictures, and those that were hanging in the houses of the rich were mostly so-called 'Old Masters.' If only they had dinginess and plenty of varnish they were satisfactory."[60] There is little reason to believe that prospects for painters were much better in the early sixties. In 1860, the *Boston Transcript* reported that during the entire year local artists had been able to sell only fourteen paintings to Boston collectors, all but two of which sold for less than $100.[61] During the same period, the trustees of the Boston Athenaeum turned down Charles Eliot Norton's request that the collection of James Jackson Jarves —dominated by the work of so-called Italian primitives—be purchased for the modest price of $20,000. Boston's narrow definition of an "Old Master" precluded even this minor effort on behalf of cultural charity.[62]

Boston's niggardliness in art matters was symptomatic of aesthetic barriers, which Hunt and his small band of advocates had to face as well. Boston, like New York, was thoroughly smitten with the forceful precepts of John Ruskin, whose books and lectures were scrutinized by a wide range of the local populace throughout Hunt's tenure as Boston's leading advocate of contemporary French painting. Because Ruskin's theories of truth to nature made almost anyone a critic, the ranks of the art audience grew as never before, filled with what William Dean Howells called "the good folks who get themselves up on Ruskin and try so honestly hard to have some little ideas about art."[63] A large exhibition of modern, mostly Pre-Raphaelite, art from England was shown in Boston and New York in 1857 and, despite an inferior selection of words, received considerable attention in both cities largely because the show was dominated by artists who seemed to embody Ruskin's teachings. Few of the paintings shown demonstrated an interest in pure landscape and, of course, visual attractiveness was downgraded in favor of Ruskin's pictorial sermons.[64]

A more pervasive source of Ruskinian influence

was the plethora of illustrated periodicals that seemed to blossom all over Boston during the 1860s —*Harper's Weekly, Hearth and Home, Our Young Folks,* and other such popular publications. Often illustrated by English artists, their stories were usually heavy on plot and light on inventive treatment, with poetical attractions buried under a thick starch of moral and intellectual stew; in short, a literary complement to Pre-Raphaelite art in America. In addition, Hunt's freewheeling aesthetics had to overcome a Ruskin-inspired determination to make art socially useful. Unfortunately for Hunt, the ranks of his opposition were constantly supplied with new recruits from the Boston school system, which during the sixties taught art according to rules laid down by England's South Kensington Museum, a Ruskinian institute for industrial designers.[65]

Nevertheless, Hunt's newly adopted city offered him several advantages. Boston had always harbored a large number of upper-class intellectuals and businessmen (many, like the collector Martin Brimmer, of French Huguenot extraction) who, as Charles Dickens had noticed during his visit there in 1854, were given to flaunting their capacity for new ideas before their narrow counterparts in New York. Also, Boston had no artistic elite of painters to perpetuate the Ruskinian gospel, a function well served by several National Academy members in New York.

Exhibitions of both international and local art in Boston before the 1870s were—the Athenaeum's British show notwithstanding—usually infrequent and very small. The only regularly scheduled, large shows were the annual exhibitions of the Boston Athenaeum where from 1852 on several of Hunt's paintings were shown to the public. Winkworth Allan Gay, who had visited Barbizon even earlier than Hunt and Babcock, was a more frequent exhibitor than either of these gentlemen, showing mostly views from the environs of Paris, including Fontainebleau.[66] Probably the first Millet painting (owned by Martin Brimmer) to be shown publicly in Boston went on display in 1854 at the Athenaeum;[67] by 1860, three more had been shown. Paintings by Troyon and Diaz were also hung during this period, but on the whole, the Athenaeum exhibitions through the early sixties can best be characterized as essentially road shows for New York artists painting in the more acceptable academic mode.

A less qualified asset for Hunt and contemporary French art in Boston than occasional exposure at the Athenaeum was the city's apparent preference for smaller, more intimate, and less expensive pictures—coupled with a general distaste for the academic "machine." It is true that Church's "Andes of Ecuador" was a much-heralded feature of the Athenaeum show in 1855 (and Hunt's entries were not), but, on the whole, Boston's tastes were less ambitious and showy. This sort of homey preference is best typified by the Bostonian author Samuel Fiske, whose fictional creation Mr. Dunn Browne in 1857 compared the peaks of Switzerland and humble fields of Holland. "After all the ecstasies people go into over the picturesque, romantic, and sublime, give me a good honest Dutch landscape, with some fat cows and a few rows of cabbage in it."[68]

The attitude of Fiske's Mr. Browne is typically utilitarian and, of course, meant to be satirical as well, strongly reminiscent of the earlier satires on Dr. Syntax's search for "The Picturesque." But in the joke lies a large measure of truth. The feeling for sublime vastness, "coming like a blast, bending and leveling everything before it," as Washington Allston described it, must have been alien to the customary responses of Bostonians familiar only with the more insulated vistas of lower New England. At the same time that the aesthetical systems of The Picturesque, The Sublime, and The Beautiful were being transposed into landscape paintings often evoking the optimism of Manifest Destiny, expansion and the opening of the transcontinental railroads were gradually shifting the economic center for the country westward. Foreign and domestic trade was slowly drawn from Boston to New York and points west. All along the Eastern seaboard disillusioned aristocrats withdrew from society, par-

ticularly during the post-Civil War years. Unable to accept their loss of power and prestige and bewildered by the vast, shambling republic with its scandals, corruption, and greed, many of them sought refuge through trans-Atlantic flight to England or France, trying to grope their way back to the old European culture that had sustained them for generations. For many who stayed at home, an art founded on optimistic middle-class tastes—as mid-nineteenth-century painting in America was—must have seemed either outdated or irrelevant. Styles that tend to imitate nature are likely to be associated with "good adjustment," what Wilhelm Worringer called that "happy pantheistic relationship of confidence between man and the phenomena of the external world."[69] The panoramas of Church and his Hudson River school colleagues proclaimed Nature's goodness and promise, their sublime vistas celebrated with typical drama and hope by New England's most famous preacher of the century, William Ellery Channing, in his 1856 "Song of the Open Road."

I inhale great draughts of space,
The east and the west are mine,
    and the north and the south are mine.
I am larger, better than I thought.

Inevitably, as visual ambitions contracted and a species of wistful melancholy displaced the ebullient openness of Channing's "great draughts of space," the scaled-down nature of Barbizon painting would find more favor in Bostonian parlors than in the large drawing rooms and galleries of New York mansions.[70]

No examination of the Barbizon spirit and its parallels in the life of Boston can ignore the most cataclysmic event of the 1860s—the great War between the States. When it began in the spring of 1861, both sides foresaw a short conflict, something along the lines of the Mexican War in duration. Volunteers rushed forth to offer their services in this, the last of our traditional "romantic" wars. Their enthusiasm and that of those who stayed behind was short-lived. As the war dragged on past even the most pessimistic deadlines and only conscription could replace the mounting casualties, the conflict was recorded in all its ugliness and grandeur by the sharp eye of photographers like Mathew Brady and Sam Cooley, as well as by a perceptive group of illustrators—none of whom captured better the monotony of the war's leisurely pace than Boston's own Winslow Homer.

As the tension of the war burned away and demythologized much of the country's idealism, humanitarian ethics were gradually replaced by those of the marketplace. Many ardent reformers who had thrived in Boston found themselves exhausted and forgotten—even the old site for Brook Farm was used as a military encampment during the conflict.[71] Small wonder then that there was surprisingly little demand for art devoted to Civil War subjects when at last the war was ended.

Summarizing the effects of the Civil War on the diverse masses of America during the sixties is a difficult task indeed, and it is no easier to examine critically the possible changes wrought by "this strange, sad, war," as Whitman described it, on so seemingly remote an endeavor as landscape painting. But ignoring for the moment subjective changes in the outlook of the postwar landscapist, it is instructive to note that the same group of Americans who first anticipated the war's dispiriting effect, the intellectual community, also provided Boston with its earliest patrons of Barbizon art.

Modern commentators like Lewis Mumford, Aline Saarinen, and Russell Lynes have developed a stereotype of the tycoon of the Brown Decades, one that has him cramming his gaudy parlors with bric-a-brac and Barbizon paintings encased in fat gilded frames. This stereotype is somewhat misleading in terms of the original patrons of Barbizon art in this country. By way of elaborating on this premise, one has only to consider the backgrounds of some of these early patrons. Most were from the Boston area and took their cue from Hunt. Martin Brimmer, Edward Wheelwright (an art critic for *Atlantic Monthly* during the late 1870s), and, of course, Hunt himself have been mentioned already. All,

though men of means, were more interested in the state of their minds and of the arts than in the state of their fortunes. Another important devotee of Barbizon painting, possibly by the early fifties when he knew Hunt in Paris, was Thomas Gold Appleton (1812–1884), a restless raconteur who was reputed to have crossed the Atlantic forty times before the Civil War.[72] A yachtsman, poet, gourmet, and spiritualist, well known for his witty debates with Dr. Holmes and James Russel Lowell, "Tom" Appleton was a man who "loved all kinds of art and artists, beginning with cooks and ending with Corot and Millet."[73] He had no fixed occupation and found the pursuit of money distasteful, even suggesting in one of his many essays ("Windfalls") that "a gallows placed at either end of Wall Street might be useful."

A generous sharing of his wit and wealth seemed to Appleton to be a more worthy calling than any sort of private enterprise.[74] A fellow collector in Boston, Thomas Wentworth Higginson (1823–1911), was cut from similar cloth, though he was much more of a zealot for social reform (abolition and woman's suffrage especially) than Appleton. A resident of Cambridge much of his life and a classmate of Hunt's at Harvard, Higginson was first a reform minister in Newburyport; later a leader of the first black regiment in the Union Army; and, by the end of the war, an essayist for several magazines, including the *Atlantic Monthly*. An agreeable, graceful writer with a keen perception of man and nature, Higginson's natural history essays contained a definite impulse toward the aesthetic and away from the philosophic or moral appreciation of nature fostered by Emerson's idealism and Thoreau's mystic search for "God in Nature." In his collected essays *Outdoor Papers* published in 1876, Higginson observed that "the direct ethical influence of natural objects may be overrated. Nature is not didactic, but simply healthy." Higginson was only one of several members of his family who began to purchase Barbizon works from Seth Vose in the 1860s and who still have considerable holdings in the Boston area today.[75]

The most conspicuously successful among these early patrons of Barbizon art was Quincy Adams Shaw, a wealthy globetrotter from Boston who probably heard about Millet as early as 1851 from Hunt, his former Harvard classmate. By the time Shaw concluded his purchasing of Millet's works about thirty years later, he had amassed the second largest collection in the world of the Frenchman's *oeuvre*—enough to require an entire gallery in the Museum of Fine Arts in Boston, in which the collection presently resides.[76]

From the above discussion of some of Barbizon's earliest advocates in America, a typical silhouette can be sketched: born in the Boston area in the 1820s with attendance at Harvard in the forties; well read and well traveled (in Europe more so than in his native country); financially sound but not to an extravagant degree; philanthropic towards all forms of the arts; receptive to the missionary advice of Hunt.

An important early exception to this profile was yet another New Englander, George A. Lucas (1824–1909), a civil engineer from New Haven whose first trip to Paris in 1857 led to his permanent residence there. His first love among French artists and undoubtedly the impetus for his consistent patronage of Barbizon art was Antoine Barye, a noted sculptor of animals and occasionally a landscapist around Barbizon.[77] Lucas had introduced Barye to William Walters, a Baltimore railroad magnate and financier whose notable gallery in Baltimore included not only casts of Barye's complete works but a choice collection of Barbizon paintings as well. Walters received much of his best advice from Lucas, as did Samuel Avery in the next decade when that important Barbizon collector turned from his pursuit of American masters to the collecting of French painting. Lucas gave his counsel without fee, and his attraction as a go-between was no less enhanced by the easy entrée he had into the studio of almost every major French painter of the day (Corot and Daubigny called him "mon petit américain").[78]

The loyalty of such collectors to Hunt was un-swerving, and through Hunt extended to dealers in the Boston area (Vose, Doll and Richards, and Williams and Everett) who sold French paintings and paintings in the "French manner," including works by Inness and the many pupils of Couture in the area. In 1867, Clarence Cook struck a rather unfair blow against the Boston group, particularly their leader, in this appraisal of Hunt's popularity:

It is the mere whim of half-cultured rich people, who follow their leader as sheep do, and spend their money for anything they are told to: people who show just what their culture and love of art are really worth by buying Mr. Hunt's pictures, and letting Mr. Jarves' precious collection be scattered to the winds. . . .[79]

Cook's contempt was probably aroused by the second and last show in 1867 of paintings from the collections of the Boston establishment, held under the auspices of the Allston Club founded in the previous year by Hunt, Gay, and yet another Couture pupil, Albion Bocknell. The feature of the Allston Club's first show was the first major work by Gustave Courbet to be bought in this country, *La Curée* (*The Quarry*, fig. 24, now in the Museum of Fine Arts, Boston). Courbet was a conspicuous public figure in France where he was the subject of great scorn and condemnation for both his art and his politics, but there is nothing in *La Curée* to offend even the most hardened tastes of Boston audiences. A highly synthetic work—it is actually several canvases stitched together—it may have seemed to be little more than a large work in the English sporting art tradition, with certain liberties taken in the rather flattened foreground space. The Courbet was announced in a huge 8- by 6-foot banner for the exhibition, a banner that also served to proclaim that here was a show dominated by modern French art collected by artists and patrons from the Boston area. At least seventeen of the works in the first exhibition were by Barbizon painters, making it the largest public display of their work ever shown in Boston.[80] By way of a "manifesto" announcing his support for the Barbizon men and his disdain for those who thought

Figure 24. Gustave Courbet. *La Curée*. Collection:
Museum of Fine Arts, Boston.

but which like the red man, must disappear before the strides of our mighty western civilization . . . it is not worth while to be alarmed about the influence of French art. It would hardly be mortifying if a Millet or a Delacroix should be developed in Boston. It is not our fault that we inherit ignorance in art; but we are not obliged to advertise it.[81]

Successful as occasional, large-scale displays could be in circulating new styles and ideas, Hunt was a far more formidable figure in the less public sectors of Boston's cultural life. He was, almost as much by default as by dint of talent, the city's finest portraitist, probably the best there since Stuart, who had died over a quarter of a century before. As a portrait painter Hunt followed the Couture recipe (although with greater emphasis on informality of pose), but his most effective outlet for propagating the Barbizon faith was through the lessons he began conducting in his Summer Street studio about 1863. Never one to do anything in a half-hearted manner, Hunt, like the French, believed that it was the duty of the recognized artist to teach others. Cajoling, surprising, and berating his students, he pleaded with them to be free, to work from memory rather than from the model only, and to treat their art as a work of love. The large, eager contingents of ladies who made up most of his classes responded with obedience and fervor, but their studio samplings, with few exceptions, must have demonstrated to their master that freedom is more creative in the finding than in the seeking.[82]

The principal flaw in Hunt's teaching was simply that, although he himself had the benefit of over twenty years of training and keen observation, he allowed his students to become—as one critic put it—"intentionists" who produced improvisations characterized by good intentions rather than technical power.[83]

Hunt's studio instrument was charcoal, a medium he had first learned to use in Couture's classes, acquiring a veritable reverence for its effectiveness after his studies with Millet (figs. 25, 26). Quick,

their work a futile effort, Hunt wrote a letter a few years later to the editor of the *Boston Advertiser* in reply to a Harvard professor who severely criticized the predominance of French art in Boston shows. The following excerpts from this significant apologia demonstrate that Hunt fully expected French art to have a salutary effect on the future of American painting and not be a shrine unto itself.

The standard of art education is indeed carried to a dizzy height in Harvard University when such men as Jean-François Millet are ranked as triflers. A public exhibition of *art work* of the gentlemen educated in this advanced school (if the fruit answers the expectations of the tree) would make the university notion of art more clear to the world, and be of service to those of us whose early advantages in art study were necessarily limited by the incapacity of such teachers as Millet and other well known names of his nationality, —a nationality which has always held high rank in art, summary, almost "democratic" in its accessibility to all, charcoal was essentially an expressionist medium and thus complemented Hunt's theories. Because it was particularly valuable in works done from memory, where "so much is forgotten," Hunt wanted his students to transfer the same technique used in charcoal drawing to oil painting, an adaptation already perfected by Couture and some of the Barbizon painters (Millet, Daubigny, and Rousseau in his later works). An interesting insight into the obvious relationships between the appearance of Hunt's paintings and the effects of charcoal drawing is indicated, for example, in an observation by James Jackson Jarves, who found the former's portraits "vaporous, diaphanous, and unpronounced in outline, in fact, too unsubstantial, but singularly clear, broad, and effective, nothing little or forced."[84] Hardly the Ruskinian advocate that Jarves was, Hunt told his students to look at their subject "through half-shut eye-lids"—a studio variation of the procedure formerly used by students of nature who had relied on the so-called "Claude glass" to tame the discordant demands of nature's endless detail.

Most of Hunt's pupils were women with time on their hands and money to spend on paintings recommended by Hunt. He also had a few male pupils. One was a painter of animal subjects, Frank Rogers, who achieved a measure of notoriety by posing his dog "in a steady position for ten to fifteen minutes."[85] None of Hunt's students made much of a mark on the art of the period, but Hunt's munificence towards younger painters in Boston was of considerable importance in establishing the city as a center for contemporary painting in the French manner. When J. Foxcroft Cole (1837–1892), a native of Maine and a student of Lambinet in Normandy, arrived in Boston in 1863, Hunt quickly bought four of his paintings and, according to Helen Knowlton, took "a lively interest in his work."[86] Cole was sufficiently encouraged to go back to France, where he studied with Jacques at Barbizon from 1865 to 1867. Jarves, another strong supporter of this now forgotten painter, claimed that Cole's

painting "gives to landscape its long needed poetical, sympathetical element, expressed chiefly in delicate gradations of color, and quiet slumberous

Figure 25. William Morris Hunt. *Untitled.* Anonymous collection.

Figure 26. Jean-François Millet. *Farmyard by Moonlight,* 1868, cat. no. 9.

Figure 27. J. Foxcroft Cole. *A Normandy Pastoral: Near Honfleur,*
1875. Collection: Museum of Fine Arts, Boston; gift by
subscription and Everett Lund.

distances, indicative of the mysterious tenderness and repose of nature."[87]

Cole's mature work is primarily composed of landscapes with cows, the latter increasing in proportionate size and importance after his study with Jacques. One of the finest of his works in this idiom, painted in his typical buttery manner, is *A Normandy Pastoral Near Honfleur* (1875, fig. 27). Delicately balanced throughout the ground level by an interlacing of diagonals, it demonstrates at least a second-hand acquaintance with Dutch landscapes, perhaps through Troyon, who launched his own career as a painter of animals on the same Normandy fields in 1852 (fig. 28). Unlike Troyon and Hunt, however, Cole was usually content to paint in a lighter mood, with summery greens and yellows undaunted by cloudy skies, the sort of persistent pleasantness that stamps his works, irrevocably perhaps, as lightweight clichés.

Another artist befriended by Hunt in the sixties, Thomas H. Robinson (1835–1888), was also a specialist in landscapes with animals, with greater emphasis given to the latter—usually oxen, cows, or the smaller domestic animals. His *Oxen Ploughing* (fig. 29) is a typical example of Robinson's true interests. Dark, burly beasts dominate the picture space with their methodical indifference while an insignificant, poorly drawn farmer seems but an afterthought in the composition. Even the landscape is barren and understated, a mere track of mud for the oxen's sullen performance.

Robinson's work was included in the Allston Club exhibitions at Hunt's behest, but rarely was much money realized from its sale. He is, in fact, a more interesting figure in his role of agent in Europe for the art dealer Vose in Providence, and later for the St. Botolph's Club in Boston. He was also a busy intermediary in Paris for Hunt's legion of collector-friends.[88] An ingratiating fellow with a perceptive eye for salable art, Robinson was dubbed "sailor" by Corot because of his frequent trips abroad. In France, this eager Bostonian had ready access to the studios of Courbet, Delacroix, and almost all of the Barbizon painters.

Figure 28. Constant Troyon. *Pasture in Normandy*, 1852, cat. no. 14.

Figure 29. Thomas H. Robinson. *Oxen Ploughing*, cat. no. 78.

3. Critics and Patrons in America Before the Centennial

The earliest breakthroughs to America's eventual welcome of the "modern" French landscape were a small series of events that accomplished little more than to put a few dents in the armor of public and private ignorance. William Morris Hunt's early efforts in Newport and Boston, as outlined in the previous chapter, broke important ground to be sure, but even these first tentative steps toward acceptance could not claim a broad base of support.

By 1850, the landscapes executed in Italy by Claude Lorraine and Nicolas Poussin two centuries before were well known and admired among the small elite of painters and patrons in America. With the exception of Diaz and Tryon, however, the contemporary French artists who labored in Fontainebleau and the nearby provinces were virtually unknown, even to such Hudson River painters as John Kensett and Jasper Cropsey, who themselves had visited Fontainebleau in the late 1840s.[1] Since the Barbizon painters were largely ignored in their own country until about the same time, it is hardly surprising that awareness of their work by American critics and artists was equally limited.

The diverse and interrelated reasons for the generally conservative reaction of Americans to French art—indeed, to contemporary European art as a whole—is a study in itself, having much to do with national ignorance, indifference, and the prevailing feeling that a work of art should be, after all, *work*. French "slovenliness" (when found outside the Academy circle, of course) carried the taint of sloppy craftsmanship and lack of patience. Against this background of preferred principles and beauty of common consent, French art and Barbizon painting in particular would be judged by mid-nineteenth-century Americans. Not unexpectedly, the painterly bravura of Couture and the landscapists from Fontainebleau was often characterized as too "materialistic"; that is, too attentive to originality and style for its own sake. A leader in the American attack on Barbizon painting was a highly influential periodical, *The Crayon*, published by a group of Ruskinian disciples from 1855 to 1861. An early article entitled "Originality" singled out Rousseau, Diaz, and Dupré for extraordinary ridicule:

Messrs. Dupré and Rousseau paint by means of a singular sprinkling of little spots, as if they were workers in mosaics. They, of course, achieve a wonderful success. M. Diaz, if we may use a vulgar expression, "chucks" his pallet against his canvas, and adroitly takes advantage of the stain thus produced. Up goes the shout again, 'A new style of painting.'[2]

A reviewer of the Boston Athenaeum exhibition held during the summer of 1855 singles out work by Hunt (probably *The Fortune Teller*, now in the Boston Museum of Fine Arts) as being painted "in the morbid manner, so popular in France" and mentions an "earnest, though affectedly feeble peasant group" by Millet.[3] The feature of this show was Frederic Church's newly famous panorama *The

Andes of Equador, which must have made the Millet-inspired simplicity and low-key palette of Hunt's painting look "morbid" indeed.

For *The Crayon,* landscape meant American nature, and the periodical's nationalistic spirit surfaced whenever Hunt and his fellow students in France were suspected of selling their birthright for an imported style. Yet, seeing Barbizon and Barbizon-related paintings in the limited context of the Athenaeum galleries was quite different from seeing the sort of full-scale "retrospective" provided by the Paris exposition of 1855. Here, a reviewer for *The Crayon* was afforded the opportunity to see what mediocre French painting was really like (there were some 6,400 works in the show, more than a thousand of them French). In so large a display, even a Diaz seemed "beautiful in tone" and while Rousseau presented obvious difficulties, the critic was not dismayed by them: "They [Rousseau's paintings] are like photographs or like scenes seen in a dark mirror . . . he seems perfectly indifferent about his choice of subject matter but he endues everything with quiet poetic sentiment. No one labors harder and more conscientiously."[4] Only Corot ("cold and unreal") receives a failing grade, despite the fact that along with Troyon and Rousseau, he had won a first-class medal.

In June of 1856, *The Crayon* published a lengthy summation of the prevailing critical attitude toward nature painting in France. Titled simply "French Landscape" and written by poet-painter Christopher Cranch, it abounds in the clichés about French art already familiar to *Crayon* readers. Nonetheless, Cranch's treatment of the subject is unique at this time because it was written from the viewpoint of an important seer of American transcendentalism who was also a minor Hudson River school painter. Cranch shared the transcendentalists' emphasis on the organic, as well as their conviction that the creative act and the critical act were inseparable— a statute they shared with Ruskin. With this in mind, one can better understand why Corot is cited as an example of how "the French landscapists fail when they endeavor to go beyond mere literal meaning of Nature and enter the realm of ideal landscape." Whereas the American landscapist, Thomas Cole, was a "poet on canvas," Corot was only a "ghost of what a poet should be . . . leaden, colorless." Cole's avidly romantic selection of subject matter and expressive color was still, eight years after his death, the standard by which truly romantic painting was judged. Cranch would assume a different stance later in his career, and his concluding remark here is substantially at odds with current opinion: "Their works make you say 'this is Nature—this is truthful' rather than 'this is poetic and suggestive.'"[5]

The sentiments expressed by Cranch, William Stillman, John Durand, and other contributors to *The Crayon* were more informative than most of the early criticism available in local newspapers or periodicals like *The North American Review* or *Sartain's Union Magazine,* but were still not far from the mid-nineteenth-century norm. In most cases, critics were most easily impressed by a painting's representational qualities and/or its evocative potential, i.e., grandeur of conception. With the early exception of John Neal, the Philadelphia critic, who preferred "bold, unlabored effects" in painting, "an off-hand free sketchy style, with high finish" like that of Gilbert Stuart,[6] most artists and critics agreed that expressive content geared to ingratiating subject matter was more important than formal qualities. When the latter were considered, they usually inspired comments on correct enframement of figures or objects, true perspective, and so forth.

The aesthetical systems of the English perfected in the late eighteenth century, decades before they were embellished by Ruskin, were the standard referents of the American critic and for many painters as well. The books on such pictorial ideals as The Sublime, The Beautiful, and The Picturesque, written by men like Burke, Knight, Price, and Gilpin, and the associational psychology of Archibald Alison (whose *Essays on Beauty* was a favorite of Thomas Cole's) convinced their readers that however unruly raw nature could be, a systematic mode of picture-making could solicit a response in the viewer that was appropriate to the scene depicted. In France and Italy, painters like Claude, the Poussins, and Salvator Rosa had practiced the aesthetics of The Picturesque long before they were systematized by the English, and by about 1840 the Barbizon artists had developed a form of romantic naturalism that successfully disguised precepts of landscape organization—though they were by no means eliminated. The usual response of American critics with a strong bias against the more informal trends in picture organization or paint handling was to deplore "French license" when they were confronted with these new methods and techniques. Neither *The Crayon* nor any other organ of the period can be said, however, to have maintained an exclusively anti-French bias.[7] For example, the *Bulletin of the American Art-Union*, until its demise in 1851, defended American painting against French encroachment largely for nationalistic reasons occasioned by the threat of Goupil's imports into New York.[8] It also criticized the "lascivious" character of French academic paintings, but at the same time, in a highly unusual article printed in the issue for November 1849, it could offer grudging praise for the glittering technique of Diaz:

Diaz . . . looks at what is constantly in operation before him—the principles of nature. Shade is in itself a picture. . . . He sees everything in the external world in reference to its color. . . . Diaz gives himself up to the color for color's sake . . . he aims alike in all subjects to realize the subtle beauties of color as they are developed through the influence of light in the rarer or the more commonplace in Nature.[9]

Horace Greeley's *New York Tribune*, which by the early 1860s would feature the pointedly anti-French polemics of Clarence Cook, also supplied during the fifties many anonymous reviews—mostly by George William Curtis, an editor for *Harper's Monthly*—that took on William Morris Hunt and his "morbid French manner" as a prime target. A Hunt painting called *Girl and Rabbit*

(present whereabouts unknown), included in the National Academy show for 1856, elicited from the *Tribune* reviewer a report that in this painting Hunt had carried his French style "to its extreme":

. . . it would be difficult to conceive of anything more thoroughly repulsive and disagreeable on canvas. The girl does not look like a girl, nor the rabbit like a rabbit. The picture looks as though it were in the last stages of decomposition. It is perversely and designedly bad—as bad a thing as a man of talent could possibly accomplish with his brush.[10]

Despite these and other setbacks in the critical arena, Hunt could take solace from the slowly growing respectability of Barbizon art during the 1850s and the important role that he and his Boston comrades had played in this development. Nevertheless, their word-of-mouth proselytizing and occasional purchases were the major evidence of American patronage of Barbizon art during the fifties, and only one private dealer in New England, Seth M. Vose of Providence, Rhode Island, had the foresight to invest on a large scale in Barbizon painting. Vose was a former clerk who took over his father's art shop in 1850, selling prints, artists' supplies, and occasionally a few paintings to the limited clientele in Providence. It is difficult to determine the actual extent of Vose's first attempts to sell modern French painting: however, his overall commitment was apparently made early and was quite substantial. According to his son, Seth Vose imported his first Corots in 1852 and his first Troyons in 1854. By 1857, he also had works by Millet, Dupré, Daubigny, and Rousseau.[11]

Vose's first speculations must have been considered audacious, even suspicious, by those aware of them—particularly by the auctioneers in New York, where many of the first Barbizon paintings to arrive in this country were collected. A report of one of Vose's visits to a New York sale mentions this remark made by a seller when he came across one of Vose's favorites: "Here, where's that Boston man? Here's another of them what-d'call-'ems of yours."[12]

At first, Vose would ask friends to come to his shop to admire the work of the Barbizon men, especially the paintings of Corot, for whom he had a special fondness. He later recalled to Clarence Cook that "they came, but they laughed so at my pictures and made such fun of my taste that I took all of the Corots down and put them away, and did not show them again for a long while, except to those who asked particularly to see them."[13] Of the few who came specifically to see his French paintings, most were from the Boston area. One of the earliest arrivals was William Morris Hunt, who, while at Newport during the late fifties, happened by to purchase some artists' supplies. By accident, he parted the curtains and entered the gallery in the rear of the store where Vose "hid" his Barbizon paintings. Hunt's discovery was of profound importance both for himself and for Vose. He had discovered a dealer who could secure Barbizon works for him and his many acquaintances, and Vose himself was sufficiently encouraged by about 1860 to open private exhibition rooms on Washington Street in Boston (he also retained his Providence gallery until 1897, at which time he moved permanently to Boston). (Fig. 30.)[14]

While Vose, Hunt, and several Bostonians were making friends and finding purchasers for Barbizon art, the art market in New England during the mid-century was by no means imbued with the competitive heat that characterized similar pursuits in New York City. While the modern French school made considerable inroads into the taste of New Yorkers during this period, a succession of financial crises militated against purchases of all but the "safest" Frenchmen, such as Meissonier, Sheffer, and other members of the academic elite in Paris. There are no records from the 1850s to indicate that the general public in New York had any opportunity to view large concentrations of Barbizon paintings, although there were a few noteworthy events where persons with sharp eyes could seek out small collections. A major example of such an event was the large showing—110 paintings and drawings— of the collection of the Honorable August Belmont,

Figure 30. Photograph of the S.M. Vose Gallery, Providence, Rhode Island, ca. 1880.

a former minister to The Netherlands, held in the galleries of the National Academy of Design during the winter of 1857–1858. "Do not fail to see it" warned the reviewer for *The Crayon*, extolling with uncharacteristic enthusiasm the French works in the show. French art, he wrote, "comes to us from a land where Art is beyond price: where money fails to tempt Art from the hands of comparative poverty . . . where artists have represented the people."[15] Predictably—for this time and place at least—the artists of "the people" were found to be romantic painters of animals and figures, such as Horace Vernet, Rosa Bonheur, and Meissonier. The small representation of Barbizon painters (two Jacques, two Troyons, and a Rousseau) were ignored by both *The Crayon* reporter and, it may be assumed, the general public.

The kind of international potpourri of Belgian, Dutch, German, and French art offered by the Belmont Collection may have been unique for the time inasmuch as it represented the private holdings of a single, major collector. Its diversity, however, was quite typical of the many displays of imported paintings shown in New York during the fifties. The two principal purveyors of French art in the city were the Paris-based firm of Goupil and Company and the auctioneers at Leeds and Company. Neither dealer managed to provide more than a limited exposure of Barbizon paintings, and that only because the school's smaller works or "studies" could fulfill the growing demand for relatively cheap cabinet pieces—"fancy, fine, little pictures" as one of Goupil's catalogs of 1858 described them, referring to three landscapes by Dupré.[16]

Given the bias in favor of paintings that qualified as cabinet pieces in terms of their size and sentiment, it is not surprising that several of Diaz's rococo figure pieces were praised by dealers and sold on the New York market while his less decorative, Rousseauesque landscapes were rare items indeed.[17] The most popular painter at Goupil's, the one who most closely approximated in his landscapes the simplicity and directness of Barbizon, was undoubtedly the Normandy painter Émile Charles Lambinet (1815–1877), whose restrained, lyrical renderings of the French countryside were available in large numbers and at very reasonable prices (averaging about $120 each). When Goupil and Company put its entire Flemish and French holdings on display in February 1861, no less than ten of the paintings exhibited were by Lambinet. They ranged in price from $70 to $212.[18]

Lambinet's favorite subject, the fields along the upper Seine, usually painted in a restricted, cool palette of middle grays and blues with deep greens (see fig. 31), may well have eased the route to later success in America for Corot and Daubigny, just as the silvery, vaporous landscapes of the Hudson River painter Thomas Doughty would later remind many Americans of the late style of Corot.[19]

In addition to the rise of dealers in foreign art, the favorable climate for sales of foreign works of art that was to prevail in New York during the later decades of the nineteenth century was anticipated, to a large extent, by three major occurrences in the 1850s: the demise of the American Art-Union in 1852, which robbed native artists of one of their most successful markets; the increasing acceptance of works by contemporary foreign painters, a trend already begun by the late 1820s;[20] and the steady rise of the profit motive in ascribing *value* to works of art, a development that worked against all but a few American painters. Several financial depressions, particularly the disastrous "Crash of '57," kept the general activity of the marketplace more subdued than it might have been,[21] despite the presence in New York of America's wealthiest men, including John Astor, Cornelius Vanderbilt, and William Aspinwall. As the new millionaires began to feel that their fortunes were secure enough to allow them to pursue art without restraint, however, the whole tenor of eastern patronage was to change from a cautious plodding among "secure items" to a frenetic scramble for art and art objects from all over the globe. Despite its humble beginnings in America, Barbizon art would soon be a principal benefactor of this country's first "art rush."

Figure 31. Émile Charles Lambinet. *Landscape with Hayrick and Buildings.* Collection: National Academy of Design, New York. Photograph, Frick Art Reference Library, New York.

4. The Sixties at Home and Abroad

Whether the Barbizon example was important or merely peripheral to the art of Inness and his luminist contemporaries in America, their exposure to and admiration for French landscapes probably seemed more daring when first they came upon them. During the fifties, as we have already seen, national pride and a general suspicion toward French style tended to bias the taste of the aspiring artist as well as that of his public. During the sixties, however, the success of the French teaching methods at the École des Beaux-Arts as well as at several of the more informal centers around Paris lured ever-increasing numbers of young Americans across the Atlantic. The variety of instruction available, augmented by the treasured examples from the past in the Louvre, undoubtedly bewildered many of these young students, most of whom were even less prepared for the struggles ahead than were their predecessors.

In addition to the advice available from the Barbizon painters, another art colony at Écouen, led by the sentimental genre painter Edouard Frére, accommodated such Americans as J. Wells Champney, George Boughton, Henry Bacon, and James Thom.[1] By the mid-1860s, Brittany also became a major "resort" for American painters, although among its more ardent visitors only two New Yorkers—F. A. Bridgman and William Picknell—achieved any measure of success.[2]

Barbizon was a far less comfortable place to visit than Écouen or Brittany, though it was at least a frequent "watering hole" for several Yankee travelers of the period. For most of these, the trip was as much a pilgrimage to sites hallowed by the work of the by-now famous "Men of 1830" as it was a summer respite from the academic routine in Paris. Some, like J. F. Cole, William Haseltine of Philadelphia, and Albion Bicknell from Boston, cultivated many friendships among the Barbizon painters in Paris and admired their exhibited work there or in Luxembourg, while they yet remained true to a safer, more traditional view of landscape painting.[3] A most unique visit by an American "pilgrim" was made in the winter of 1860 by William Stillman, formerly an ardent disciple of Ruskin and the first editor of *The Crayon*. In February 1861, Stillman wrote to Charles Eliot Norton this significant confession of past errors and present delights:

I have studied the French painters hard this winter especially Rousseau who has taken quite an interest in me and treated me like a pupil as does Troyon. . . . I am learning what color is and how to get it and you will I believe find me much improved both in color and aerial qualities. I regret now my last year's experience, my study in England and my summer with Ruskin. The English artists know almost nothing of the art of painting and Ruskin I am sure is principally and fundamentally wrong on all practical questions and his advice and direction the worst things a young artist can have. . . .[4]

Another visit, a brief one made by an artist who had no sympathy for French art, was that of Thomas

Moran (1841–1921), an English-born landscapist then residing in New York, who went to see Corot in the fall of 1866. Later, in 1889, he noted that he found the elderly Frenchman painting at a rate of three a day "those gray pictures that you see in every American auction." Moran's relentless pursuit of the grand effect may have wavered slightly when Corot confided to him: "When I was painting good pictures, nobody would have them, but now that my eyes are poor I can't seem to paint enough."[5]

However frequent these visits to Barbizon may have been, a general survey of the work of most Americans who went there indicates that they were either indifferent to, or unaware of, the struggles of those younger landscapists in France later dubbed the *impressionistes*. The possibilities for contact were there inasmuch as Monet, Renoir, Bazille, and Sisley all worked at Chailly near Fontainebleau between 1863 and 1867.[6] In addition to this chance proximity, Daubigny and Corot—especially the former—were frequent defenders of the new group by 1866. Their presence on the Salon jury of that year helped gain acceptance for Sisley, Bazille, Pissarro, and Morisot—the last two former pupils of Corot's.

The first group exhibitions in Paris of the impressionists did not take place until 1874; during the sixties, almost none of the American travelers in Paris chose to stray far enough from the mainstream to cope with the puzzling works of these young men—not to mention the far more difficult challenges posed by Manet or the young Cezanne. Mary Cassatt, who arrived from Boston in 1866, is a well-known exception, although only her role as a go-between for several Barbizon paintings sent to the United States in later years need concern us here. One other exception, and a figure closer to painting in the Barbizon manner, is a little-known artist from Boston, Mark Fischer (1841–1923). After some lessons from Inness, Fischer arrived at Gleyre's studio in 1861, a year before Monet, Renoir, and Sisley attended the same class.

Fischer may well have visited Fontainebleau after Monet exalted its charms to his fellow pupils at Gleyre's. At any rate, after 1872 Fischer was in London, where his competent brand of the new technique (fig. 32)—fresh and vibrant but somehow unexceptional—was so successful that he spent the rest of his life there.[7]

One inescapable aspect of Fischer's work in respect to his training with Inness is its complete lack of his mentor's sense of drama. Fischer's essential optimism and joyous palette are symptomatic of a fundamental difference between Inness and the Barbizon painters on the one hand, and the impressionists on the other. Monet's use of Fontainebleau as a picnic backdrop for *Dejeuner sur l'herbe* was a prophetic gesture for French landscape in the mid-1860s, a throwback to the fetes of the eighteenth century that all but Corot and Diaz among the Barbizon painters would assiduously avoid. Fischer's sweet and sunny views partake of this return to a more festive mood.

Fischer's future teacher, George Inness, decided in 1860 to leave New York for New England.[8] Unlike William Morris Hunt, whose studio was then in the heart of Boston, Inness opted for the quiet seclusion of Medfield, Massachusetts, a rural village a few miles outside of Boston. An epileptic for most of his life, Inness's condition had apparently

Figure 32. Mark Fischer. *Boys Bathing.*
Anonymous collection.

[48]

Figure 33. George Inness. *Christmas Eve*, 1866, cat. no. 52.

worsened in 1859 and, while his stay in Medfield lasted only about three years, it brought him the sort of physical and emotional relief he constantly sought throughout his career, away from the crowded pressures of the New York art world. The motifs he employed with greater frequency than ever in his Medfield landscapes—small, solitary figures and winding streams and paths that seem to lead nowhere in particular—were effective surrogates for his own search for escape through nature (fig. 33).[9]

As his acceptance of his high-strung personality grew stronger, so too did Inness's paintings. The promise of new conviction and maturity in *Clearing Up* was sustained throughout the sixties, interrupted only by occasional lapses into his "old-master" formulas.[10] Critical acclaim began to come his way in a degree heretofore unknown to the artist at the same time that his feelings toward his art turned increasingly inward, to content more than form. Inness's field of vision, however, remained essentially panoramic in scope and he used his major landscapes during the sixties to declare manifest hope and promise, reflecting his firm belief that all would be set right with America after the bitter experience of the Civil War had passed away.[11] The iconographic trappings of the previous decade were dispensed with, and, in their place he created a

Figure 34. George Inness. *Peace and Plenty,* 1865. Collection: The Metropolitan Museum of Art; gift of George Hearn, 1894.

private Eden from an assemblage of idea and actuality that went far beyond simple pastoral pleasantries. For example, a large scene in the Franconia region of the White Mountains entitled *Sign of Promise* (1862, now destroyed) was described in the November 20, 1863, issue of the *New York Post* as "a commingling of vaporous clouds and azure sky, murmuring stream and quiet meadow, field and forest, hills and mountains, and over all the rainbow of hope, following the storm, gives glorious promise of peace and joy to come." With minor variations, this inventory of effects could serve to describe dozens of landscapes by Inness from the Civil War period, including *The Light Triumphant* of 1862 (present whereabouts unknown),[12] *A Passing Shower* (1860, Hall Foundation, Canajoharie, New York), and Inness's most famous work, *Peace and Plenty,* painted over *Sign of Promise* in 1865 and now in the Metropolitan Museum of Art in New York (fig. 34).

Painted shortly after the close of the Civil War, *Peace and Plenty* has been reproduced so often that it has become, like Constable's *Hay Wain,* a hackneyed metaphor for pastoral escape. Such a judgment does a disservice to one of Inness's most successful classically conceived compositions, a work that amply demonstrates how far he had come in his distillation of Barbizon art. Surely, the peculiarly American sense of site and scope in *Peace and Plenty* has no resounding parallel in the Barbizon repertoire; only the remarkable control of tonal values in the fading golden light of the sunset and the muted yellows and greens of the trees and hill, suggesting a remembrance of certain late works of Rousseau, could indicate otherwise. In fact, the warm glow of the vanishing sun, capable of evoking promise and sadness, strongly recalls the description of a Rousseau evening scene that Henry James saw in Boston a few years later. "It is not an American sunset, with its lucid and untempered splendour of orange and scarlet, but the sinking of a serious old-world day, which sings its death-song in a muffled key."[13]

Inness's preference for manipulating light for romantic, moralizing purposes places his mature works closer not only to those of Barbizon painters like Rousseau and Millet, but also to earlier American landscapes painted by Thomas Cole and Asher Durand. In this regard Inness differs significantly from his pre-impressionist contemporaries in America—men like John Kensett, Martin Johnson Heade, Fitz Hugh Lane, and Sanford Gifford—who form the nucleus of what some American art historians now describe as the luminist phenomenon in American landscape painting. Because the American luminists and Inness have been credited, for varying reasons and to varying degrees, with preparing the way for the advent of impressionist painting in America, it is particularly instructive at this juncture to compare a few representative examples from the period in order to appreciate more fully the alternatives to Inness and the Barbizon method.

A close study of Inness's *Peace and Plenty* and Heade's *Salt Marshes, Newport, Rhode Island* of about 1863 (fig. 35) demonstrates Inness's willingness to maintain the rugged, Rousseauesque qualities of his original "impression" in the studio work while Heade's rather hesitant painterliness still adheres to the surface of the canvas, altering neither the basic shapes of his forms nor the luminist space that surrounds them. Although the origins of the ever-wandering Heade's very personal style are difficult to establish, the mathematical precision of his receding planes and the exacting way that light and shade delineate them suggest a close study of classical landscapes as well as the more topographical "romances" of the Dutch, in particular those of Ruysdael and Van Goyen.

Both Heade and John Frederick Kensett have been the worthy recipients of recent large-scale retrospective exhibitions. A reviewer of the Kensett show at the Whitney Museum noted in bewilderment something of the mystery of the artist's lyrical vision, which he admitted was "hard to talk about

Figure 35. Martin Johnson Heade. *Salt Marshes, Newport, Rhode Island,* ca. 1863. Collection: Museum of Fine Arts, Boston.

Figure 36. John Frederick Kensett. *Shrewsbury River,* 1859. Collection: The New-York Historical Society, New York.

because it isn't either linear or painterly, it's just clear."[14] Indeed, the haunting stillness of one of the most popular works from that show, Kensett's *Shrewsbury River* of 1859 (fig. 36) seems almost to apply the processes of elimination to nature that so-called minimal art presents today. Unlike Inness and Heade, Kensett's penchant for compositional understatement and his avoidance of strongly asser-

[51]

tive natural forms allowed precision and delicacy to act as foils for breadth and space. The resulting finish was a sort of metallic gloss that makes even Heade seem by comparison to be a *bravura* technician. For Kensett, who did not try to grow within a coloristic tradition, color meant value rather than hue and did not demand the analysis undertaken by LaFarge at Newport or the symbolic intensity developed by Inness. In this respect, the approach of Kensett seems to parallel much of the stress on value in Hunt's studios, and, to a limited extent, the tonalist renderings of the young Corot and his older contemporaries of the 1820s in France.[15]

Of all the second-generation members of the Hudson River school who in their maturity turned to painting in a manifestly luminist mode, Sanford Gifford (1823–1880) would seem to be the one with the greatest opportunity to adopt a compromise based on exposure to Barbizon intimacy and painterliness. Gifford spent his early career painting romantic dramas modeled on those of Thomas Cole, but his attitude toward the role of nature in his art began to change in 1855 when he visited Paris and the Exposition Universelle. Impressed with the work of Troyon and even more so of Rousseau, he wrote in his *Journals* one of the earliest eulogies of Barbizon painting by a New York-based artist:

In the French landscape everything like finish and elaboration of detail is sacrificed to the unity of the effect to be produced. Every "prettiness" of execution is ignored utterly. Nothing is allowed to interfere with that unity. . . . The subjects are mostly of the simplest and most meager description; but by the remarkable truth of color and tone, joined to a poetic perception of the beauty of common things, they are made beautiful.[16]

Gifford, however, was no rebellious spirit and, despite a trip to Barbizon in May 1856,[17] chose to translate his intense love of light effects in a lengthy series of pictorial essays that might best be described as simplicity of effect on a grand scale. *In The Wilderness* of 1860 (fig. 37), one of his most successful efforts in the "luminist" mode, amply exhibits just what "unity of effect" meant for Gifford.

He certainly knew that it was a concept articulated and approved by most of the major landscapists of the century, though one far easier to talk about than to realize in practice. Gifford chose to concentrate not so much on light's effect on natural objects as on "the veil or medium through which we see it."[18] The color of the sky, in the case of *In The Wilderness* a pinkish orange, is not only the keynote of the picture, it almost *is* the picture. Barbizon art provided nothing more than technical reinforcement for Gifford's "veil" paintings. His keen sense of finish throughout—Corot's "slovenliness" offended him—shows how difficult it was for Gifford to shed traditional restraint. Still, at a critical turning point in his development, Gifford learned from Barbizon art, as apparently he could not learn from Cole or from English art, the value of subtlety for its own sake, of a new idealism based more on essentially abstract problems and less on shopworn precepts governing compositional rules and worthy intentions.

With Inness remaining home throughout the sixties, the only American in Paris during this decade who would prove to be a major contributor to the future development of American landscape painting was Winslow Homer (1836–1910). There is no evidence to show that Homer sought any instruction in Paris beyond what he could glean from his wanderings through the International Exposition of 1867—where he had two of his paintings on display, including his famous *Prisoners At The Front*—and trips to local museums and galleries. For European critics, Homer's work had a uniquely American flavor to it, in part because, as his biographer Albert Gardner expressed it, "so many other Americans were practicing in the currently fashionable French, misty manner."[19] As far as this observation goes the critics were right, for Homer's sense of narrative and the sharp lucidity of his light and line were not salient Barbizon characteristics. Yet, Homer did number among his few close friends several admirers of Barbizon painting. Bostonian J. F. Cole was Homer's fellow worker at Buford's printing firm in 1855 and his

Figure 37. Sanford R. Gifford. *In the Wilderness*, 1860. Collection:
The Toledo Museum of Art; Gift of Florence Scott Libbey, 1951.

frequent companion in Paris and Normandy as well. During the early sixties, Homer's fellow lodgers in the Studio Building in New York included such admirers of Corot as Homer Martin, John LaFarge, and Charlotte Coman ("famous in her day for her skill in painting landscapes in the silvery gray manner of Corot.")[20] Another acquaintance from his early days in Boston as well as from the Studio Building in New York was Alfred C. Howland (1838–1909), a pupil at Düsseldorf who later became friendly with Corot, Rousseau, and Millet.[21]

From his secondhand exposure to Barbizon ideals, Homer may have derived his interest in peasant subjects while in France, as well as his broad, summary touch in several farm scenes painted during the seventies (fig. 38). Any discussion of Homer's alleged borrowings from French art, however, must perforce assign equal credit to impulses within this inscrutable Yankee that render any foreign affinity in his art more instinctive than imitative. This is particularly apparent in the more intriguing parallels in Homer's paintings to Japanese prints, the impressionist vision, or the works of Manet and Courbet, whose one-man shows at the fairgrounds

he may well have attended in 1867.[22] Nevertheless, as the earlier reference to some of Homer's early acquaintances indicates, his knowledge of Barbizon art was probably more fully formed than that of any other. The Athenaeum exhibitions that included Millet are reflected in many illustrations from *Harper's* and *Every Saturday* in the early sixties, although Homer's *Girl with a Pitchfork* (cat. no. 44) suggests something more akin to the frank naturalism of Courbet. Homer himself offers us only his paintings to unravel the puzzle, and somehow it seems inappropriate to the vigor and directness of his work to approach them as historical mysteries. In fact, it was to his friend, the Francophile J. F. Cole, that Homer offered his famous dictum, "If you want to be an artist, never look at paintings."

Homer did look, however, and he learned more than he cared to admit. Unlike his American compatriots in France at the time (including Thomas Eakins, who saw more in Spanish and Dutch art than in the art he studied during his French training), Homer found confirmation rather than discovery in the paintings to which he was exposed. As one Frenchman recently described Homer's sojourn in France, "Homer crossed Paris with a

Figure 38. Winslow Homer. *Two Girls with Sunbonnets in Field,* ca. 1877.
Collection: Cooper-Hewitt Museum of Decorative Arts & Design, New York.

finger on his lips . . . that is why he used his eyes all
the better, studied more closely, and felt and understood all the more deeply."[23]

Not even the aloof Homer could have failed to
see that the crucial years of 1866 and 1867 represented the apogee of Barbizon popularity in France.
While Émile Zola mocked the shortsighted juries
who rejected Manet and his impressionist friends,
all of the Barbizon artists were copiously represented
at the International Exposition and at the Salons.
Troyon was given a large retrospective show in
Paris in 1866, and the following year brought a
similar honor to the aging Rousseau, who had been
received into the court of Napolean III in 1866.
(Rousseau was chosen, shortly before his death, to
head the jury for the International Exposition.)

William Morris Hunt, who could appreciate this
belated acclaim more than most Americans, announced to John LaFarge in Paris, "Well, our men
have won."[24] The victory was by no means a complete one. Critical taboos in France and America
remained alive and resistant, but now even the
detractors of the Barbizon painters were forced to
acknowledge their presence as a significant force in
the mainstream of Western landscape painting.

5. Barbizon and the Unifying Impression

While Hunt and a small group of patrons and painters from Boston carried the Barbizon banner during the 1860s, only the provocative creations of George Inness provided consistent exposure in New York for American painting in any way indebted to the Barbizon painters. Gradually, new adherents joined the ranks, starting in the late sixties with the work of two New York residents, Alexander Wyant (1836–1892) and Homer Dodge Martin (1836–1897). Both of these men, with Inness, would eventually be greeted by critics as a troika of the avant-garde, the harbingers of a kind of painting to be called "impressionism" in France. More than mere bridge builders and camp followers, Wyant and Martin deserve—and are beginning to receive —recognition in their own right as provocative interpreters of the American landscape. Of the two, Wyant was by far the more productive and successful, the artist whose lineage seems more unmistakably native in its origins.

Raised in Defiance, Ohio, and trained as a sign painter in nearby Port Washington in the early fifties, Wyant made his first trip to Cincinnati in 1857. There he managed to view an exhibition that contained a few works of George Inness.[1] Unswayed by the more ambitious and better known productions of Church and Albert Bierstadt—or simply ignorant of their work—Wyant was sufficiently aroused to travel to New York in 1858 to seek out Inness and determine as best he could the future direction for his own art. Wyant secured an intro-

duction from Inness to the wealthy Cincinnati patron Nicholas Longsworth and, by 1863, was able to move back to New York. Here, his protean course was changed again by a show of Düsseldorf paintings held in the city in the same year.[2] He was quickly impressed by the discipline and effort so indicative of stern, Düsseldorf training. Disregarding the example of several important Inness paintings—including *Sign of Promise*—that he must have seen in New York, and equally oblivious to French painting in local exhibitions, Wyant decided to raise money for a trip to Germany. In 1865 he left for Hans Gude's studio in Karlsruhe.

Wyant's experience in Gude's classes was beset by problems all too typical of those of the many Americans who had preceded him in Germany— eager anticipation gradually diluted by restrictive teaching and professorial posturing, language difficulties, and lonesomeness.[3] He forced himself to leave for England in March 1866, a full five months before his originally intended departure. Wyant studied several seventeenth-century masters in the National Gallery in London and took a long look at the work of J. M. W. Turner, whose color and fury seem to have been beyond his grasp. He was far too quiet and undramatic a soul to sympathize with Turner's flamboyant romanticism. The paintings and sketches by Constable appear to have had the most profound effect on him, an experience paralleled by that of several Barbizon painters, among them Rousseau, Dupré, and Jacques. Wyant's admira-

Figure 39. Alexander Helwig Wyant. *Mohawk Valley,* ca. 1866. Collection:
The Metropolitan Museum of Art; gift of Mrs. George E. Schanck in memory of
Arthur Hoppock Hearn, 1913.

tion for Constable's natural vision, a vision too common for Ruskin but otherwise admired throughout Europe by the late sixties, was described several years later by Wyant's first biographer:

If Claude was the first painter to 'set the sun in Heaven,' Wyant like Constable and his predecessors in Holland, seldom saw the sun; the vision is beyond, and the flying clouds indicate the spirit of change, the introspection and brooding mystery of the North.[4]

The most representative work of Wyant's early mature style and still one of his most famous canvases is the *Mohawk Valley* (fig. 39), generally believed to be a work dating from late in 1865, possibly painted shortly before his trip to Germany. In style and composition *Mohawk Valley* is Hudson River picturesque at its best; a rugged foreground of scalloped waves of water, deeply carved rocks, a tall *repoussoir* spruce tree framing a ruglike valley, and a river winding its way to infinity. Thinly painted throughout with tightly controlled greens, browns, and grays, the *Mohawk Valley* lacks only what we might reasonably expect the introverted

Wyant to ignore: the glorifying possibilities of a bright sun to bless this vast setting.

Gradually Wyant's touch broadened, his angle of vision narrowed, and his mood became more intimate. The first examples of this transition can be found in a number of views painted in Ireland before his return to America.[5] Here and in several efforts back on home soil, his changeover often proved less than successful. For example, his *Landscape* (fig. 40, now in the Art Institute of Chicago), which dates no later than the early seventies,[6] appears deliberately to set Wyant's brooding melancholy against the array of pictorial conventions normally employed towards a more optimistic end. The spotlighted foreground provides highly textured reds and yellows of autumn, with giant pines and birches receding, with only a slight loss of detail, into a long, sublime stretch of shadowy cliffs and distant hills. The light seems neither natural nor symbolic, and the contrast in mood suggests more a combination of Cropsey and Kensett than any Anglo-French remembrances.

What is most significant about the Chicago *Land-*

Figure 40. Alexander Helwig Wyant. *Landscape*. Collection: The Art Institute of Chicago.

scape and several other Wyant paintings from the early seventies is that he appears to be making every effort to develop his art within a style much closer to an American idiom than most authorities would have us believe.[7] If nascent rebellion were truly harbored in his mind, Wyant's eventual escape was accelerated by a stroke suffered during a disastrous Western trip in 1873. His right hand was rendered useless and, while teaching himself to paint with his left hand, he was forced to reduce the size of his landscapes even as their mood became more somber and intimate in feeling. After he had secured quarters in the YMCA building in New York (which he would leave in the summers to vacation in the Lake Champlain-Adirondacks area), Wyant scumbled and glazed his way to a measure of success that surely would have evaded him if his accident had occurred during his earlier, more conservative years.

During the first crucial years after his stroke, Wyant's paintings—and Inness's at the same time—came closer than ever before to the spirit of the Barbizon school. Wyant's subtlety of color, sugges-

tive more than explicit, fascinated that group of viewers who, for similar reasons, were so impressed with the late work of Corot. Wyant was pleased by the comparison[8] and further affirmed his affiliation with the Barbizon group by exhibiting a painting called *In The Spirit of Rousseau* (present location unknown) at the annual show of the National Academy in 1879.

During the final two decades of his life, Wyant's favorite compositions were usually either vertical canvases of forest interiors or elongated horizontal flatlands accented with small copses of trees and bushes and alternating patterns of light and shadow under cloudy skies (fig. 41). Art dealers and patrons no doubt found in both types echoes of a Barbizon flavor: Rousseau and Diaz reflected in the forest interiors; Corot and Rousseau most markedly in the horizontal works. Wyant's woodland interiors, like those first popularized in American by Durand, are decidedly more elegant in design and never as thick and impenetrable as the scenes of Fontainebleau or the Bas-Bréau executed by Rousseau or Diaz. And, of course, his horizontal views of fields and

Figure 41. Alexander Helwig Wyant. *Keene Valley*. Collection: The Brooklyn Museum, New York.

trees (which must have seemed more congenial to him in view of the strains imposed upon his draftsmanship by his disability) are remarkably close to numerous landscapes by Inness painted as early as the late sixties; for example, Inness's *Cloudy Day* of 1868 in the Smith College Museum of Art. Unlike Inness, who was some twenty years older, Wyant rarely suffered from stigmas incurred by the foreign flavor that critics discovered in his silent, uninhabited landscapes. This was more than a simple matter of good timing; Wyant's less pretentious art undoubtedly seemed, like the artist himself, less remote than that of Inness—challenging only in terms of small subtleties that reward the patient viewer. Despite a lifelong preference for charcoal studies,[9] Wyant never completely eliminated details, thus providing a reference point that all but the most progressive critics could appreciate.

He did not live long enough to worry about doing battle with the brighter, more "modern" landscapes of the impressionists. Indeed, Wyant's light, wet touch went as far as many of his patrons cared to have native impressionism advance in America.

Wyant and Homer Dodge Martin were born in the same year, 1836, but the latter enjoyed early advantages in his training not available to the Ohio-born painter. Raised in Albany, New York, Martin experienced the same absence of success in various businesses that had earlier plagued Inness in Massachusetts; however, Albany did provide Martin with a brief formal education in art, first through the advice of the noted sculptor, Erastus Dow Palmer, and later through a few weeks of training with James MacDougal Hart, a Düsseldorf-trained painter of conventional Hudson River panoramas. Along with Hart, Martin's early acquaintances included two artists who would make their reputation in France as well as America—George Boughton and Edward Gay.[10]

Albany, unlike New York, was a city that had earnestly preserved its long Dutch tradition. But Martin was endowed with a temperament ill-fitted to the stern demands of either traditional landscape or traditional training. Like Albert Ryder, whose personality and creative impulses were so similar to his own, he was fond of reading and reciting romantic poetry and of listening to music by the best of the romantic composers.[11]

Both in Albany during his teens and later during his first years in New York City in the early sixties, most of Martin's initial efforts were wide, sweeping vistas in the style of the Hudson River school. Many seem to affect the soft stillness already heralded in the work of John Kensett, albeit with Hart's livelier interest in a brighter range of colors. Thinly textured and small in touch, they nevertheless prophesy a dominant feature of most of Martin's work—his love for "wide, well balanced spaces," simple arrangements of large masses free from the dynamic trappings of baroque composition. According to his biographer, Frank Mather, Martin's affinity for simple relationships was confirmed by the sight of a Corot brought to Albany in the late fifties. The fundamental difference between the two painters remained unshaken, however, for as Mather points out, "Martin retained his love of color, never sacrificing it to tone in the manner of Corot."[12]

With few exceptions Martin's paintings were increasingly derived from memory, often from charcoal sketches or oil studies made in the Adirondacks during the summer. He actually reversed the usual procedure for outdoor studies, searching the outdoors for compositions while trusting his memory for details.[13] Improvising "natural" effects was inevitable with such a routine—strong evidence indeed of the decline of the outdoor-to-studio relationship so indispensable to Martin's Hudson River school acquaintances.

His temperament and working habits would seem to qualify Martin for a major role in the development of French tastes among American landscapists. Such was not the case, however—at least, not for a long while. Martin produced only a few truly important paintings of the sort that are seen and studied by many. He also had long fallow periods when, to the dismay of family and friends, he did almost no painting at all. Although he enjoyed the support of John LaFarge, who shared quarters with him in the Tenth Street Studio Building during the late sixties, he had only a small circle of patrons until very late in his life (the vogue for Wyant and especially that for Martin was mostly posthumous).[14] LaFarge was well traveled and knowledgeable about the latest happenings in foreign painting, whereas Martin was not able to make his first trip abroad until 1876. Martin admired LaFarge, whose advice may have influenced his decision to visit not only Barbizon during his initial European visit, but also Saint Cloud, a favorite haunt of Corot's.

Only a few drawings and paintings have survived from Martin's trip through Saint Cloud and Barbizon,[15] but his course had already been set, perhaps by the exhibition at the Philadelphia Centennial Exposition of 1876 of one of his finest landscapes, *Lake Sanford,* a painting later bought by the Century Association in New York (fig. 42). A brooding, low-key picture, *Lake Sanford* is uncharacteristically limited in color. Nevertheless, it shows that when he willed it, Martin's vision could extend far and wide, but rarely without that special kind of melancholy overcast we associate with Wyant and Inness. Even the winding lake and vast distances here are upstaged by a thin, bare tree silhouetted against a sky of thick gray clouds. The surrounding grounds seem overcome by fire or decay with no trace of human habitation. It is certainly one of Martin's many paeans to "The Sublime" in American landscape, yet his love of the simple and bittersweet in nature exposes his progressive instincts as well.

While in Europe, Martin also visited Holland and finally London, where he made the acquaintance of Whistler. Martin's preference for tonal harmonies

Figure 42. Homer Dodge Martin. *Lake Sanford,* 1870. Collection:
The Century Association, New York. Photograph, Frick Art Reference Library, New York.

rendered more in the service of art than of nature was no doubt confirmed by his friendship with Whistler, though he was too cultivated by tradition ever to transform himself into the full-blown aesthete that Whistler had already become. Nevertheless, Martin was regarded by 1880 as one firmly in the camp of the new breed of "art for art sakers." A lengthy review of Martin's work in the *Art Journal* of that year explained his rather puzzling style with long passages from Corot's letters ("By-and-bye, I shall paint my dreams"), but went on to explain in a rather breathless passage the American's failure to achieve full kinship with the now-renowned Frenchman:

It can scarcely be said ... that in the department of

absolutely pure painting—in that department where Nature's services as an ally are dispensed with, so far as the pictorial impression intended to be conveyed is concerned; where the artist depends solely upon his art for the strength and value of the emotions that he excites—Mr. Martin is either most frequently found or most felicitous when found.[16]

Martin returned to Europe in 1881, taking his wife with him to the fishing village of Villerville in Normandy. He was so entranced with the area that he spent the next eight years there, painting and sketching the same sites that had already been studied by many French artists, including Boudin, Seurat, and Corot. Always the contemplator rather than the activist, Martin's sense of painted poetry deepened, his details became ever less insistent, and

Figure 43. Homer Dodge Martin. *The Mussel Gatherers*, 1886, cat. no. 65.

the elegiac mood of the ancient villages in the region readily answered to his quest for withdrawal in nature. *The Mussel Gatherers* of 1886, probably painted in Normandy (fig. 43), is typical of Martin's understated impressions of that area's raw coastline. A first glance offers little more than a gloomy dunescape under a dense sky with two fisherwomen—figures suggesting neither heroic toil nor artful insertions in the composition, but merely hinting at the nature of the locale and revealing something of the scale of the scene. Vague reminders of Boudin's color and touch in his seaside view of the same vicinity are discernible in *The Mussel Gatherers*, but the resemblance is a far from compelling one. Martin's study of generalized hues drawn more from the mind than the eye and his

predilection for silhouette rather than topography seem to have been inspired in greater part by acquaintance with the landscapes of his friend La-Farge, particularly LaFarge's Newport scenes of the early sixties. In fact, while still in Normandy, Martin painted a Newport scene (fig. 44), the semi-abstract qualities and total lack of pictorial trappings of which remind one immediately of such earlier LaFarges as *Bishop Berkeley's Rock, Newport* (1865, fig. 45), not to mention certain Whistlers from the mid-sixties (the landscapes from Trouville, for example, which Martin may have remembered from his 1876 trip to Whistler's studio).

Few American landscapists developed as slowly, not to say sluggishly, as Martin, and certainly echoes of the aestheticism of LaFarge and Whistler, some

Figure 44. Homer Dodge Martin. *Wild Coast, Newport,* cat. no. 66.

Figure 45. John LaFarge. *Bishop Berkeley's Rock, Newport,* 1865. Collection: The Metropolitan Museum of Art, New York; gift of Frank Jewett Mather, Jr., 1949.

twenty years after the fact, were not untypical of his slow progress. Neither, for that matter, are these echoes unusual aspects of late-century romanticism in American painting, as attested by Inness in his late work and by men like George Fuller, Dwight Tryon, John Twachtman, J. Francis Murphy, and other artists who came into their maturity during the last two decades of the century. These were painters of lyrical sentiments unencumbered by objective analysis who turned the style of our pioneer landscapists, in Edgar Richardson's words, into "a primarily decorative impulse, a thing of taste and charm, rather than discovery or power."[17]

Inness, Wyant, and Martin are the best known today of those landscapists of the late-nineteenth century who developed styles that critics were quick to associate with the bittersweet mood of Barbizon art. They were by no means the only ones, however, nor were they necessarily the most successful in the public arena. Their younger contemporaries include a nearly forgotten substrata of landscapists who seemed to have one developmental strain in common: an early exposure to Barbizon art that often resulted in outright imitation—of

Figure 46. J. Appleton Brown. *On the Coast of France,* 1875, cat. no. 19.

Corot and Rousseau especially—with later changes in style to accommodate challenges to older ways of seeing and coloring imposed on them by the work of the French impressionists.

When the break with the Barbizon approach was as markedly apparent as it was with J. Appleton Brown (1844–1902), the effect of the newer style could be almost overbearing. Raised in Boston, Brown enrolled in 1867 as a student of Émile Lambinet in Paris, some seven years after Foxcroft Cole had frequented the same studio.[18] Brown was already a devotee of Corot during his student days in Boston, and the two years and more that he spent in Paris only enhanced this admiration. *On the Coast of France* (1875, fig. 46) is one of Brown's more successful displays of the sort of cool, subtle color and unassuming composition that led the critic Samuel Benjamin to chide him for his "discouraging servitude to Corot."[19] When Brown decided to change tactics in the late seventies, the transformation was more a switch in palette, to vivid autumn reds and lush springtime greens,[20] than the result of new scientific awareness of light and color. Before long, he proceeded from his long-standing allegiance to Corot to a bright and cheerful manner that earned him the nickname "Appleblossom Brown."

Brown's new style with its extravagant pastel colors was unique for a latter day adherent of Barbizon painting, because it represented a mood wholly different from the brown, barren woodlands that characterize so much late-nineteenth-century landscape painting in America. In fact, many painters of this period, including such followers of Inness as Carleton Wiggins, Henry Ward Ranger, and Leonard Ochtman, as well as J. Francis Murphy and Wyant's pupil, Bruce Crane, all made a veritable specialty of late-autumn scenery. They replaced the joyous cacophony of Jasper Cropsey's Hudson Valley autumns with a mellowness that metaphorically approximates the muted tones of the "Brown Decades."[21] In this respect, Dwight Tryon (1848–1925) was a more representative figure than Brown, more poetically somber and severely self-limiting in scope.

Tryon received his rather brief training from 1877 to 1879 from members of both the first and second generation of Barbizon painters in Paris,

Figure 47. Dwight W. Tryon. *May*, 1898–1899. Collection:
Museum of Art, Carnegie Institute, Pittsburgh.

Charles Daubigny and Henry Harpignies. Although he later claimed to have "received little help from them," his early work in Europe and his later addiction to lyrical tone poems in autumn twilight indicate otherwise.[22] His Paris studies were augmented with lessons from Antoine Guillemet, a former pupil of Corot and Daubigny, and by extensive travel throughout France, Italy, Holland, and England— where, like Wyant before him, Turner's "epic poetry" fascinated him.[23] Tryon managed to show three paintings in the Salon of 1881 and then returned to America, spending most of the remainder of his career commuting between New York and South Dartmouth, Massachusetts.

Tryon's deep roots in Barbizon painting were

joined to a poised, restrained temperament that eschewed the overtly picturesque and depended almost entirely on impressions from memory. By about 1890 he had developed to its full potential his most characteristic approach to landscape, a modest impressionism devoted more to subtle nuances of atmosphere than to the empirical examination of natural light and color. His favorite theme, one he returned to repeatedly throughout his maturity, was a woodland scene evenly balanced by horizontal divisions of grass and shrubbery and verticals of tall, thinly dressed trees aligned with the precision of a close-order drill, often with their leafage all but evaporated in the moist twilight especially favored by Tryon (fig. 47). As appropriate to their lack of emphasis on a specific site, Tryon's canvases were usually titled merely according to the month or season and, like those of Wyant and Martin (a good friend), his fields and meadows are rarely complicated by the presence of man or beast.

Tryon shared with Martin, Inness, Thomas Dewing, and other members of the "liberal wing" of American painting many of the same patrons: Potter Palmer, N. A. Montross (whose Fifth Avenue gallery also promoted the work of Albert P. Ryder), and Thomas B. Clarke, Inness's most avid collector. However, the most telling support he received came after about 1889 from Charles Freer, a man best known for his immense holdings in Oriental art. For Freer, Tryon's paintings (along with those by the few other Americans he collected, Whistler, Dewing, and Abbot Thayer) embodied the same spiritual qualities he found in his Oriental vases and screens.[24] Tryon's tremulous trees, misty airs, and elegiac mood measure quite accurately a taste for fragile beauty that typifies much turn-of-the-century art in America. The Oriental sense of refinement in this art has been seen as the heart of its appeal (as it must have been for Freer). It is certainly no accident that for critics of this era, words such as "exquisite," "poetic," "lyrical," and "precious" replaced at this time more traditional terms of approbation like "strong," "true," and "solid."

The popularity of Corot (and pseudo-Corots) and the increasing interest in the art-for-art's sake aestheticism of Whistler, Walter Pater, and others no doubt contributed in large measure to this phenomenon, although, as Barbara Novak, John McCoubrey, and other students of American art have reminded us, the "amorphous dream" in American painting was always with us—as far back as the Italian reveries of Washington Allston.[25] For the new lyricists of late-nineteenth-century America, withdrawal into a more interior, dreamlike world did not demand, as it did for the later surrealist painters, that the dream be objectified with concrete metaphors, but rather that the evanescence of the dream be retained on canvas. Indeed, many

of the most evocative works of Martin, Tryon, and Murphy, defined by swift, short strokes of paint, seem to portray views rendered during a brisk walk, passing thoughts that belie the deliberate precision of their technique.

However successful these practitioners of late-century "dreamscapes" may have been in the commercial and critical arena, they still had to take second billing to the more sophisticated and detached paintings that make up the late style of their titular leader, George Inness. Older, wiser, and more complex, Inness, during the last decade of his life (from 1884 until his death in 1894), produced a remarkable series of landscapes that form what most observers define today as his "signature style" as well as his strongest claim as a prophet of American modernism. Nevertheless, as Inness explained it, such works were more the result of a very old aesthetic battle in America—between the two conflicting poles of the subjective and objective or the real and the ideal[26]—than of any sort of demonstrably new awareness of form and content on his part. Inness devoted much of his thought and unruly prose to such meditation on this problem, and, by 1878, proposed this quite impossible solution: "If a painter could unite Meissonier's careful reproduction of details with Corot's inspirational power, he would be the very god of art."[27]

Inness, of course, opted for "inspirational power" over "careful reproduction," but a close study of his late works (fig. 48) shows that his selection was more of a reconciliation between the two choices than one might at first assume. Indeed, his firm, almost mathematically precise placement of forms and space, with those distant parallels in the classical tradition that Corot and Rousseau were also wont to observe, is one of the distinguishing qualities that perforce sets his work apart from the "passing thoughts" of most of his younger contemporaries (with the exception of the rigid Tryon).[28] The manner in which so much of his sense of ordered composition was now the result of the flow and flux of warm, glowing color harmonies instead of the more traditional illusionistic devices

Figure 48. George Inness. *Sundown*, 1894, cat. no. 55.

may tend to disguise Inness's delicate constructions. Neverthless, as Paul Valéry said of Corot, "Structure is there behind the veil: not absent, but at one remove."[29]

In keeping with his increased awareness of the manifestations of Swedenborg's "spiritual world" in the earthly world, Inness progressively minimized the role of man in these later years. Human elements may be absent altogether or confined below the horizon line where their presence attracted less attention. Like the trees, shrubbery, and occasional flecks of flowers surrounding them, Inness's farmers and solitary strollers seem anchored to the earth more by a common spirit than by gravity. Indeed, Inness's summary treatment of vague forms is a telling postscript to Jules Castagnary's reaction (in his review of the Salon of 1857) to Corot's nymphs and cupids: ". . . a mere breadth has set them upon the grass." Inness's late work recalls Barbizon art in still other ways. The penchant for the strong, isolated silhouette against twilight or moonlight skies (a predilection that Inness shared with his fellow Americans, Albert Ryder and Ralph Blakelock) appears with equally intense, vivid coloration in the late landscapes of Théodore Rousseau—whom Inness had acclaimed "perhaps the greatest French landscape painter."[30] (Compare figs. 1 and 33.) Like Rousseau and Diaz before him, Inness, in the last dozen years of his life, made a near specialty of interior forest scenes. Though he was less overtly coloristic than Diaz, he shared with both Frenchmen a fascination with the effect of a hidden sun penetrating to the bark of selected trees, an effect of transient glimmer amidst dense gloom (fig. 49).[31] Inness, who had all but abandoned panoramic views by the late seventies, undoubtedly found these forest interiors especially congenial to his taste, inasmuch as his approach to art itself was becoming increasingly interior at the same time.

Given the intensely personal equation drawn by Inness to fit his conception of the unity of the spirit and the material—a concept later defined by much of the post-impressionist aesthetic in Europe—how much of Inness's late work can offer insights into

Figure 49. George Inness. *Sunset In the Woods,* 1891. Collection: Corcoran Gallery of Art, Washington, D.C.

his Barbizon heritage? Inness was, after all, very much his own man through much of his maturity, and the final decade of his life only served to heighten this independence. But in the synthetic terms which conditioned the artist's thinking, many striking recollections of Barbizon paintings can be found in his late work. Even Millet, to whom he has only rarely been compared, offers a few rather suggestive clues to the study of Inness. Although the latter showed little interest in Millet's paintings of laborers in the fields (no doubt he found them too literal and obvious as subject matter), the Frenchman's soft-edged treatment of nature and Inness's late style have much in common.

One of the most interesting examples, in terms of difference and similarity, of the vision they shared in common can be shown by a comparison of one of Millet's best known landscapes, *The Spring* of 1868–1873 in the Louvre (fig. 50), and Inness's *After a Summer Shower* of 1894, now in the Butler Collection of the Art Institute of Chicago (fig. 51). Ironically, each painting dates from its creator's final year. Perhaps for this reason the similarly dramatic ploys (passing showers, silhouetted rainbows, dark foregrounds with a raking light shining on distant

Figure 50. Jean-François Millet. *The Spring,* ca. 1868–1873. Collection: The Louvre, Paris.

Figure 51. George Inness. *After a Summer Shower,* 1894. Collection: The Art Institute of Chicago; The Edward B. Butler Collection.

fields) give both works an uncommonly didactic, almost valedictory quality.

The twenty years that separate these two landscapes are particularly important when one notes that the richly colored drama of Millet, with its Ruysdael-like trappings, represents the sort of literal drama that Inness was increasingly disclaiming in his late art. The thinness of touch and unusually pastel colors (pinks and light blues) throughout the middle ground in the *Summer Shower* may be a hint at some sort of accommodation on Inness's part to the impressionist pallette—a détente nipped in the bud by his sudden death the same year.

Several other artists of somewhat lesser interest could be added to the aforementioned painters in order to round out a group portrait of their contributions. Many of them, including Charles Davis, Alexander Van Lear, Charles Dewey, Frank DeHaven, and Charles Warren Eaton, labored long into the twentieth century, content to work within a single context with little notice paid to the many new "isms" introduced to this country during and after World War I. The cosmopolitan bent of American collectors and critics during these artists' younger days and the residue of Barbizon inspiration in much of their work helps us to at least sketch in the outlines of an American impressionism. Shunning, however, the uncomplicated joy and empirical fervor of their French counterparts, they offered a new subjectivity that, as Frederic Sherman said of Homer Martin, insisted on "certain inescapable intimations of the important fact that the poetry of the earth is never dead."[32]

6. *Post-Centennial Critics and Patrons*

The elaborate Centennial celebration held in Philadelphia in 1876 was by no means a high-water mark in the popularity of Barbizon art in America, but without question the exposition as a whole did serve to accelerate the pace of American internationalism in the arts. Within only five years, a series of events were to firmly establish the hegemony of French art and art training in this country. Although the benefits from this ascendancy were to be shared by the Barbizon painters and their American adherents, such an outcome seemed improbable at the time of the Centennial. The largest foreign contingent in the exposition, and also one of the most highly praised, was that of Great Britain.[1] Barbizon painting was conspicuous only by its absence; in the American galleries, the Boston followers of William Morris Hunt were largely ignored and George Inness was not represented at all. The most successful medal winners were the painters of the Hudson River school, although their future as viable directors of American landscape painting was already in doubt.[2]

With its wide-ranging displays of crafts and machinery, the Philadelphia extravaganza did manage to demonstrate that art and culture were compatible with that most precious of American obsessions—progress. In the year before the exposition opened, *Appleton's Journal* noted that "as a means of culture, art is overrated."[3] Whether this opinion was a minority one at the time is impossible to tell, but the increasing interest in art at all levels of

society in America had certainly quickened in the period between the Civil War and the Centennial. Advocacy for this pursuit found its strongest voice in the art periodical, no longer a rarity on the American scene. That writers about art had a vested interest in the subject is implicit in this proud announcement appearing in 1880 in the newly created *American Art Review:*

Within the last ten years, a great change has taken place in public sentiment. The arts are no longer regarded as comparatively unimportant to our national growth and dignity, and ever increasing enthusiasm has replaced languid interest or indifference. Our cities have their museums, their art schools . . . and our libraries their multiplicity of books upon art subjects whose circulation equals if it does not surpass books on other topics.[4]

During the decade and a half after the Civil War the number of magazines devoted solely to the arts trebled, despite the fact that most of the more perceptive criticism found its way into periodicals of wider interest.[5] In these, presented on the same pages with household hints, political matters, and gossip, art criticism became—typographically at least—an integral part of the American experience.

The evolving information explosion should be kept in mind as a complement to the critical afflatus that blossomed dramatically about the time of the Centennial Exposition. The true leaders of the exposition were a new breed of critics; young, well-traveled, thoroughly cosmopolitan, and, for the most part, French-oriented in their views on art matters. Born in the generation that followed such critics as Tuckerman, Cranch, Jarves, and Cook, the most important among the new critics were Samuel Greene Wheeler Benjamin (1837–1914); William Crary Brownell (1851–1928); John C. Van Dyke (1856–1932); and Eugene Benson (1839–1908). These and others (Charles de Kay and Millet's pupil, Edward Wheelwright, for example) were also important in the rise to popularity of Barbizon art because their mixed bag of prejudice and perception was heavily weighted in favor of the then modern French idea of an art based on imagination, memory, and brilliant technique. It is on just such a foundation that the term "impressionism" first entered the American critical vocabulary. Samuel Benjamin used it in 1878 as a designation for all great painters who have effectively combined the real and the ideal in their art, including Turner, Corot, Velasquez, and the Japanese.[6] Although acknowledging that modern impressionism in this broader context was a significant aspect of French painting, Benjamin failed to mention a single painter of the group that is referred to today as "impressionist" (although the name had already been applied in France to members of this group). Inness was designated by Benjamin as the leader of the American impressionists (though he would shortly deny any such role),[7] and the reader soon realizes that for Benjamin, French impressionism—even at this late date—was, in fact, Barbizon painting.

Benjamin was quick to note that the "unfinished look of impressionism" was held by many to be an inability to harmonize the objective and the subjective, a criticism peculiar to the whole sketch versus finish controversy. He reasoned, nevertheless, that an artist who finds himself in this predicament "is yet so far right because he is endeavoring to interpret the wholly imaginative and intellectual side of art." In supporting imagination, however indecisive, as a virtue unto itself, Benjamin placed his name

firmly in the camp of the more advanced American critics of his day, most of whom possessed more facile minds than his. Even a theorist as unruly as George Inness was encouraged to publish his own views on such matters during the years 1879–1881. Though his advice hardly served to clarify matters, Inness's well-earned success as a painter no doubt helped his cause in the battle of—as he liked to describe it—the forces of spiritual truth (idealism, imagination) against materialistic (realistic) concerns.[8]

Most of the artists whose work typified Benjamin's definition of impressionism were no more than forty years of age when the Centennial exhibition took place. The fifty-one-year-old George Inness was a notable exception. However vehement his protests against having been labeled an "impressionist," he could at least take solace from the fact that the old, tiresome comparisons of his work to that of the Barbizon painters was at last abating. Even the proposed connection of his latest work with that of the impressionists, broadly based as it was, served to emphasize rather than deprecate Inness's formidable powers of invention. By 1882 his landscapes were finally given the sort of in-depth analysis they deserved in a lengthy article for *Century Magazine* written by Charles de Kay (Henry Eckford), a polished and perceptive critic who understood and was sympathetic to Inness's art.[9] Shunning the usual analogies to Claude, Constable, Turner, and Rousseau, de Kay found Inness's newest style—typified, for example, by *The Rising Storm* (fig. 52)—the workings of a man with a system abetted by "pure dramatic imagination" and a slight touch of madness.

Overwhelmed by the beauty of a scene, the play of light and shade, the balance of clouds, distant hills and nearer masses of forest, he has dashed his paint on with hardly a line of pencil or charcoal to guide him, working in that rapt condition of mind during which the lapse of time is not felt, in which the mind seems to extend itself through the fingers to the tip of the brush, and the latter, as it moves on the prepared surface, seems to obey the general laws of nature which fashioned the very landscape that is being counterfeited at the instant.[10]

De Kay's obvious relish for an art akin to pure expression that depicted nature "in its great outer, rather than in its little inner, form" was an important early milestone in the growing interest in America in the psychological aspects of the creative process. The post-Centennial art criticism supplied by *Harper's, Scribner's, Atlantic Monthly, The Nation,* the aforementioned *American Art Review,* and several other digests, pamphlets, and newspapers, came to the attention of a public whose appetite for art was being met in all sorts of new ways. More and better reproductions, more public museums and public galleries—these were a few of the major features of the new quest for art, not to mention that most curious but predictable specimen of the late seventies, the "art factory" (where stenciled landscapes could be had by the dozens for only a few dollars apiece).[11] The surge of interest in art at all levels of American society helped not only to broaden the base of patronage, but also to weaken the old strictures against subject matter that failed to elevate the mind or glorify the country. Technique ceased to be an italicized word in American criticism and nature was no longer written with a capital N.

In ways that were at once salutary and regrettable, Barbizon art played a major role in this transformation. William Brownell, a leading authority on matters French and a close friend to LaFarge and Martin, perceived the transformation primarily in terms of the toppling of an old guard and its subsequent replacement with fresher faces and more progressive ideas. Brownell was especially pleased with the show of the "radical" Society of American Artists at the Kurtz Gallery in New York City during the fall of 1878. This exhibition featured the work of LaFarge, Martin, Hunt, and the recent Munich Academy alumni, Frank Duveneck and William Merritt Chase. Brownell noted with barely disguised delight that it was a "veritable chamber

Figure 52. George Inness. *The Rising Storm,* ca. 1879, cat. no. 53.

of horrors" for the old standbys at the National Academy.[12] Radical techniques were no longer an anomaly supported by Boston alone; the "latest" methods had now hit New York full force. Brownell found the flashy, Rembrandtesque brushwork of the Munich students exceptional for its "sense of what is pictorially impressive." For their "grasp of the poetic" (always a standard shibboleth in American criticism), however, he reserved plaudits for men like Hunt, LaFarge, and Martin. To critics who still regretted the French insistence on style, Brownell haughtily warned that "mere intelligence assuming the privileges of genius is never an agreeable spectacle to the educated person."

Clarence Cook had previously suggested in a "Letter to the Editor" in the March 30, 1878, issue of the *New York Tribune* that Hunt was the perpetrator of the painterly style practiced by the younger artists at the first exhibition of the Society of American Artists.[13] He was equally alarmed that the ideas of the French school were more available than ever before in New York at that time. Hunt's *Talks on Art* was published in Boston and London in 1878 and Couture's *Entretiens d'atelier* were given

Figure 53. Jean-François Millet. *The Angelus*. Collection: The Louvre, Paris.

an English translation in the following year (the dedication reads "À l'Amerique"). Even before the Centennial, Boston's influence was being felt in New York.[14] By 1881, with the publication in Boston of Edna Cheney's *Gleanings in Art,* the patronizing attitude of Bostonians toward conservative painting in New York acquired a certain historical propriety. In this book, one of the first written by an American that pretended to be a survey of Western art, the chapter on American painting omits, with the exception of Cole, all reference to the acknowledged masters of landscape and genre. Appropriately enough, French painters —especially Millet—are extravagantly praised, while the treatment of established English painters is deprecatory in tone.

American enrollment in the *écoles* of Paris was so large by 1880 that local students attempted to have Americans barred from award competitions. When the Americans broke from their classes for the summer, many took the two-hour journey to Barbizon where, according to a reporter for the *Century,* "every house . . . is more or less of a shrine."[15] None of the old regulars then remained at their former haunts in Barbizon except for William Babcock, whose hut was still full of Barbizon memorabilia. Among the French, only Jacques, Dupré, and Daubigny were still alive in 1880 and all were in their final years and far from Barbizon. But the names and reputations of all of the Barbizon "originals" found new and greater acclaim in their absence, especially in American auction rooms and galleries. Millet's *The Angelus* (fig. 53), which fetched no better a price than $500 as late as the early 1870s, opened at auction in New York in 1880 at $20,000.[16] Even his pastels now commanded prices as high as $4,000. Corot was given his first comprehensive exhibition in 1881 at Vose's Westminster Gallery in Providence. Had he been alive to see it, Corot would have been amused to find paintings that were earlier grabbed up for a pittance from disappointed importers netting prices of around $6,000 apiece. So bullish was the market for Barbizon paintings that the Paris newspaper *Figaro* alleged that a rather desperate French dealer came to America in 1880 with a $200,000 letter of credit to buy Troyons, but had to return home empty-handed.[17]

The decade of the 1880s also witnessed the first substantial buildup of art collections away from the Boston-New York axis, which contained extraordinary holdings of Barbizon paintings. Among the more important were the Borie, Gibson, and Johnson collections in Philadelphia; the Coale Collection in Saint Louis; and the Potter Palmer Collection in Chicago. The eighties also witnessed the dispersal of some of the country's largest concentrations of Barbizon paintings, the Mary Morgan Collection at the American Galleries (1886), for example, at which fifty-nine paintings by the original group (including eleven by Millet and seventeen by Diaz) were sold, or the Capen-Warren sale at the same site three years later, at which 159 French imports were sold, nearly half of them Barbizon works imported by Vose.[18]

From the highlights mentioned briefly above, a picture of late-nineteenth-century taste begins to emerge that warrants study in its own right. Nevertheless, one can reasonably ask what the inflated market prices have to do with the true nature of American criticism during the same period, particularly since the best writers on art tended to see beyond the vagaries of the marketplace, treating art as a purified piece of culture undefiled by the whims of the consumer. The most appropriate answer to this question is that the same shows and sales occasioned most of the best criticism written at this time. As sales boomed and large shows were launched in those centers that could support such undertakings, art became not only a pursuit but a cause of newsworthy "events"; its audience appeal increased accordingly.

A more coldhearted analysis of the role of money and glamour vis à vis aesthetic judgment was offered by Vose's agent, Thomas Robinson, a man responsible for the importation of hundreds of French paintings then on the market. In a letter titled "In Defense of French Art" written to a Boston editor who had expressed regret at the incipient clamor for Barbizon and French romantic painting, Robinson assured the editor that "the only valid test of the merit of paintings after people have had time to study them and let their enthusiasms cool, is the money value which connoisseurs and collectors throughout the world put on them."[19] As an unsuccessful artist himself, Robinson might have wished for different standards; as a dealer's agent, he was far closer to the facts of life.[20]

7. Artful Animals and Pleasant Peasants

I think I could turn and live with animals, they are so
    placid and self-contain'd;
I stand and look at them long and long.
They do not sweat and whine about their condition;
They do not lie awake in the dark and weep for their
    sins;
They do not make me sick discussing their duty to God.
       WALT WHITMAN, *Song of Myself*, Sec. 32

By describing his love of animals in terms that emphasize their negative virtues rather than their services to man, Walt Whitman addressed himself to a peculiar fascination that the beasts and fowl of the earth have long held for Americans. When artists such as the Audubons and Alexander Wilson produced their justifiably famous studies of animals in the middle of the nineteenth century, their objectivity and scientific exactitude went even further than that of their fellow landscapists of the same period. However, just as the land had to be cultivated and almost conquered before it was deemed a worthy subject for the painter, so too the vast audience for animal paintings in the later decades of the century had to be cultivated by the development of a less utilitarian, more subjective outlook toward the animal kingdom than that current earlier in the century.

Gradually, as all aspects of life in nature's realm came to be regarded as worthy of respect and study, a remarkable abundance of articles appeared in the eighties and nineties in magazines such as *Popular Science* and *Scientific American* with titles such as

"Do Fishes Remember?," "Do Birds Reason?," and "The Religious and Aesthetic Sensibilities of Animals."[1] At the same time the theories of evolution promulgated at mid-century by Darwin and Spencer were finally "discovered" by the growing number of persons in this country who were concerned not only with an animal's appearance, but with its behavior and habits as well. For many such persons, the romantic bombast that helped to popularize many of the animal paintings of Europeans like George Stubbs, Delacroix, and Géricault was largely ignored in favor of the more therapeutic qualities of sentimentalized farm genre. Native attempts to capture the more ambitious qualities of the former mode were far from successful. Indeed, when a rather pallid variety of American animal genre was introduced to America about 1845 by Thomas Hewes Hinkley and Arthur Tait (not to mention the morality tableaux of William H. Beard), even its best effects seem suggestive of the science museum mock-up, long on observation but short on artistic accomplishment. On the other hand, the countless "animalscapes" produced by the American progeny of Barbizon painters (Troyon and Jacques, especially) satisfied a deeper personal need shared by most viewers of these works. The scenes of familiar domestic beasts served as an antidote for the sense of nostalgia and loss experienced by the thousands who had left agrarian backgrounds to seek their fortunes in the growing cities of the eastern and midwestern United States.

Figure 54. Jean-François Millet. *Bringing Home the New-Born Calf*. Collection: The Art Institute of Chicago.

Figure 55. Eugène Verboeckhoven. *Sheep*. National Collection of Fine Arts.

The farm animal as subject matter for art was basically an urban phenomenon, just as it was in France. Such paintings did not always display the sweet glow of innocence and light, however, especially when such qualities were even vaguely compromised by the presence of the farm worker. A conservative critic at the Salon of 1864 in Paris, disturbed by Millet's *Bringing Home the New-Born Calf* (fig. 54), summed up the reservations many Americans would have voiced about similar efforts by their fellow countrymen: "The animals who populate the fields become friends and if the human figure is met with, it plays such an impersonal role that it concerns us only as if it were a creature not like ourselves."[2]

To be sure, the root origins of the "animal rage" are more Dutch and Flemish than Barbizon. Most of the Hudson River school painters were conversant, usually through engravings, with the work of the seventeenth-century Dutch masters of animal painting—from the placid, carefully composed scenes of cows and herders of Albert Cuyp and Adriaen van de Velde to the rugged, less artful creations of Paulus Potter. One of the most ubiquitous exhibitors at shows of foreign art in New York from about 1855 to 1880 was a Belgian named Eugène Verboeckhoven (1799–1881), who specialized in paintings of large cows and oxen classically grouped before perfunctorily arranged landscapes (fig. 55). Verboeckhoven and his brother Louis produced a seemingly endless series of animal paintings—"cermantile imbecilities," Inness called them—and in the spirit of Reynolds's *Discourses*, many American critics found the popularity of these scenes to be a barometer of native taste that the country could well do without. One angry critic for *The Crayon* even blamed their popularity on the theories of Darwin and his colleagues:

New theories of the creation assert that animals came before man—were this open to discussion from our pen, the first argument we would advance on the affirmative side would be one based upon the 'natural selection' of the Americans in the works of art.[3]

No foreign painting was better known in the fifties than Rosa Bonheur's huge *Horse Fair* of 1853, now in the Metropolitan Museum of Art.[4] Its notoriety, however, which was based on numerous engravings after it as well as on public exhibition, would prove an exception to the general trend

Figure 56. Constant Troyon. *Going To Market*, 1860.
Collection: The Metropolitan Museum of Art;
bequest of Isaac D. Fletcher, 1917.

Figure 57. Paulus Potter. *The Young Bull*. Collection:
Mauritshuis, The Hague.

toward scenes of more domesticated animals. The far more pervasive influence of Barbizon painting was something quite different (as indeed were Miss Bonheur's paintings after she moved to her studio *cum* stable near the outskirts of Fontainebleau in 1859). With Troyon, Jacques, and—by the early sixties—Millet leading the way, the Barbizon painters focused on the farm animal acting naturally in familiar surroundings; paraphrasing Millet's definition of beauty, these creatures were beautiful because they were "in place." As befits their docile nature, these loungers' role in their rural arena is a more sedate one than that of the rearing horses of Delacroix and Bonheur. Yet they still serve as vehicles for some marvelously rich painterly effects. The broad, sumptuous impastos of Troyon's cows and the woolly fluff of Millet's sheep were constantly praised by Hunt, Thomas Robinson, J. F. Cole, and other American artists.

Troyon, who won more medals for his pure landscapes than for his more numerous paintings of animals, was equally successful in the re-creation of atmospheric effects, especially the cool mist of early morning light. This facet of Troyon's work heightened the sense of intimate communion of animal and environment and was undoubtedly his most singular contribution to painting in the nineteenth century. A comparison of Troyon's *Going To Market* of 1860 (fig. 56) and Paulus Potter's most renowned work *The Young Bull* (fig. 57) demonstrates the more salient aspects of Troyon's achievement. The Potter is a minutely rendered portrait of a huge red bull complete with wet nose and whiskers, with serious, wondering eyes fixed guardedly on the spectator. Unlike the Troyon, there is no light or air anywhere and shadows are neglected altogether; in short, a lack of academic expedients adds to its rugged appeal while diluting its claim as landscape art.[5]

The above comparison is no less instructive—though hardly all-encompassing—than the analysis of a large segment of American paintings later in the nineteenth century that deal with similar subject matter. Indeed, it appears that many American ani-

Figure 58. William Henry Howe. Study on door panels for *Monarch on the Farm*. Collection: Lyme Historical Society—Florence Griswold Association.

Figure 59. Carlton Wiggins. *Evening after a Shower*, cat. no. 89.

mal painters tended to pick and choose between the style of Troyon and Potter or, in effect, to arrive at compromises between these two possibilities. For example, the best known works of Carleton Wiggins (1848–1932), William H. Howe (1846–1929), and Hunt's pupil John Bernard Johnston (1847–1886) are essentially bovine portraits executed on the scale of Potter's *The Young Bull*, but brushed in with the softening impressionist stroke of Troyon. Howe, who late in his life was honored by the French government for his bovine paintings, produced the most bizarre example of this genre—an illusionistic barn stall transposed into the door panels of a Connecticut dining room (fig. 58). Johnston's career was too short-lived to permit the building of a solid reputation, but Wiggins, a student of Inness's at Eagleswood and an exhibitor in the Salon of 1881,

was, in the last two decades of the century, an enormously popular painter of animal-landscapes who often commanded more than $10,000 for his larger paintings (fig. 59).[6]

A more coherent illustration of the Franco-Dutch compromise noted in Johnston and Wiggins can be found in the development of Thomas Craig (1849–1924) of Philadelphia and Rutherford, New Jersey. Craig's reputation, like that of most animal specialists of his day, was primarily regional in scope (he was little known east of Philadelphia). He still managed to maintain a long, productive career specializing in scenes of cows in dramatically lit pastures. Craig is, in fact, something of an art historian's delight inasmuch as his career divides itself into three roughly equal parts. First were landscapes with small accessory cows; then scenes in which cows and landscapes are more or less equally balanced (fig. 60); and finally, during the height of the "cow craze," bovine portraits with only slight hints of the open air.[7]

The roll call of aspiring animal-landscapists in

Figure 60. Thomas Bigelow Craig. *The Mill Pond,
Rutherford,* cat. no. 22.

America during this period could be extended to
dozens of other specialists, including Peter Moran
(1842–1915) in Philadelphia, Henry Rankin Poore
(1859–1940) in New Jersey, and Charles Pierce
(1844–1920) in Boston. To name them all would
only serve to further emphasize the ubiquity of the
genre. What seems most unfortunate about the general run of their work is simply that, despite the
popular overstated notions then current about the
socio-religious significance of much Barbizon painting (promoted by Sensier's biography of Millet),
there is little evidence that any artist in this country
capitalized on the full spiritualizing potential of
the animal theme. Few Barbizon works exhibit
these possibilities more completely than a little-
known masterpiece by Millet owned by William
Walters, *The Sheepfold, Moonlight* (fig. 61). Soberly
colored in browns and grays with occasional touches
of blue and violet, this is a painting abounding in
biblical allusions—The Good Shepherd, The Sacri-
ficial Lamb, the leadership of their "flocks" by
Moses and Christ—subjects always popular in religious circles in America,[8] but never previously
thus developed in painting. None of the confec-

tionery flavor of Troyon's *Going to the Market* is
to be found here. Instead one finds a slow, winding
procession of sheep, blessed by the glow of a three-
quarter moon and presided over by the spectral
figure of the herder, whose leadership provides full
opportunity for the moving flock to form itself
naturally into tightly knit, faceless mounds of wool.[9]
With the exception of a few late etchings by Samuel
Palmer in England or the humble efforts of Dutch
artist Anton Mauve, the Millet pastoral mood, direct
and always a little disturbing, was rarely duplicated
in nineteenth-century Europe, let alone in America.

That American painters sought safer ground in
parlor-room pastorals instead of in works reflecting
the simple, expressive dignity of Millet's paintings
is evidenced not only in the Americans' treatment
of subject matter but in the manner in which
decorative pastoral scenes by both French and
American artists were enshrined in glaringly inappropriate frames of gilded fleurs-de-lis. In a similar
vein, the attitude of Americans toward the human
instruments of rustic toil during most of the nineteenth century seemed to support Emerson's warn-
ing in "Nature" (1836) that "you cannot freely admire a noble landscape if laborers are digging in
the field hard by." The reason for a change in this
attitude is easy to understand. The 1848 Revolution
in France and the tone of the art it helped to spawn
—in Millet and Courbet especially—proved to
many American visitors that the "digging" itself was
a noble undertaking and a fit subject for the painter.
Nevertheless, when American artists returned home
from their European sojourns, they obviously found
it all but impossible to convey the sentiment and
pathos of Millet's toilers in the guise of the American Farmer. One such traveler, Samuel Isham, a
writer, French-trained artist, and enthusiastic admirer of Millet, pinpointed the problem in his *History of American Painting* (1901): "He [the American Farmer] was too independent, too sophisticated; his machinery, his reapers and threshers
lacked the epic note; they were new like his clothes,
his house, all his surroundings."[10]

The lack of the "epic note" in agrarian life in

Figure 61. Jean-François Millet. *The Sheepfold, Moonlight.* Collection:
The Walters Art Gallery, Baltimore.

America did not, however, preclude a rather lively patronage in this country for paintings with peasant subjects. A national temper that prided itself on the freeing of its slaves as well as on the concept of its homeland as a refuge for the oppressed was reason enough for many Americans to detect a strong democratic character in the peasant paintings of Millet. When the aging Walt Whitman in 1881 visited the collection of Quincy Adams Shaw in Boston, he spent "two rapt hours" there among the Millets, seeing in *The Sower,* particularly, "that last impalpable ethic purpose" which, to his mind, was also the primary purpose of a truly American literature.[11]

In *The Sower* Walt Whitman felt that he finally understood the meaning of the French Revolution, but in his poetry, he also saw a healthier, more promising side to peasant life.

Now I see the secret of the making of the best persons
It is to grow in the open air, and to eat and sleep with
    the earth.[12]

As a young art critic in New York in the early fifties, Whitman's ideals had been more didactic than this, but he had changed and so had his country.[13] America was by now better prepared to welcome other renditions of the peasant theme, less fatalistic than Millet's and with far more appeal to America's traditional respect for sentiment.

The most interesting example of American sentiment in peasant subject matter can be found in the short-lived but auspicious success of George Fuller (1822–1884). Fuller's themes and technique no doubt owed much to Barbizon-inspired revolutions in taste, but, as with Inness, due consideration should also be given to Fuller's unusual background and personality. He had three successive careers:

Figure 62. George Fuller. *The Dandelion Girl,*
cat. no. 35.

first, as a moderately successful portrait painter;
next, as a tobacco farmer (from 1860 until the col-
lapse in 1875 of the market for that product); and,
finally (the shortest and by far the most illustrious
of his several careers), as a painter of dreamy-eyed
peasant girls set against suffocating brown and
ocher landscapes.

Before taking on the responsibility for the family
farm in Deerfield, Massachusetts, Fuller in 1860
went on a long trip to Europe, visiting England
with William Stillman then continuing on to France,
Germany, Italy, and Holland. Like Inness before

him, he firmly believed in the effectiveness of
museum visits over formal training and, during the
fifteen years that followed his trip abroad, he had
ample time to ruminate on paintings by the masters
he most admired. Although Millet, Titian, and Rembrandt were special favorites, he also admired lesser
artists on rather opposite sides of the sentimental
spectrum—Friedrich Overbeck in Rome and Pierre
Édouard Frère in Paris.[14]

In 1876, Fuller's new, highly personal style first
gained recognition for him. During that year, a
group of Hunt's pupils visiting Deerfield happened
upon Fuller's studio; returning to Boston, they
brought his work to their mentor's attention.[15] Soon
after, an exhibition of Fuller's work at Doll and
Richards proved an instant success. For eight years
(until his death in 1884), Fuller was widely praised
and exhibited in New York and Boston. His ardent
supporters included William Dean Howells, John
Greenleaf Whittier, and, of course, Hunt. Fuller's
appeal was twofold. It encompassed first of all an
ad hoc technique, replete with scrapings, finger
rubbings, and an almost obsessive inclination to
"old master" his forms beneath layers of tinted
glazes[16] resembling the time-darkened Titians so
often praised by Jarves. It also embodied a simplicity in subject and conception—despite the fact
that his themes were often taken from intricate
romantic novels (Hawthorne was a particular favorite). Fuller avoided the lucid rhetoric of form
that one might expect from a painter of literary subjects. His peasant girls, such as *The Dandelion Girl*
(fig. 62), neither toil like Millet's nor pose heroically
in the manner of the "Salon laborer," nor are they
quite the arcadian dreamers of Corot's idylls. Their
innocent, waiffish stares are the stuff that anxious
dreams are made of, evoking what Frank Mather
called "hesitancies and frustrations of personalities
too finely wrought for such a struggle as Fuller himself had faced."[17]

Fuller's "painted poetry" was keyed on a brown,
enveloping mist, an autumn melancholy that anticipates Inness's late style and the look and feel
of October twilight in New England, "when the air
shimmers with a luminous dust that has been

[80]

Figure 63. George Fuller. *The Tomato Patch*, cat. no. 36.

crushed up from dried leaves."[18] The soft-edged peasants and gloomy landscapes (fig. 63) he painted are the antithesis of scenes of similar subjects painted by other artists, such as the Frenchman Jules Breton (1827–1906), whose heroic interpretations of life near the soil were, in this country, rivaled in popularity only by Millet's paintings. Breton's robustly immodest biography was published in America in 1890 and his *Song of the Lark* of 1884 (fig. 64, now in the Art Institute of Chicago), was one of this country's most lavishly reproduced works well into the twentieth century.[19]

Song of the Lark, the popularity of which once rivaled Millet's *The Angelus* in America, is typical of one of Breton's two favorite peasant themes (religious processions being the other). A pretty, sturdily constructed girl stands in the forefront in vaguely classical pose, returning the lark's song with one of her own. A harvest moon—another Breton staple—glares over the horizon, and the foreshortened fields show little evidence that the young gleaner has much work to look after. She is the archetypal Salon peasant, little concerned with the dramatic realities of her existence. As Millet remarked about these damsels without distress, "M. Breton paints girls who are too pretty to stay in a village very long."[20]

For his part, Breton found Millet worthy of great praise, but recoiled at his "savage" countrysides and his "overburdened workers."[21] From the beginning of his career, Breton was a great admirer of David and French classicism and even his most cheerful peasants take on the hieratic look of tinted statues, a textbook example of *juste milieu* compromise. Millet himself may have suggested this alternative when, during a discussion with Breton at the Salon of 1853, he remarked, "Why should not painters have the right to choose . . . one, the rough potato, the other, the morning glory that twines itself among the corn."[22]

Those Americans in Paris who sought a style suitable for the depiction of peasant life preferred the "morning glory" to the "rough potato." One might expect to find an exception in the work of

Figure 64. Jules Breton. *Song of the Lark*, 1884, cat. no. 1.

Figure 65. William Morris Hunt. *The Little Gleaner*, 1854. Collection: The Toledo Museum of Art; gift of Arthur J. Secor, 1923.

Figure 66. William Morris Hunt. *Gleaner*, 1865. Collection: Museum of Fine Arts, Boston.

William Morris Hunt; yet, despite his study with Millet and his unwavering respect for Millet's devotion to the peasant, Hunt was too much of a portraitist and too much of a Brahmin ever to adopt Millet's unsentimentalized directness in his own work. Hunt's *The Little Gleaner* of 1854 (fig. 65) is far closer in its sweetness and comfortable melancholy to Breton's successful painting of the same title from the Salon of the preceding year, despite Hunt's use of Millet's warm, soft tones. Another *Gleaner* (fig. 66), executed in 1865, is essentially a study in ideal portraiture, a fertility goddess painted in the manner of Couture and the spirit of classical art. These and the many landscapes that increasingly engaged Hunt's attention in the seventies form a part of his Barbizon reminiscences, but his peasant portraits remain distillations of a people that he probably never understood.

Far more ambitious in such undertakings than Hunt and closer to Breton's "morning glory" ideal was a Philadelphia-born painter, Daniel Ridgeway Knight (1845–1924), whose productive and remarkably successful career demonstrates all too well how misunderstood the Barbizon aesthetic had become in the late-nineteenth century. Knight was so enamored of French peasant life that about 1870 he

Figure 67. Daniel Ridgeway Knight. *Hailing the Ferry,* 1888. Collection:
The Pennsylvania Academy of the Fine Arts, Philadelphia; gift of John H. Converse, 1891.

bought a home and studio at Poissy on the Seine, where he resided for the remainder of his long life. For sheer loyalty to a single area of land and people, Knight was something of a latter-day John Constable—but there the similarity ends abruptly. Knight had been a pupil of Gleyre's and Meissonier's in Paris but, unlike some of Gleyre's students (Monet, Renoir, Sisley), he was always a thorough-going conservative. The work illustrated here, *Hailing the Ferry* (fig. 67), suffices to define the fundamentals of hundreds of his works. They are always peopled by rosy-cheeked rustic belles resting, greeting neighbors, pouring water, knitting —almost never indulging in strenuous activity.[23]

From his Poissy cottage, Knight turned out scores of these works for a wide-ranging clientele in France and America, rarely able to keep up with the demand on his services. As a technician, he had none of the impressionistic bravura of Breton or his younger contemporary Léon Lhermitte (1844–1925) who, unlike Knight, demonstrated to many American buyers that academic correctness in peasant genre need not rule out palpable space and form (fig. 68). The silvery grays and browns affected by Knight remind one superficially of Corot or Jean Cazin, as does the moist, luminous film that covers his skies and rivers.

The peasants that populate the canvases of Knight and his fellow American Frederick Bridgeman (1847–1927), as well as those of Breton, Lhermitte, and the short-lived Jules Bastien-Lepage,[24] have in common one feature that, in varying degrees, keynotes the severe criticism heaped today upon this unfortunate phase of American taste. Their peasants are essentially play actors, dressed in costume and only slightly closer to the soil than Marie Antoinette when she impersonated a farm maiden in her Versailles cottage. Their general character, hinting at but rarely dwelling fully on social commentary, was admirably defined in this American appraisal of Breton's "democratic feeling":

Whatever the surrounding evil, for the artist the sun is always at the zenith. His business is to put whatever part of nature he paints—human nature as well as other —in the best possible light. . . . The reformer's zeal, much less his discontent, admirable elsewhere, is inconsistent with the repose of spirit which wins beauty to the side of the artist. . . . Unless an artist sees peasants as potential Apollos and Madonnas he can not paint them.[25]

Without a peasant class of their own, Americans opted for something more easily digestible than the Barbizon ideal projected by Millet and Jacques. Only one American artist devoted to rustic subjects seemed sufficiently endowed with the French artist's rare combination of raw simplicity and dramatic design to merit the title of "The American Millet." Horatio Walker (1858–1938) managed to approximate Millet's struggles during his own lifetime in North America. Although this native of Canada found his subjects among the hardy French peasants on the Isle d'Orlèans near the St. Lawrence River, he was not to enjoy much recognition until he took a studio in New York in 1878. In Canada, under the most inhospitable conditions, he could view

Figure 68. Léon Lhermitte. *The Vintage*. Collection: The Metropolitan Museum of Art; gift of William Schaus, 1887.

peasant life as Millet had viewed it, as the heritage of the ages.

Walker had no fear of the homely theme (his first success in New York was a painting of a hog).[26] Fortunately, his broad, translucent technique provides a viable counterpoint to his occasionally puerile subjects, such as *Ave Maria* (fig. 69). Obviously indebted to Millet's atypically sentimental *Angelus*, Walker's *Ave Maria* features a gloriously tinted sunset glinting along the edge of a roadside Crucifixion, the finely chiseled figure of the dying Messiah hanging in mute contrast over a nondescript peasant boy and his indifferent oxen.[27]

For modern tastes, Walker is undoubtedly more effective in his many attempts to re-create the timeless struggle of man and beast to forge a living, or at least an existence, out of the unyielding pastures of the remote Isle d'Orlèans. Despite the elemental

Figure 69. Horatio Walker. *Ave Maria,* cat. no. 84.

simplicity of these paintings, Walker was anything but a primitive. A traveler in England, France, and Holland before his arrival in New York, he was, like Inness, self-taught both from extensive visits to galleries and museums and from long, firsthand observation of many varieties of rustic life. His horses, cattle, and oxen are well drawn, albeit shabby, beasts, while his peasant workers are rendered without distinctive features in the manner of Millet and Robinson, with no attempt to match the Frenchman's monumental power.

The sun rarely shines in full display over Walker's desolate landscapes and his workers often toil amid snow and mud. His peculiar brand of truth draws some of its strength from the fatalism of Millet, though it is more earth and animal centered—the mere fact that man is even there seems heroic enough for Walker. His painstaking technique was lavishly praised in his lifetime; with four gold medals before 1900 and membership in over a dozen artists' societies,[28] he was exceeded in collected honors in America at the turn of the century only by such esteemed artists as John Singer Sargent and William Merritt Chase. This is proof enough that the work ethic, rendered sympathetically, could still command attention in the increasingly jaded society of industrial America.

8. *The Early Nineties: Triumph and Displacement*

The World's Columbian Exposition held in Chicago in 1893 was primarily designed to display and promote, as its Centennial predecessor had before, a successful marriage between the arts and industry. For William Dean Howells, the site of the exposition was a great, white city clothed in magic, an American Altruria filled with "pillared porches" commemorating the yielding of "nature . . . herself to the enlightened will of men."[1] But whereas advocates of populist-realism like Howells and Hamlin Garland hoped that such enlightenment could be accomplished on native-born terms, they found instead a celebration of the thoroughly cosmopolitan character of late-nineteenth-century fashions in dress, architecture, and painting.

The millionaires of America who helped further these ends no doubt agreed with the banker in Howell's Altrurian essays that "what the great mass of the people . . . needed was some standard of taste."[2] Standards per se were difficult to discern through the eclectic maze represented by the fair with its Grecian buildings, art glass, and academic painting from several nations. In the American painting section, the most popular work was Thomas Hovendon's large, sentimental tableau *Breaking the Home Ties*, but among the most talked-about and fashionable group displays was a loan exhibition entitled "Foreign Masterpieces Owned by Americans." This exhibition represents one of the most triumphant—and incongruous—moments of Barbizon popularity in America.

"Foreign Masterpieces" was overwhelmingly French. Organized by Mrs. Potter Palmer of Chicago, the exhibition included loans from such prestigious collectors as Cornelius Vanderbilt and Charles Yerkes of New York, railroad magnates Jay Gould and William Crocker (who lent Millet's *Man with the Hoe*), Chicagoans Henry Field and the Potter Palmers, and several others of similar means and cultural persuasion.[3] The "best taste" was conspicuously represented by all of the original Barbizon group, with Corot and Millet enjoying, respectively, about a four-to-one and two-to-one advantage over the other French artists represented. If one subscribes to the oft-stated theory that Barbizon art provided nostalgic escape for the new industrial, bourgeoise society, then we might readily assume, given the position of the lenders, that a strong back-to-the-soil sentiment motivated these scions of American industry. Although nature rendered mildly rather than with raw power was a popular feature of the landscapes of Corot, Daubigny, and Diaz, the appreciation of their art was probably enhanced as well by the alternative they posed to the hardier "democratic" attraction exerted by Millet. Indeed, the absence of "materialism" in their stance before rural nature was the sort of sedative that the busy tycoon could find only in atypically sentimental Millets like *The Angelus*. In a panegyric on Corot in his *Art Thoughts*, James

Jackson Jarves had predicted as much.

Corot can never be popular in France, for he is too removed from the common characteristics of the nation . . . he is not materialistic enough. His solitude is too calm. . . . To soothe, to give repose, to evoke sentiment, such is their [his paintings'] mission.[4]

The soothing properties of Barbizon art notwithstanding, the investment motive—as we have already seen—was a primary concern for the "lions" of the marketplace. In the eyes of many, the Barbizon rage had also expanded the production and sale of fraudulent paintings and forgeries. Five years before the Columbian Exposition the *New York Evening Post* had investigated an alleged domestic "Corot factory," and a Frenchman (E. Durand-Gréville) visiting America to survey his countrymen's art in local collections had given up in dismay upon finding not only spurious Corots, but Millets and "Diazs without end."[5] In his militant muckraking, Sheridan Ford put the blame squarely on the shoulders of Barbizon collectors, who, he asserted, "jostle elbows to pay inflated prices for even ephemeral sketches."[6] Ford realized as well that the quest for works by the men from Fontainebleau also involved a de facto slight against the fervent efforts of Americans then painting in their own Barbizon-related idiom. "Create a school the peer of the Barbizon and plant it on Manhattan Island, and it is safe to say that the dealers would either sneer at its pretensions or plod on in blissful ignorance of its existence."[7]

The problem for men like Wyant, Martin, and, to a lesser degree, Inness, as well as for their younger adherents, was not wholly commercial; in their Barbizon proclivities lay the seed of a new idiom, French impressionism, that would replace them in the studio and the marketplace. Durand-Ruel realized as much in his impressionist shows in the late eighties in Boston, Chicago, and New York, and presented his new entourage with a smattering of the more familiar Barbizon paintings (most notably Corots and Daubignys) that he had successfully defended earlier in his career.[8] In exalting a flight from civilization and the overthrowing of the

conventions of the "civilized" landscape, the Barbizon painters—inevitably it would seem—had created a new convention, limited in its selection of motifs, too understated to provide for full expression. A striking example of the new awareness of the school's limitations, in this case by a noted critic, was provided by Hamlin Garland in a report of a visit he made to the 1893 loan exhibition at Chicago:

I walked through the loan exhibition with a man who cared nothing for precedent—a keen, candid man; and I afterward visited the entire gallery with a painter— a strong and earnest man, who had grown out of the gray-black-and-brown method.

Both these men shook their heads at Inness, Diaz, Corot, Troyon, Rousseau, and Millet. The painter said, a little sadly, as if surrendering an illusion, "They do not represent nature to me any more. They're all too indefinite, too weak, too lifeless in shadow. They reproduce beautifully, but their color is too muddy and cold."

The other man was not even sad. He said, "I don't like them—that's all there is about it. I don't see nature that way. Some of them are decorative, but they are not nature. I prefer Monet or Hassam or the Norwegians."[9]

Like Howells, Garland was a strong advocate of the "local color" school of American literature (he lectured on its behalf at the exposition), and found in impressionism similar qualities: a sense of vivid actuality, vigorous individualism, and a disdain for the "mystery" and "sentiment" of nature. Garland's favorable response to the impressionists was couched in terms similar to the early defense of Barbizon art in America—a typical example of the evolutionary role of time and semantics in American criticism.

Garland's essay on "Impressionism" was probably, as Rewald put it, "the first all-out defense of the movement to be written in English."[10] In the true spirit of a manifesto, he treats the new force as a radical break with the past, using his Exposition dialogue to downgrade the important contributions of the Barbizon painters (even though "local color" in the literary sense was an important part of their aesthetic). It is important to note here that apart from Childe Hassam, the American painters who were then working in an impressionist style did not embrace the new French manner without imposing modifications of their own. Men like John Twachtman, Theodore Robinson, Mark Fischer, and the "dark Impressionists" of the Munich school all betray, in varied ways, a residue of Barbizon feeling in their work. It is found, for example, in the insistence on a rustic ideal in Fischer and Robinson and in the Corotesque concentration on tone more than on hue in the very personal visual poetics of Twachtman. In both America and France these painters and most of their colleagues could locate and study Barbizon painting far more readily than recent impressionist works. In addition their redoubtable American predecessors—Inness, Wyant, Martin, and LaFarge—were all receiving rather extraordinary attention in the nineties.

Coincident to these end-of-the-century developments in American landscape painting, it is interesting to note also that not until 1900 was an art colony formed in the United States that was at least vaguely similar in structure and outlook to that formed in Barbizon over a half century before. This colony was organized at Old Lyme, Connecticut, a small town on the Connecticut River near Long Island Sound, with the house of Miss Florence Griswold serving as its headquarters. Miss Griswold's warm hospitality established her home as Old Lyme's worthy counterpart to Ganne's Inn at Barbizon.[11] Henry Ward Ranger (1858–1916), who had formerly studied with Diaz and Corot, gave the colony its first spark in 1899, though his nominal leadership was soon usurped by Childe Hassam, who arrived in 1903. The quiet, meditative quality of Ranger's woodland scenes (fig. 70), however, continued to be the prime attraction for those visitors not susceptible to the dazzling surfaces of Hassam's many sun-filled views of the town and its gentle, rural surroundings.

In addition to Ranger, artist-migrants from New York whose intermittent presence at Old Lyme helped earn for the town the title "American Bar-

bizon" include Henry Rankin Poore, William Howe, Bruce Crane, Carleton Wiggins, and Louis Dessar (figs. 45, 58, 59, 71). The holiday atmosphere within the group and the lovely, storybook appearance of Old Lyme and its environs were hardly conducive to the intensely serious search for nature's mystery that motivated the first artists in Barbizon. Yet, divested of the retrospective considerations and critical clockwork that force us to check to see if our American artists are on the proper historical schedule, we can still appreciate the low-keyed joy, sincerity, and occasional hypnotic charm of these modest canvases from the Old Lyme group.

A detailed investigation of this moment of change in American landscape painting would go well beyond the scope of this study. It should include, apart from an examination of changes in painterly concerns, a thorough study of the role of photography as a catalyst in any such transformation. In terms of Barbizon popularity, photography certainly shortened the life of its artistic forerunners, including the Hudson River school in America, many of whose adherents welcomed photography as an aid.[12] At mid-century, photography, with its increased refinement in methods of control (such as the development of the wet-plate process and the soft-focus lens), generated a serious reappraisal of the artist as an agent for the reproduction of images. By the mid-eighties, however, the situation had changed drastically. As the improved skill of the photographer transformed the merciless objectivity of the photograph and made it more of a truly "pictorial" art, it became incumbent upon the landscapist to emphasize those aspects of his art as yet unchallenged by photography, particularly color vibration and related methods of surface animation.

The Barbizon painters were among the first groups of artists to demonstrate an awareness of the possibilities of the camera as both recorder and poetizer of nature. Millet found photography useful merely as a means of transcribing pose and details, but Rousseau and Daubigny were derided by such critics as Baudelaire, About, Zola, and Stillman for the photographic qualities of tone and values in

Figure 70. Henry Ward Ranger. *Connecticut Woods*, 1899, cat. no. 76.

Figure 71. Louis P. Dessar. *Return to the Fold*, cat. no. 31.

their landscapes.[13] Corot was never subjected to such attacks, despite the superficial similarity of his late style, with its blurred images of forest glades, to contemporary developments in wet-plate processing. The lack of critical hostility to Corot's effects can perhaps be attributed to the preference of the French for a dreamier look in photographic views than that offered, for example, in the more precise views of the English pictorial photographers.

American opinion was unaffected by the negative reaction of French critics to the works of Corot's comrades at Fontainebleau until the appearance of the impressionists' landscapes. The effect of these was to make the Barbizon approach to nature seem less vital and cogent than ever before. As Garland's dialogue implies, "newness" had much to do with this shift, for impressionist art met the challenge of photography on its own grounds. Many early critics thought, erroneously as it turned out, that impressionism was as much a new science as a new art;[14]

in this respect, its very currency made it an effective complement to photography, while its strength of color and light effects provided, conversely, additional strengths not matched by the photograph. In neither area could Barbizon painting compete for the attention of the aspiring artist or the forward-looking patron.

If Barbizon art suffered by comparison with impressionist and post-impressionist painting vis à vis pictorial photography, it nevertheless contributed a curious footnote to the development of the new science in Europe and America. For even as the pictorial photographer (i.e., the photo-maker as artist) attempted to duplicate many of the technical conventions of Barbizon art, he often perpetuated, at the same time, the Barbizon spirit in his choice of subject matter. Indeed, while a thriving market in city views made great strides in the last quarter of the century, the labors of the fields were only slightly less popular as subjects. The hero of Peter

Figure 72. Peter Emerson. *Poling the Marsh Hay.*
Photograph in Emerson's *Life and Landscape on the
Norfolk Broads* (London, 1886).

Emerson, a London photographer, who was perhaps
the most successful specialist in rustic scenes, was
none other than Millet—"Millet the Great" as he
called him.[15] Emerson's weighty folios of the English
outlands were very popular in America despite their
expense, a circumstance due in no small measure
to the way he presented his farmers in the "characteristic" postures of Millet's laborers. The example
in figure 72, from Emerson's *Norfolk Broads* of 1888,
is typical of his resourceful simulation of Millet's
figures (although the composition recalls more
strongly Bastien-Lepage or Breton). The delicate
placement of figures, the artful smudging, and the
moist look of soft-focus selection may seem today
to be questionable practices for the photographer
of rustic life. To their credit, however, these peculiar transmogrifications of Barbizon ideals serve to
remind us that, as Robert Herbert put it so suc-
cinctly,

... the only *meaningful heritage* of Barbizon art lies in
the *paintings* themselves. Because we can see the colors
and brushstrokes the artist used, we can feel his ges-
tures as he laid them down on his canvas. If we study
a painting with love, we can feel the artist beside us,
moving his hands. [italics mine][16]

The "meaningful heritage" of nature painting in
America had not been completely forgotten during
the final years of the century; rather, it had been
reconditioned by the formulation of a new aesthetic
and the surrendering of some of our more cherished
illusions. From the earliest attempts to examine and
record American nature in paint and verse from the
1820s to the present, landscape viewing and landscape painting have meant different things to diverse segments of American society: a medium for
cultivation or exploitation, spiritual and physical
refreshment, or simply a remote backdrop for the
"granite forests" of our growing cities. In 1835
Thomas Cole readily acknowledged the taming role
of the axe and plow, but still could state with certainly that "the most distinctive, and perhaps the
most impressive, characteristic of American scenery
is its wilderness."[17] Most of the early explorers
would have agreed, albeit with certain allowances
for material gain. Yet Cole was a composer of
nature as well as an explorer of sorts. Although he
extolled the "natural majesty" of the Hudson Valley
he was quick to add that it also presented "an unbounded capacity for improvement by art."[18]

For Cole, "improvement" meant the good taste
of an enlightened civilization capable of encourag-
ing and understanding the artistic temperament
that alone could bring forth "consequent associations of God the Creator." In retrospect, his call for
creative privilege on behalf of divine revelation was
a harbinger of the improvisations of the last third
of the century, a more secularized use of nature
in the service of art than even Cole would have
thought unlikely.

In theory, Cole's approach to nature painting was
not that different from the Barbizon artists: go to
nature first with humility, communicate a sincere
response, and generalize, as Inness put it, "without

losing that logical connection of parts to the whole which satisfied the mind."[19] Nevertheless, the generation of artists that grew into maturity some twenty years after Cole's death could survey their surroundings and find far less of Cole's hallowed wilderness, a great deal more art to learn from, and, eventually, belated support from an aesthetic richer in creative license—far less insistent on literal truth than the English aesthetics and early American literature that nourished Cole. As early as 1860, when William James was still a teenage student of Hunt's, *The Crayon* predicted that the aesthetic climate would eventually shift when the "researches now being made in psychology shall be matured," and all previous systems of beauty disappear "like the chaff before the wind."[20] This prophecy was partially fulfilled by Hunt's *Talks* and his advocacy of Barbizon art, both of which rendered Beauty more accessible, and less (compared to Allston's *Lectures*) dependent on the experience of subtle intellects. Americans did not suddenly cease their insistence on "reading" a work of art for its message —Millet especially, as well as Troyon and Jacques, exerted a strong literary appeal in this country.[21] This appeal, however, was but one side of the Barbizon coin. The attraction for Americans of Corot, Diaz, Dupré, and, to a lesser degree, Rousseau, originated in implicit rather than explicit suggestion. In France the same dichotomy was eloquently defined at mid-century by Baudelaire, an admirer of Corot and Daubigny, who though Millet's "fine visual qualities" spoiled by pedantry and pretentiousness.[22]

The weakening of those "materialistic" concerns that Inness so vigorously fought was undertaken with an urgency matched only by the fervent appeal to a national conscience by the art of the Hudson River school. American literature and the critical controversies that surrounded it demonstrate a similar antididacticism, summarized in a dialogue written by George Santayana in 1890 in the words he assigned to a "liberal critic": "There is something brutal and fatuous in the habit we commonly have of passing the parts of nature in review and pro-

nouncing them good or bad according to the effect they have on our lives."[23] Although Santayana was addressing himself to the critical disclaimers of Walt Whitman's genius, his indictment also refers obliquely to the nature poetry and prose of Bryant and Cooper, as well as to their counterparts among the Hudson River school, such as Thomas Cole and Frederic Church. Just how dated the moral operas of Hudson River painting had become by the final years of the century can be readily observed in any number of comparisons. None is more telling than an examination of two paintings of our most hallowed natural monument, Niagara Falls, one by Frederic Church, painted in 1857 (fig. 73), and another by Inness, executed in 1889 (fig. 74).

In both cases, the artists have accepted the panoramic possibilities of the hallowed site (although such a format was generally anathema to Inness in his later years). The artistic promise of this natural wonder, however, was decidedly different for both men. "The true use of art," according to Inness, was "first, to cultivate the artist's own spiritual nature, and secondly, to enter as a factor in general civilization."[24] Church would probably have reversed these priorities, especially as they applied to American civilization. He understood our natural history, and the artist's obligations toward it, in Ruskinian terms. His rocks are etched by time and the Creator; his water bubbles, boils, and evaporates much like the cycle of life itself. Church's rainbow is a marvel of trompe l'oeil painting, a more effective symbol of divine revelation because of its veracity. The lesson of nature's energy, its unlimited diversity, its "human nature" if you will, this was Church's *expression*.[25]

Nature harmonized Church's Niagara vista through the sum of its parts; for Inness, acting under the influences of a more introverted personality and a unique adaptation of Barbizon principles, harmony was an even more synthetic alliance with nature. Through the medium of Inness's broad, dry brush (many of whose hairs are still imbedded in the murky green and brown paint), all potential "facts" of the scene are generalized and detached

Figure 73. Frederic Edwin Church. *Niagara Falls,* 1857.
Collection: Corcoran Gallery of Art, Washington, D.C.

Figure 74. George Inness. *Niagara Falls,* 1889. National Collection of Fine Arts.

from nature by Niagara's mists. The enforced unity that results parallels Inness's admiration for the "pure ideas" of Corot and Daubigny,[26] ideas which influenced so many of Inness's like-minded followers. The clear light of Church's panorama, illuminating the age and the "new youth" that D. H. Lawrence called "the true myth of America,"[27] has been dimmed by Inness's ethereal screen—even the rainbow seems but an improbable afterthought. The double meanings of symbol and fact are blurred beyond recognition, replaced by a single, sonorous "sensation." It is not too fanciful to speculate that Whistler, if he had brought suit against Ruskin in America instead of England, could have referred to Inness's *Niagara* in his own defense.

The mystical, quasi-theological aesthetics that Inness so diligently tried to embody in his late landscapes required, for most Americans, a tinge of European culture if their evocative potential was to be more fully understood (or even tolerated). Certainly the organization of nineteenth-century critical theory, which supported the inseparability of the visual and the conceptual, beginning with Immanuel Kant in Germany and supplemented by, for example, Whistler in London and Conrad Fiedler in Rome and Munich, was hardly a homegrown product. By the 1890s, however, the writings of John LaFarge and George Santayana skillfully demonstrated that the philosophical rectitude for a new art need not depend exclusively on Europeans or expatriots.

In a series of lectures on problems of aesthetics delivered at Harvard from 1892 to 1895 and published the following year as *The Sense of Beauty*, Santayana admitted that "resemblance is a source of satisfaction," but added that for true "stimulation" of the mind, art must be something more.

Science is the response to the demand for information, and in it we ask for the whole truth and nothing but the truth. Art is the response to the demand for entertainment, for the stimulation of our senses and imagination, and truth enters into it only as it subserves these ends.[28]

An occasional painter himself and one who undoubtedly knew the art life of Boston well, Santayana rarely referred to painting per se in *The Sense of Beauty*. He did, however, choose to make an exception in a short examination of landscape painting that he divided into two categories: "impressionism" (in the generic sense used by earlier American critics), and "discursive landscape," the latter presumably including the art of the Hudson River school, which "collects so many glimpses and gives so fully the sum of our positive observations that its work is sure to be perfectly intelligible and plain."[29] Various devices are at the artist's command to divest himself of the weighty demands of "discursive" painting, one of which, according to Santayana, is the "unhumanized scene," free from the constant reminder of man's presence. The uninhabited landscapes of Rousseau, Daubigny, and a host of Americans (Wyant, Martin, Tryon, and Murphy, especially) are given a new rationale in Santayana's analysis.

The indeterminateness of the suggestion of an unhumanized scene was previously felt as a defect; now we feel it rather as exaltation. We need to be free; our emotion suffices us; we do not ask for a description of the object which interests us as a part of ourselves.[30]

Santayana was the paradigm of Emerson's typical philosopher, a man more interested in "reasons for believing than in believing itself." He judiciously avoided absolute judgments and his first treatise on aesthetical matters cannot be defined as the *resumé ideal* of the art life of his youth. Nevertheless, he did manage to perceive very real and cogent distinctions between the naturally beautiful and the artistically beautiful. During the same years when theories of both aesthetics and evolution were most hotly debated, *The Sense of Beauty* articulated with rare insight and organization the ambivalent feelings of both progressive and traditionalist toward philosophic ideals for which they felt a certain temperamental kinship, and the naturalistic position to which they were logically attracted but emotionally repelled.[31]

The Barbizon landscapists provided practical support in their writings and, more important, in their elegiac landscapes, for a resolution of just such a conflict. At the same time that old-line patriarchs of culture like Charles Eliot Norton and Henry Adams were reacting to this late-century dualism with a despair that bordered on the nihilistic, Barbizon art provided for many a thoroughly logical retreat into one's most interior thoughts. Shortly after the turn of the century, John LaFarge described Barbizon melancholy in words that formed an apt addendum to Santayana's defense of the "unhumanized scene."

The melancholy born of failure in fitting the issues of the world to one's own desires turns naturally into contemplation of that over which we have no control—that nature which continues undisturbed by the vicissitudes of man.[32]

By emphasizing the artist's detachment from nature as a viable means of realizing her most important secrets, the Barbizon painters posited an art that elevated imaginative ideals while it avoided what the new breed of critics disparagingly referred to as "mere transcripts of nature." Most attempts by American artists to expound at length on the application of the ideal to ordinary practice were anything but successful. Inness was the most conspicuous case in point, and even Hunt's *Talks on Art*, popular as they were, could not set the matter straight. Inconsistency was the bane of Inness's art and theories; for Hunt, it was part of his reckless charm and his pithy aphorisms tend to be most instructive when extracted from the context in which they appear.[33] It remained for another Barbizon sympathizer of long standing, John LaFarge, to provide in his *Considerations on Painting* what Hunt could not—a treatise by an artist of genuine intellectual depth dedicated to the same ideals that Hunt and his circle had long before espoused.

Considerations on Painting, published in 1896, was originally a series of lectures delivered by LaFarge in 1892 and 1893 at the Metropolitan Museum in New York. The very titles of some of his lectures —"Personality and Choice, Suggestion and Intention, Sincerity"—sound like the outlines of Hunt's classroom sermons. LaFarge, however, brought to his task not only greater intellectual equipment, but an eclectic taste even more "un-American" (to use Henry Adams's unfortunate term) than that of Hunt.

Borrowing liberally from the associationist theories of Herbert Spencer, and possibly from the *Principles of Psychology* (1890) of his former Newport colleague, William James,[34] LaFarge gave new shading and substance to previous laments by contemporaneous critics about the lack of spontaneity in mid-nineteenth-century American painting. Citing the examples of Delacroix, Millet, Rousseau, and Corot, he ridiculed the adverse judgments previously heaped upon these men by "literary critics of pictures." For LaFarge, art began "where language ceases," a distinction that most Hudson River painters would, to say the least, have found distasteful. Painting and literature in LaFarge's view had in common only one property, "expression"— the "correspondence between the sensations of the soul and the sensations of the body."[35]

In proposing art as an expression of sensation, LaFarge and Santayana (who devoted an entire chapter to "expression" in *Sense of Beauty*) were in complete agreement. Neither felt, to use LaFarge's words, that art was "a lawless game." And yet the laws had certainly changed, or at least they had been modified by new ideals. Most important, the moralizing rhetoric that had been a touchstone for American naturalism from Thomas Cole through the later Hudson River school had been muted by psychological imperatives established by the artist himself, who devoutly desired communion with sympathetic beholders.

Notes

Chapter 1

1. In addition to the term "Barbizon school," other terms with some currency in America included "the school of Fontainebleau" (a label that unfortunately causes some confusion since it also is used to describe a group of sixteenth-century "mannerists," mostly Italian, who decorated the new palace at Fontainebleau built by Francis I); "the generation of 1830," which normally included the romantic painters Gericault, Delacroix, and—because of his age—Corot; and "the Fontainebleau-Barbizon school," which was a compromise favored by a few American critics in the 1890s. In addition to the main core of the Barbizon group discussed later in the text, various other painters were also associated with the original members, though mostly through their choice of similar subject matter. These painters included George Michel (1763–1843), who favored Montmartre and Saint Denis and left no record of his stay in Barbizon; Honoré Daumier (1808–1879), who was a close friend to Millet, Daubigny, Diaz, and (especially) Corot, and who visited Barbizon frequently, though he was best known as a painter and caricaturist of life in Paris; and Gustave Courbet (1819–1877), often connected with the group because of his rural origins, his broadly painted landscapes and peasant scenes, and, of course, the multiple possibilities offered by the term "realist," which he liked to apply to himself. Other Frenchmen who were generally considered to be part of the second generation of the Barbizon school include François Louis François (1814–1897), Henri Joseph Harpignies (1819–1916), Jules Breton (1827–1906), Jean Charles Cazin (1841–1901), and Léon Augustin Lhermitte (1844–1925). This is by no means an exhaustive listing, nor does it include a host of other European followers, especially those from Holland, Belgium, and England.

2. Charles S. Smith, *Barbizon Days* (New York, 1903), p. 16. Cooper's praise does not appear in any of his published writings, including *Gleanings From Europe*, which contains a rather lukewarm description of the Fontainebleau area. Nevertheless, for a new edition of Cooper's *Last of the Mohicans*, the Swiss painter Karl Bodmer sought out J.-F. Millet at Barbizon in 1850 to help with proposed illustrations. Several of these collaborative lithographs were finished, but were never published. See B. P. Draper, "American Indians, Barbizon Style," *Antiques* 44 (September 1943): 108–110.

3. Smith, *Barbizon Days,* pp. 15–16.

4. With occasional variations, the story of this initial discovery of Barbizon by touring artists can be found in several sources. Especially useful are Émile Michel, *La Forêt de Fontainebleau dans la Nature . . . et dans l'Art* (Paris, 1901); Prosper Dorbec, *L'Art du Paysage en France* (Paris, 1925); and Jean Bouret, *The Barbizon School and 19th Century Painting* (Greenwich, Conn., 1973).

5. See the chronology of the Barbizon painters in Robert L. Herbert, *Barbizon Revisted,* catalog of an exhibition held at the California Palace of the Legion of Honor et al., 1962, pp. 75–82.

6. John Rewald, *The History of Impressionism* (New York, 1961), p. 18. The Comte de Nieuwerkerke (Alfred Émilien) was director general of the museums of France during the Second Empire and superintendent of the fine arts, a post especially created for him by Napoleon III.

7. Herbert, *Barbizon Revisted, passim,* (esp. pp. 64–65).

8. Quoted without date in Alfred Sensier, *Jean-François Millet* (Boston, 1881), p. 119. The role of nature as refuge in Millet's art is somewhat belied by

the following remark about Millet made by Corot to Sensier: "A good heart but his pictures are to me a new world—I don't know where I am; I am too fond of the old" (p. 143).

9. Quoted by Rewald, *Impressionism*, p. 18, from "Homage à C. F. Dennecourt" in *Fontainebleau, paysages, legendes, souvenirs, fantaisie*, ed. F. Desnoyers (Paris, 1885). These remarks appear to have special references to the work of Millet and his "peasants with pipe in mouth." In 1855, the Barbizon painters were especially successful in the Universal Exposition in Paris, but Millet was represented by only one painting. Corot, whose dreamy glades are closer to Saint-Victor's preferences, won a first-class medal, as did Rousseau and Troyon.

10. British influence was first experienced in France in the realm of topographical illustrations. Even before the 1824 Salon, Girtin, Turner, Pugin, and others had published views of Paris and its environs. The fact that French scenery was worthy of attention by landscapists was especially important for Jacque, Daubigny, and Dupré, all of whom had illustrated travel books earlier in their careers. These Anglo-French relationships have been discussed in many sources; summaries can be found in Dorbec, *L'Art du Paysage*, pp. 38–78, and Herbert, *Barbizon Revisited*.

11. John E. Canaday, *Mainstreams of Modern Art* (New York, 1959), p. 121. Similar conclusions can be reached about art derived from much of nineteenth-century naturalism, including that of Courbet and the Barbizon painters. Sir Kenneth Clark has also noted this deterioration: ". . . just as classicism tends to emptiness and lack of vitality, so naturalism tends to vulgarity. It is the popular style, the style that can be understood without effort or education; and as with all forms of luxury, the saving of intellectual and spiritual effort creates an insatiable appetite for more (*Landscape into Art* [London, 1949], p. 86).

Chapter 2

1. William M. Hunt, *W. M. Hunt's Talks on Art*, series 1 (Boston, 1875), p. 33.

2. Henry James, *Autobiography*, F. W. Dupee ed. (New York and London, 1956), p. 287.

3. The most reliable and recent source for Hunt's early years is Gibson Danes's "A Biographical and Critical Study of William Morris Hunt, 1824–1879" (Ph.D. dissertation, Yale University, 1949). See also Helen M. Knowlton, *The Art-Life of William Morris Hunt* (Boston, 1899).

4. Knowlton, *Art-Life*, p. 6. Hunt's predecessor as Boston's leading artist, Washington Allston, admired contemporary German painting to a degree matched only by Hunt's dislike for it. Concerning the German master Wilhelm Kaulbach—much praised by Allston—Hunt wrote that his works were "all literature!" There was, in Hunt's view, "nothing there to stimulate or develop the perceptions, and everything to suppress instinct and enthusiasm. One learned neither to see nor to feel, everything was a task, a parrot's training." (*Talks on Art*, series 1, p. 93). Allston died during Hunt's first trip to Europe (1842), and with him went the strong intellectual bias in Boston toward art that this exceptional mind had helped to establish.

5. Knowlton, *Art-Life*, p. 7.

6. Couture's enormous moral allegory, *The Romans of the Decadence*, was, after its display at the Salon of 1847, the most notoriously popular painting of its day in France.

7. Albert Boime, *The Academy and French Painting in the Nineteenth Century* (London, 1971), pp. 161–180.

8. *Voyage a travers l'esposition des beaux-arts* (Paris, 1835) quoted in Boime, *The Academy and French Painting*, fn., 40.

9. Hunt, *W. M. Hunt's Talks on Art*, series 2; comp., H. M. Knowlton (Boston, 1894–1895) 2:32. See also Couture's *Methode et entretiens d'atelier* (Paris, 1867), pp. 235–237. Couture's hoarding of sketches for incomplete projects were shown in a posthumous exhibition in 1880 where an unsympathetic critic labeled them "The Apotheosis of the Incomplete" (C. H. Stranahan, *A History of French Painting* [New York, 1888], p. 290.)

10. Albert Boime, "Thomas Couture and the Evolution of Painting in Nineteenth Century France," *College Art Bulletin* 51 (1969):48.

11. Cf. Alain de Leiris, "Thomas Couture The Painter," in Jane Van Nimmen and Alain de Leiris, *Thomas Couture: Paintings and Drawings in American Collections* (University of Maryland Art Gallery, 1970), pp. 11–25; ". . . in the art of Couture, style is strictly defined and limited by technique, and is in fact technique and 'method' " (p. 14).

12. Robert L. Herbert, *Barbizon Revisited,* catalog of an exhibition held at the California Palace of the Legion of Honor et al., 1962, pp. 39–40, 78–79.

13. Information on Gay was kindly provided by Mrs. Marcia Mathews of Atlanta, Georgia, who is preparing a publication of the sketchbooks by Gay made during his travels in Japan in 1877–1881. According to Mrs. Mathews, there is no correspondence or other records which give information about his Barbizon exposure, including his study with Troyon.

14. John I. Baur, ed., "The Autobiography of Worthington Whittredge," *Brooklyn Museum Journal* 1 (1942): 21.

15. Reference here is to Millet's *Oedipus Being Taken From a Tree* shown at the Salon of 1847 (now in the Louvre). (See Joseph C. Sloane, *French Painting Between the Past and the Present* [Princeton, 1951], pp. 144f.)

16. Babcock never returned to America and died in Bois d'Arcy in 1899 (Marchal E. Landgren, *American Pupils of Thomas Couture,* catalog of an exhibition held at the University of Maryland Art Gallery, 1970; p. 22).

17. Will H. Low, *A Chronicle of Friendships, 1873–1900* (New York, 1908), pp. 108–109. See also Edward Simmons, *From Seven to Seventy* (New York and London, 1922), p. 190. Simmons learned, apparently from Millet's widow, that Babcock often raised the ire of the Frenchman by collecting drawings discarded by Millet from the latter's garbage: "Nothing daunted, he would retreat like a dog with a bone."

18. The first version of this painting was chosen for purchase by Louis Napoleon from the Salon of 1852, but it had already been spoken for by an American collector (present whereabouts unknown). The version illustrated here was bought by Martin Brimmer of Boston in 1853 and was one of the early donations to Boston's Museum of Fine Arts. (*American Paintings in the Museum of Fine Arts* 1 [Boston, 1969]: 156, cat. no. 587.)

19. Danes, "Study of William Morris Hunt," p. 24.

20. Knowlton, *Art-Life,* p. 21.

21. Ibid., p. 10. Knowlton refers to the exhibition of this work at the Salon of 1852, which is incorrect (cf. "Explication des ouvrages . . . Paris, 1852," which does not list any works by Millet). The version that Hunt probably saw first was shown at the winter Salon of 1850–1851. The version shown here and bought by Hunt was the first of three on this theme, all executed early in 1850. The Salon painting is now at the Provident Trust Bank in Philadelphia and a third version is also in a private collection in America. (See Herbert, *Barbizon Revisited,* p. 150.)

22. From Jules Castagnary's "Salon of 1859," quoted in Sloane's *French Painting,* p. 70.

23. Hunt, quoted in the catalog *The Sale of Paintings and Drawings at Warren Chambers* (Boston, 1898), p. 1.

24. For example, *The Sheep-Shearers* (Museum of Fine Arts, Boston) was bought by Hunt straight from Millet's easel to pay the latter's paint bill at Deforge's art store. This painting was subsequently sold to Martin Brimmer, then a pupil at the École. (Knowlton, *Art-Life,* pp. 10–11.) Brimmer was a Harvard student who had gone to Paris for treatment of a leg ailment and stayed there to study at the Sorbonne and collect paintings. Several decades later he was a moving force in the founding of several New England museums including the Museum of Fine Arts, Boston, and the Farnsworth Museum at Wellesley. (See George Silbee Hale, "Martin Brimmer, A Memoir," *The Publications of the Colonial Society of Massachusetts* 3 [Cambridge, Mass., 1897].)

25. Twenty years later another American visitor to Millet's Barbizon home, Wyatt Eaton, noted that Millet's spartan studio contained casts of antique torsos and reliefs from Trajan's Column as well as heads by Donatello and Luca della Robbia, and a cast from the arm of one of Michelangelo's *Slaves* (see Wyatt Eaton, "Recollections of Jean-François Millet," *Century Magazine* 38 [May 1889]: 91.)

26. Knowlton, *Art-Life,* p. 18.

27. The steady development from drawings to completed canvas in Millet's method is examined in detail by Robert Herbert in his "Millet Reconsidered," in *Museum Studies* 1 (The Art Institute of Chicago, 1966): 29–65.

28. Hunt, quoted in Knowlton, *Art-Life,* p. 12.

29. For example, this definition of beauty in Hunt's *Talks on Art,* series 1, "Beauty is that little something which fills the whole world and is neither contained in a straight nose, a long eye lash, or a blue mountain. Some see it in a leg of mutton; others in a compound fracture." (p. 53).

30. Edward Wheelright, "Personal Recollections of Jean-François Millet," *Atlantic Monthly* 38 (September 1876): 264.

31. Innes to Ripley Hitchcock, 1884, Goochland County, Virginia. This letter, the most important autobiographical source for the artist, is reprinted in its entirety in *George Inness of Montclair*, catalog of an exhibition held at the Montclair Art Museum, 1964.

32. "Art Matters," *New York Tribune*, May 1, 1852.

33. As early as 1848, a critic for the *Literary World* reviewing the annual exhibition at the National Academy claimed Inness's *Evening* was an "imitation of the sunsets of Claude Lorraine" and his *Diana Surprised by Acteon* was a "literal copy of that master Titian in the National Gallery in London" (*Literary World* 7 [1848]: 25).

34. George Inness, Jr., *Life, Art, and Letters of George Inness* (New York, 1917). Inness found these qualities as well in the older members of the Hudson River group, Thomas Cole and Asher Durand. "There was a lofty striving in Cole, although he did not technically realize that for which he reached. There was in Durand a more intimate feeling of nature. If, thought I, these two can only be combined. I will try!" (p. 14).

35. Inness to Samuel Gray Ward, November 30, 1852, Houghton Library, Harvard University.

36. *The Knickerbocker Magazine* 33 (April 1849): 158.

37. Nicolai Cikovsky, Jr., "The Life and Work of George Inness" (Ph.D. dissertation, Harvard University, 1965), p. 173.

38. Two of the paintings reviewed by the *Knickerbocker* in 1849, *Early Recollections* (private collection, New York City) and *The Old Mill* (the Art Institute of Chicago) have strong echoes in them of the rural scenes of the seventeenth-century Dutchman, Meindart Hobbema. Inness was once quoted as remarking in front of one of his early canvases: "I remember that picture. I was thinking much of Hobbema when I painted it" (Elliott Daingerfield, *George Inness: The Man and His Art* [New York, 1911], p. 15).

39. Cikovsky, "Life and Work of George Inness," p. 9.

40. Nicolai Cikovsky, Jr., "George Inness and the Hudson River School," *American Art Journal* 2 (Fall 1970): 36–57. Inness, with a growing family and mounting debts, was paid $75 for this commission, which he probably would have preferred to have avoided. Later, he was able to buy the painting at a curio shop in Mexico City. (Cf. also, LeRoy Ireland, *The Paintings of George Inness* [Austin, Texas, 1964], p. 28, cat. no. 110.)

41. *The Crayon* (1855), p. 17. When James Jackson Jarves published *The Art-Idea* in 1864, he had this type of Inness's work in mind when he spoke of the artist's facility in re-creating "the drowsy heat, hot shimmer, and languid quiet of a summer's noon . . . we can breathe in his atmosphere and travel far and wide in his landscape" (Cambridge, Mass., 2d edition, 1960, p. 195). Both Durand and Jarves held similar expectations for landscape painting although contemporary European art had little attraction for the former. Nevertheless, Durand's disavowal of the historical landscape and his call for firsthand study of nature helped clear the air for the later acceptance of Barbizon painting.

42. Leo Marx, *The Machine in The Garden* (New York, 1964), pp. 220–222. An opposite point of view in terms of Inness's accommodation to progress is presented in the film "The American Vision" (National Gallery of Art, Washington, D.C.).

43. Inness to Hitchcock, 1884.

44. Inness claimed that "my forms are at my finger tips as the alphabet is on the tongue of a schoolboy" (George Calvert, "George Inness, Painter and Personality," *Bulletin of the Art Association of Indianapolis, Ind., John Herron Art Institute* 13 [November 1926]: 49).

45. Inness's mother was a zealous Methodist, his stepmother a fervent Baptist, and his step-uncle a "proselytizing Universalist." Inness dabbled in all three religions as well as in Catholicism before turning to the teachings of Swedenborg in the mid-1860s. (See Cikovsky, "Life and Work of George Inness," pp. 14–15). An early Inness biographer for *Harper's Weekly* (July 13, 1867) noted that if the artist "had not possessed an intense love of form and a wondrous sense and power of expression of color, he would have been a preacher or a philosopher in another way, for he was of a deep religious nature and an extraordinary analytical-philosophical mind" (p. 433).

46. "Dream Culture," *Star Papers; or, Experiences of Art and Nature* (New York, 1855), p. 263. Although he may have been aware of Beecher's writings in the 1850s, Inness probably did not make his acquaintance until the 1860s. Beecher owned at least one Inness by 1860 and five by the time of his (Beecher's) death in 1887 (see Nicolai Cikovsky, Jr., *George Inness* [New York, 1971], pp. 35; 150, fn. 71).

47. Cikovsky, "Life and Work of George Inness," p. 32.

48. Of the eight pictures exhibited at the National Academy in 1859 by Inness, seven were already sold, one of them to Beecher who helped the young painter establish himself with the Boston dealers, Williams and Everett.

49. For a brief comparison of Inness and Dupré, see William Howe Downes, *Masters in American Art* (New York, 1908), p. 225.

50. Inness, Jr., *Life, Art, and Letters of George Inness*, p. 46.

51. An excellent study of this stage of Hunt's career can be found in Gibson Danes, "William Morris Hunt and His Newport Circle," *Magazine of Art* 48 (April 1950): 144–150.

52. Danes, "Hunt and His Newport Circle," p. 144.

53. The relationship between LaFarge and Hunt is examined at length in Ruth B. Katz, "John LaFarge as Painter and Critic" (Ph.D. dissertation, Radcliffe, 1951); see especially chapter 4, "Landscape Painting."

54. Royal Cortissoz, *John LaFarge* (New York, 1911), p. 70.

55. Henry LaFarge's essay in *John LaFarge, Oils and Watercolors*, catalog of an exhibition held at the Kennedy Galleries, New York, 1968.

56. M. E. Chevreul's *De la loi du constraste simultané des coleurs et de l'assortiment des objects colorés* was first published in Paris in 1839 and would have been accessible to LaFarge, who was fluent in French. Chevreul's experiments, which helped build the foundation for the divisionist theories of Seurat, received their first circulation in America in *Fraser's Magazine* 52 (November 1855): 503–516.

57. Introduction by John W. Beatty to *The Life and Works of Winslow Homer* by William Howe Downes (Boston and New York, 1911), p. xxvi. Besides Hunt, several conservative critics were mystified by LaFarge's Newport landscapes. When a view of *Brenton's Cove* was shown at the National Academy in 1864, Clarence Cook felt he could find nowhere in the picture a hint of nature: "It [color] is never so completely disjoined in nature, not even where there is the most mystery and the most confusion" (*New York Daily Tribune*, April 23, 1864).

58. John LaFarge's *The Higher Life in Art* (New York, 1908), a series of lectures on the Barbizon painters given at The Metropolitan Museum of Art, is still valuable as a unique piece of formal analysis by an understanding painter and eloquent writer. He stressed among other points the relationship of Delacroix to Millet, and hence the confluence of romanticism and realism. Millet, the real hero of the book, was for LaFarge "a vision of emotional art fit to balance the record of Delacroix" (p. 69).

59. Subsequently, in 1864, Hunt moved into a larger studio in the old Mercantile Building on Summer Street. Here "his walls were covered with paintings by him and Jean-François Millet." (Knowlton, *Art-Life*, p. 36). Most of the paintings on display were destroyed by fire in 1872.

60. Benjamin Champney, *Sixty Years' Memories of Art and Artists* (Woburn, Mass., 1900), p. 78.

61. *Boston Transcript*, 1860, month and day unknown, quoted in Roger A. Welchans, "The Art Theories of Washington Allston and William Morris Hunt" (Ph.D. dissertation, Western Reserve University, 1970), p. 121.

62. Francis Steegmüller, *The Two Lives of James Jackson Jarves* (New Haven, 1951), chapter 13.

63. William D. Howells, *A Foregone Conclusion* (Boston, 1875), p. 14.

64. For a thorough review of this show, see "Art— The British Gallery in New York," *Atlantic Monthly* 1 (February 1858): 501–507.

65. See Jean Gordon, "The Fine Arts in Boston, 1815– 1879" (Ph.D. dissertation, University of Wisconsin, 1965), p. 265.

66. Through 1860, Gay, who was basically a painter of views in the old tradition, showed eighteen paintings at the Athenaeum while Hunt managed to exhibit thirteen (see catalogs for the annual exhibitions of the Boston Athenaeum [1844–1860] collected in the Fine Arts library of that institution).

67. *Boston Athenaeum—Annual Exhibition, 1855*, cat. no. 78, *An Interior* by Millet. This may be *The Sewing Lesson*, the painting that Brimmer gave as one of the first gifts to the newly formed Boston Museum of Fine Arts in 1876.

68. Samuel Fiske, *Mr. Dunn Browne's Experience in Foreign Parts* (Boston, 1857), p. 251. Similar sentiments were expressed by Hunt: "You can't represent the height of the Alps or the Sierras. We must keep ourselves within the limits of possibility." (Hunt, *Talks*

on Art, series 1, p. 61.)

69. Wilhelm Worringer, Abstraction and Empathy: A Contribution to the Psychology of Style (New York, 1953), pp. 15, 45. Cf. also the more recent Vytautas Kavolis, Artistic Expression (Ithaca, N.Y., 1968), in which Millet is connected with the peasant characteristics of pre-urban social classes: "His featureless human beings eschew middle-class subjectivity and become part of the landscape" (p. 68).

70. In general, smaller pictures were increasingly popular during the 1860s, both in Boston and New York. Probably the strongest evidence of this is the rising market in watercolors, drawings, and prints during this period. The American Water Color Society was founded in 1866 and the French-owned Etching Club came to New York in the same year. At the beginning of the decade, a commentator for the New York Daily Tribune of February 18, 1860, reported, "Large pictures are no longer wanted." A similar situation occurred in France, in which the demand for small genre paintings and landscapes about mid-century was an increasingly important trend in the marketplace, with les grandes machines appearing less frequently in the Salons (see Harrison C. White and Cynthia A. White, Canvases and Careers: Institutional Change in the French Painting World [New York, 1965], p. 84).

71. For an engaging account of the effect of the war on New England idealism, see Van Wyke Brooks, New England: Indian Summer, 1865–1915 (New York, 1940), p. 121ff.

72. See The Dictionary of American Biography 1 (New York, 1932–1933): 333–334, hereafter cited as DAB. Appleton's wanderings were funded by the fortune of his father, Nathaniel Appleton, one of the founders of the textile industry in Lowell, Massachusetts.

73. Brooks, Indian Summer, p. 18. According to his friend Ernest Longfellow, Appleton once ordered a painting from Millet that later was discovered to be the famous Angelus. Millet asked only $200 for the painting, but Appleton "countermanded the order" when the artist "was long finishing the picture." (Ernest Longfellow, Random Memories [Boston and New York, 1922], p. 101.)

74. Appleton donated his valuable art collections, which included large samplings of Oriental art, to the Boston Public Library and the Boston Museum of Fine Arts (of which he was founding member). He also had a reputation for helping needy painters wherever he encountered them (DAB 1: 334).

75. The best known member of Thomas Wentworth Higginson's family was his cousin Henry Lee Higginson, the founder of the Boston Symphony and the donor of several paintings to the Museum of Fine Arts in Boston.

76. The largest single collection of Millets, collected mostly in the late nineteenth century, was that of an Englishman, James Staats Forbes. Unlike Shaw's group of Millets, Forbes's collection has been largely dispersed. Shaw, incidentally, did not actually meet Millet until a later trip to Paris in 1860–1861, at which time he was introduced to the artist by the former Crayon editor William Stillman, then a pupil of Rousseau's. Shaw purchased a few French paintings at this time, including a Rousseau (The Quincy A. Shaw Collection, Museum of Fine Arts, Boston, 1945, p. 2), but did not begin his ambitious collection of Millets until the 1870s. No specific records related to Shaw's earliest purchase of Millet's work have yet come to light.

77. The George A. Lucas Collection of the Maryland Institute, text by Gertrude Rosenthal, The Baltimore Museum of Art, 1965. The voluminous diaries of Lucas (over 15,000 entries) record visits to the studios of Couture, Corot, Daubigny, Dupré, Daumier, Pissarro, and many others. They are currently being edited for publication by Mrs. Lillian Randall.

78. On the whole, Lucas avoided American painters in France and did not collect their work. Works by his friend Whistler were a notable exception, as were works by Hunt. Lucas owned a half-draped figure by Hunt, probably a studio piece from Couture's classes. (The George A. Lucas Collection, p. 41, cat. no. 139.)

79. "The Yale Fine-Arts School," New York Daily Tribune, August 2, 1867. Cook was an early advocate of Ruskin and a founding member in 1863 of the Society for the Advancement of Truth. Unfortunately for Hunt's reputation west of Providence, Cook considered the Boston painter to be a sort of object lesson for those who would succumb to the blandishments of the French manner; in his Tribune reviews (1861 to 1881), he mentions Hunt more frequently than any other American. For his part, Hunt may well have welcomed such critical venom. According to Ernest Longfellow, "a failing exhibition by Hunt was enlivened when one of his friends wrote a damning letter to the Transcript; next evening, an article by the same man appeared praising it extravagantly" (Longfellow, Random Memories, p. 100).

80. William Howe Downes, "Boston Painters and Painting," Atlantic Monthly 64 (1888): 388. The first

show of the Allston Club contained 100 paintings and included among the artists and owners most of the officers of the club. The list of pupils of French masters in addition to Hunt, the president of the club, and Bicknell were Thomas Robinson (pupil of Courbet), R. H. Herne (pupil of Millet), and William Babcock (pupil of Couture and Millet). Among the Barbizon painters shown, Corot (six paintings) and Millet (three) headed the list, which included Daubigny (two), Rousseau (two), Jacques (one), and Troyon (two). The 1867 show contained 115 works, with much the same lineup of artists and owners. The catalogs for both exhibitions are in the Widener Library at Harvard University.

81. Hunt, *Boston Advertiser*, June 9, 1872, quoted in Knowlton, *Art-Life*, pp. 68–69.

82. At least three of Hunt's female pupils are worthy of mention; not surprisingly, all had studied with Couture as well. Elizabeth Otis Lyman Bott (1846–1889) was a frequent exhibitor of genre and still-life paintings at the Boston Art Club during the seventies and eighties. One of Hunt's first pupils, Marcia Oakey Dewing (1845–1928), was a collaborator with her husband, Thomas Dewing, in several paintings where she provided various still-life effects. She was best known as a painter of delicate flower pieces that helped win her a bronze medal at the Columbian Exposition of 1901 (Knowlton, *Art-Life*, pp. 30–31). Among Hunt's other lady pupils, probably the one most influenced by Barbizon art was Sarah Wyman Whitman (1842–1904), a member of the Society of American Artists, and a student of Couture's at Villiers-le-Bel at the time of his death in 1879 (ibid., p. 64).

83. F. D. Millet, "Mr. Hunt's Teaching," *Atlantic Monthly* 46 (August 1880): 191.

84. Jarves, *Art-Idea*, p. 184. Like William Stillman before him, Jarves's remarks demonstrate that a disciple of Ruskin could adjust to certain effects derived more from art than nature. In a description of Millet, Jarves uses Ruskinian terminology to imply an accommodation to modern French style: "Millet represented the Pre-Raphaelitism of his country, which is superior in its *scientific* execution and has more breadth of idea and manner than the English . . . particularly in subordination of inferior parts and lesser motives to the principal . . ." [italics mine] (p. 146).

85. Knowlton, *Art-Life*, p. 68.

86. Jarves, *The Art-Idea*, p. 185.

87. The only prime source for information on Robinson's life is a eulogy written by Edward Allen, *Thomas Robinson: A Memoir* (Providence, 1888). Robinson's important but largely incalculable role in importing paintings for Vose is examined in "An American Expert," *The Collector* (January 1, 1891), typescript in the Vose Galleries, Boston, Massachusetts.

Chapter 3

1. Kensett visited Fontainebleau with landscapist Benjamin Champney in the summer of 1845 and Cropsey went there with Thomas Hicks and George William Curtis three years later. Information from John Howat, *John Frederick Kensett, 1816–1872*, catalog of an exhibition held at The Metropolitan Museum of Art, 1968, and William S. Talbot, *Jasper F. Cropsey, 1823–1900*, catalog of an exhibition held at the National Collection of Fine Arts, 1970, p. 54.

2. *The Crayon* 1 (1855): 261.

3. "Boston Athenaeum Review," *The Crayon* 1 (1855): 24.

4. "Paris Notes," *The Crayon* 1 (1855): 198.

5. *The Crayon* 3 (1855): 184. The one Barbizon painter enjoying a consistently favorable press during this period was Constant Troyon. The painting of landscapes dominated by cows and sheep to which he turned after his trip to Holland in 1847 quickly achieved for him success throughout Europe and America. *The Crayon* mentions him favorably and frequently. Cranch found Troyon's landscapes "juicy in tone" and painted with "such knowledge . . . such love," terms of approval often invoked on behalf of the Hudson River artists, although most of them had considerable difficulty in painting convincing animals in their landscapes.

6. John Neal, *Observations on American Art*, ed. H. Dickson (New York, 1943), pp. xxii–xxiii. Neal was one of America's earliest art critics and relied on instinct rather than education in writing most of his criticism. Most of his articles, which appeared in *Randolph*, *Blackwood's Magazine*, and *The Yankee* during the 1830s and 1840s, applied to portrait and historical painting rather than to the rather small school of landscape painters known to him.

7. Several of the French romantics, including Delacroix and Chasserieau, were frequently praised in *The Crayon*, as were the religious paintings of Ary Sheffer (a special favorite, perhaps, because of the Pre-Raphae-

lite look in much of his work).

8. Goupil's International Art-Union was the French dealer's counterpart to the American Art-Union. The vast array of paintings and prints offered by the former were deemed by the American group to be "faithful specimens . . . of the modern French school . . . impure in sentiment, most of them extravagant in action and exaggerated in color" ("The International Art-Union," *Bulletin of the American Art-Union* 2 [1849]: 10–15).

9. "Memoranda of the mode of working adapted by several French Artists," *Bulletin of the American Art-Union* 2 (1849): 19–20. This article also notes that Couture "works on the principle that whatever cannot be realized at heat ought to be thrown aside as a failure."

10. "National Academy of Design, IV," *New York Daily Tribune*, May 3, 1856. Hunt's studio in Barbizon was rented from a rabbit seller and *Girl with Rabbit* may have been painted from a Barbizon sketch.

11. From the cover of *French Masters of 1830*, catalog of an exhibition held at R. C. and N. M. Vose Galleries, Boston, 1908.

12. "The Listener," *Boston Transcript*, June 17, 1908. The "what-d'call-'ems" must have been largely Corots and Daubignys. This same reporter wrote that by 1881, Vose had gathered 165 pictures by Corot and 69 by Daubigny. Cf. also, "Corot Came to U.S. by Grace of Seth M. Vose," *Boston Evening Transcript*, November 17, 1934.

13. [Clarence C. Cook], "Art in Providence," *The Studio*, n.s. 6, (April 25, 1891): 1.

14. "The Memoirs of Robert C. Vose and Seth Morton Vose," manuscript in possession of the Vose Galleries, Inc., Boston.

15. "The Belmont Collection," *The Crayon* 5 (January 1858): 23. For later comments on the Belmont Collection, with rather disproportionate praise for the small group of Barbizon works, see commentary by Samuel Swift in the August F. Jaccaci Papers, on microfilm in the Archives of American Art (hereafter cited as the AAA); and "The Belmont Collection at the Rooms of the National Academy of Design," New York, 1857 (AAA microfilm).

16. *Catalogue of A Large Collection of Superb Oil Paintings of Messrs. Goupil and Co.*, May 27–28, 1858, nos. 295, 296, 297. Goupil had opened operations in New York in 1846 as a print shop called Goupils, Vibert

and Company. By 1857, the business was taken over by Michael Knoedler, who continued to use the Goupil name. Leeds and Company began operations in New York by specializing in the auction of large private collections rather than in importing art from Europe.

17. For example, Diaz's *The Lovers*, sold by Leeds from the J. F. Beaumont Collection in April 1853; a *Sketch of Lady and Dog* on sale at Goupil's in April 1856, praised in the catalog for its "magical effect of color . . . truly a Connosseur picture"; and a *Venus and Cupid* sold by Goupil and Company and Leeds and Company. Cf. also Lois Fink, "The Role of France in American Art, 1850–1870" (Ph.D. dissertation, University of Chicago, 1969), p. 190ff.

18. *Catalogue of . . . Original Pictures Being the Entire Collection Known As the French and Flemish Exhibition at Goupil's . . .* , February 6–7, 1861. Many of Lambinet's small landscapes were bought by Boston collectors as well. The Museum of Fine Arts, Boston, has six examples by this forgotten painter.

19. For example, Mabel Swan, writing about the first exhibition at the Boston Athenaeum in 1844, noted that Doughty's six paintings there featured "wooded foregrounds whose silvery tones suggest Corot" (Mabel Swan, *The Athenaeum Gallery, 1827–1873* [Boston, 1940], p. 31). Doughty's rather tentative generalizations of nature provided an early, though not very successful, alternative to the specifics of the Hudson River school.

20. Lillian B. Miller, "The American Art-Union," chapter 14 in *Patrons and Patriotism; The Encouragement of the Fine Arts in The United States, 1790–1860* (Chicago, 1966). The previously noted criticisms in my discussion of the "old-master style" of George Inness were symptomatic of the new preference for contemporaneity in art.

21. When the London art firm of Gambert and Company sent over about a hundred canvases in 1858, several of them by Barbizon painters, the critical reception in New York was favorable but the selling power of the paintings was "incredibly low." The Gambert show fared better commercially when it was removed to Philadelphia, but most of the pictures were returned to England. (Samuel Swift, "Notes on New York Collections," Jaccaci Papers, AAA; see also Fink, "Role of France in American Art," pp. 188–189.)

Chapter 4

1. An interesting account of the sentimental alterna-

tive to Barbizon ruggedness offered by Frère (a favorite of Ruskin's) and his colony at Écouen can be found in M. D. Conway, "Édouard Frère and Sympathetic Art in France," *Harper's New Monthly Magazine* 42 (November 1871): 802.

2. It is worth noting here that two art critics of the future with a decidedly French orientation, Earl Shinn (pseudonym, Edward Strahan) and Henry Bacon, were art students in Brittany. Bacon was later a commentator for *Scribner's Monthly*, writing a column entitled "Parisian Art and Artists" (1880–1881). See also Lois Fink, "The Role of France in American Art, 1850–1870" (Ph.D. dissertation, University of Chicago, 1969), pp. 231–234, 320–323.

3. Haseltine, a marine painter famous on the American market for his harbor scenes of Naples and the New England coast, visited Paris first in 1866–1867 and "often left his studio in the Boulevard de Clichy to work at Barbizon." Like Hunt, he found in Barbizon painting an antidote for earlier training at Düsseldorf. (Helen H. Plowden, *William Stanley Haseltine* [London, 1947], p. 88.)

4. Stillman to Norton, February 14, 1861, Houghton Library, Harvard University. Stillman's frequent companion in Paris was Quincy Adams Shaw of Boston, later to become Millet's most important collector in America.

5. Quoted from the *Brooklyn Daily Eagle*, August 18, 1889, reprinted in Thurman Wilkins, *Thomas Moran: Artist of the Mountains* (Norman, Okla., 1966), p. 49. Moran once painted an imitation of a Corot for the mother of the noted collector Albert Gallatin. This work, listed as *A Corot* in Moran's records, was shown to an agent at Goupil's who, according to Gallatin, "could not tell it from a real Corot." (Wilkins, p. 183).

6. In 1863, Monet deserted the studio of his cousin Toulmouche to go to Fontainebleau, finding there "a thousand things which I could not resist" (John Rewald, *The History of Impressionism* [New York, 1961], pp. 93ff). Monet's first large outdoor painting, the *Déjeuner sur l'herbe* of 1865–1866, was begun at Chailly. Renoir's first effort of a similar nature, an open-air portrait of his mistress, was painted in the same locale in 1867.

7. A few facts on Fischer's life amidst much conjecture and panegyric can be found in M. L. D'Otrang Mastai, *Mark Fischer, 1841–1923: American Impressionist,* catalog of an exhibition held at the Shore Galleries, Boston, July 1969.

8. The date usually given for his departure is 1859, but this is convincingly corrected in Nicolai Cikovsky, Jr., *George Inness* (New York, 1971), p. 32.

9. James Jackson Jarves finds him an artist "impersonating his own mental conditions at times with a poetical fervor and depth that rises to the height of genius" (*The Art-Idea* [Cambridge, 1960], p. 195).

10. For example, Inness's *Road to the Farm* of 1862 (Museum of Fine Arts, Boston), perhaps his most Hobbema-like composition.

11. Inness was an ardent Republican and probably an abolitionist as well, although his "nervous condition" prevented him from enlisting in the Union Army (Cikovsky, *George Inness,* pp. 33–34).

12. A wood engraving of this painting is illustrated in George W. Sheldon, *American Painters* (New York, 1879), facing p. 31.

13. Quoted from Henry James, "French Pictures in Boston, 1872," in *The Painter's Eye* (London, 1956), p. 45.

14. Jerold Lanes, "Kensett at the Whitney," *Art Forum* 7 (December 1968): 53. Regarding the more modern, French look of younger Americans, Lanes adds: ". . . the development of painters like Homer Martin or George Fuller or the entire work of George Inness, shows how far precept had been sacrified to concept under the influence of European currents that swamped American painting late in the century." Strangely enough, Kensett's personal collection of foreign paintings, which helped realize over $150,000 for his estate when sold at auction after his death in 1872, was dominated by works of the more acceptable modern French painters. Included were three Troyons, one valued at $1,000, and a Rousseau, also valued at $1,000. The wily Kensett managed his money with unusual acumen for an artist and may have bought these paintings as investments only. His own development showed little inclination to be swayed by more up-to-date directions.

15. Samuel G. W. Benjamin, writing eight years after Kensett's death, remarked that the artist's tender harmonies were "so marked . . . that before the great modern question of the values began to arouse much attention in the ateliers of Paris, Kensett had already grasped the perception of a theory of art practice which has since become so prominent in foreign art." (*Art in America: A Critical and Historical Sketch* [New York, 1880], pp. 63–64). The word "since" indicates that

Benjamin is referring to the work of the young impressionists in France, despite the fact that Kensett's mature work is manifestly closer to Corot's early studies in tone and atmosphere than the faceted color of impressionism. Kensett could have seen Corot's work at the Salon during his two trips to Paris and Fontainebleau (in 1840 and 1845), but no hint in his scant commentaries indicate that such was the case. Nevertheless, Kensett's long-standing popularity and his considerable output must have contributed to the favorable reception eventually accorded Corot's work in America after about 1875.

16. From Sanford R. Gifford, "Journals" 1, September 29, 1855, AAA typescript. The primary sources from which other material on Gifford is here presented are Ilya J. S. Weiss, "Sanford Robinson Gifford (1829–1880)" (Ph.D. dissertation, New York University, 1968); and, an essay by Nickolai Cikovsky, Jr. in *Sanford Robinson Gifford (1829–1880)*, catalog of an exhibition held at the University of Texas Art Museum, Austin, 1970.

17. Gifford was accompanied by an Irish landscapist named Hearne, a former pupil of Millet's. Both called on Edward Wheelwright of Boston, then studying with Millet at Barbizon (Gifford, "Journals" 1, May 18, 1856). Oddly enough, when Gifford went to Europe in 1855, William Stillman wrote in *The Crayon* 1 (May 1855): 330, that "he will spend his time of study mainly in England, certainly the best school for landscape which the day affords." As we have already seen, both Stillman and Gifford would change their positions on English hegemony before long. Like Cole, Gifford had little regard for English landscapes anyway, and felt that they offered "nothing that showed a superiority over our American school..." ("Journals" 1, June 3, 1855).

18. Quoted in an interview with Gifford in George W. Sheldon, "How One Landscape Painter Paints," *Art Journal* 3 (1877): 285.

19. Albert T. E. Gardner, *Winslow Homer, American Artist* (New York, 1961), p. 85. First considered by Lloyd Goodrich and expanded upon by Gardner, the thesis that the major feature of Homer's trip to Paris was his exposure to Japanese prints at the International Exposition has been recently disproved in John J. Walsh, "Winslow Homer: Early Work and the Japanese Print" (Master's thesis, Columbia University, 1965.)

20. Gardner, *Winslow Homer*, p. 132.

21. See William H. Gerdts, introduction to *Alfred Cornelius Howland, 1838–1909*, catalog of an exhibition held at Coe Kerr Gallery, Inc., New York, 1971.

22. The incidental relationships between Homer and Courbet have been summarized in Barbara Novak, *American Painting in the Nineteenth Century* (New York, 1969), pp. 171–172; and George Boas, ed., *Courbet and the Naturalist Movement* (Baltimore, 1938), pp. 118–122. Philip C. Beam, "Winslow Homer, 1836–1910" (Ph.D. dissertation, Harvard University, 1944) is the only biography of Homer's to propose Millet as the more important French influence on him (p. 111).

23. Yvon Bizardel, *American Painters in Paris* (New York, 1960), p. 168.

24. John LaFarge, *The Higher Life in Art* (New York and London, 1908), p. 7. Hunt had returned to Europe to renew old acquaintances with Corot and Millet in Paris, and to visit England, Spain, and Italy.

Chapter 5

1. The facts surrounding Wyant's life can be studied in greater detail in Robert C. Olpin, "Alexander Helwig Wyant, 1836–1892" (Ph.D. dissertation, Boston University, 1971); or in the more accessible catalog by the same author, *Alexander Helwig Wyant, 1836–1892*, published in conjunction with an exhibition held at the Utah Museum of Fine Arts, University of Utah, Salt Lake City, March 1968. There is no record available at this time to indicate what or where Inness exhibited in Cincinnati (see exhibition record in LeRoy Ireland, *The Paintings of George Inness* [Austin, Texas, 1964], pp. 5–6).

2. New York's Düsseldorf Gallery had been open since 1848 and reached the height of its popularity in 1863 (when Wyant arrived there) with the publication of *Gems From The Düsseldorf Gallery* (New York, 1863) by Goupil and Company. This large folio featured photos of works by most of the leaders of the school including an exciting waterfall view by Wyant's future teacher, Hans Gude. Cf. Eliot Clark, *Alexander Wyant* (New York, 1916), pp. 10–11.

3. Nine unpublished letters by Wyant to his patron, Thomas Turlay, written from Karlsruhe during the winter of 1866–1867 (now in the AAA manuscript collection) are filled with misgivings about his choice of school. For example (February 3, 1866): "To be sure there are many learned artists here in Germany but their learning is to their pictures, what dry pedantry

is in a haranguer, to Church's or Kensett's infinite suggestion and detail, or H. W. Beecher's burning eloquence." See Peter Bermingham, "Alexander H. Wyant: Some Letters From Abroad," *Archives of American Art Journal* 12, no. 4 (1972): 1–9.

4. Clark, *Alexander Wyant*, p. 16.

5. The best known of this series of Wyant's *View of County Kerry, Ireland* is in The Metropolitan Museum of Art. This work postdates *The Mohawk Valley* by about a year. See Olpin, "Alexander Helwig Wyant," p. 137, where *View of County Kerry* is compared to Constable's *Weymouth Bay* in London; and remarks of Wyant's pupil, Bruce Crane, included in John C. Van Dyke's *American Painting and Its Tradition* (New York, 1919), p. 52.

6. The Art Institute of Chicago records date this painting about 1880, which is manifestly too late. Olpin places the work with several lake paintings of the early seventies ("Alexander Helwig Wyant," p. 293, no. 74). In my opinion, its sublimity of composition and rather finicky brushwork—the academic convention of the "needle-mark" waves, for example—dates it even earlier in Wyant's career, perhaps as soon as 1868.

7. Several texts, including contemporary surveys, dismiss Wyant's style as an amalgam of French mannerisms. For example, Samuel Green, *American Art* (New York, 1966), p. 273, in which Wyant's heavy application of paint is related to the "impasto of men like Diaz de la Peña and Monticelli"; and Albert T. E. Gardner, *Winslow Homer, American Artist* (New York, 1961), p. 131, in which Wyant is dismissed as an artist who "lost himself in the forest of Barbizon and never quite managed to find his way back into American landscape." Cf. also Samuel G. W. Benjamin, *Art in America*, (New York, 1880), pp. 189–190.

8. "When an art dealer was showing some small examples of Wyant to a patron the latter remarked, 'These pictures are very much like the Barbizon men.' Wyant, informed of the remark, was appreciably pleased, and proudly acknowledged his allegiance" (Clark, *Wyant*, pp. 30–31).

9. Charles H. Caffin, *American Masters of Painting* (Garden City, New York, 1913), contains a rather Lincolnesque passage describing Wyant as a child practicing charcoal drawing on his kitchen floor, and finding in the "soft, suggestive medium" his first awareness "of the meaning of synthesis in landscape; the securing of character and tone, and the fascination of working in masses rather than outline" (p. 143).

10. The basic sources on Martin's life used here are the memoirs written by the artist's wife, Elizabeth G. Martin, *Homer Martin: A Reminiscence* (New York, 1904); Frank J. Mather, Jr., *Homer Martin: Poet in Landscape* (New York, 1912); and *The Index of Twentieth Century Artists* 4, no. 1 (New York, 1936): 321–326, which, despite its misleading title, has the largest compilation of Martin's bibliography readily available. Patricia Mandel, "Homer D. Martin: American Landscape Painter (1836–1897)" (Ph.D. dissertation, New York University, 1973) offers the most recent analysis of Martin's painting. At this writing, I have not yet had the opportunity to read this study.

11. During the early sixties in New York, Martin executed a forest interior based on the andante from Beethoven's Fifth Symphony (reproduced in William J. Henderson, Frank J. Mather, Charles R. Morey, *The American Spirit in Art* [New Haven, 1928] 12: 81). The present location of this painting is not known.

12. Mather, *Homer Martin*, p. 35. Martin's friend, George Boughton of Albany, New York, once wrote to another Albany artist, sculptor Launt Thompson, that "if Homer Martin had been his [Corot's] pupil, he could hardly paint more like him" (Martin, *A Reminiscence*, pp. 9–10). Mrs. Martin noted, "It was not until long years after that Thompson had the grace to repeat the observation to Homer, and when at last he did so, the only reply was: 'Why did you not tell me that years ago, when it would have been of some service to me?' For Homer, too, was one of Corot's worshippers from the first."

13. Mather, *Homer Martin*, p. 32.

14. Reference to Martin's limited appeal was made in the anonymous review "American Painters—Homer D. Martin," *Art Journal* 6, n.s. (November 1880), pp. 321–323. "In a certain circle of metropolitan lovers of Art, Mr. Martin has long been fully appreciated . . . yet for some reason . . . his works have not sold commensurately with their deserts" (p. 321). To this reviewer, Martin's problems seemed especially acute when compared to the successes of the "modern Fontainebleau school."

15. The Princeton University Museum has a Martin drawing inscribed "St. Cloud 25 June 76."

16. "American Painters—Homer D. Martin," p. 321. See also Dana H. Carroll, *Fifty-Eight Paintings by Homer D. Martin* (New York, 1913). Number 26, facing page 68, illustrates a work *On the Seine* that is undoubtedly from this period, and that is, perhaps, of any of Martin's works, the closest in touch and com-

position to Corot's late works. Such imitations are, however, atypical of Martin's development during the eighties.

17. Edgar P. Richardson, *Painting in America* (New York, 1965), p. 307.

18. Biographical information on Brown used here was obtained from William Hose Downes, "John Appleton Brown, Landscapist," *American Magazine of Art* 14 (August 1923): 436–439; and *American Paintings in the Museum of Fine Arts, Boston* (Boston, 1969) 1:41. The Museum of Fine Arts owns seven oils by Brown.

19. Benjamin, *Art in America*, p. 106. The records of the Vose Galleries indicate that Brown also owned a substantial collection of Barbizon paintings, including examples by Corot, Rousseau, and Daubigny.

20. For example, *The Month of May* and *New England Landscape,* both undated works probably from the 1890s, now in the Museum of Fine Arts, Boston.

21. This subdued lyricism in the work of Thomas Moran, an otherwise atypical artist, was also noted by the critics. Moran's small landscapes executed from the late seventies on in Long Island, New York, and Florida were cited in *The Critic* 8 (1886): 108, for "that beauty of subdued color and gray tone which is distinctly modern."

22. Henry C. White, *The Life and Art of Dwight William Tryon* (Boston and New York, 1930), p. 35. Tryon's study of Corot was sufficiently intense to allow him during his student days to identify a false Corot for a Paris collector, a judgment later supported by the French dealer Pettit, a leading seller of Corot's work.

23. Ibid., pp. 53–55. White offers a lengthy, rather mechanical comparison of Turner and Tryon, both as painters and personalities.

24. Ibid., pp. 76–87.

25. Barbara Novak, *American Painting in the Nineteenth Century* (New York, 1969), p. 255, notes that the "amorphous dream" was "expressed also by other artists as an ephemeral veil, glaze, stain, or mist of color that was the antithesis of indigenous clarity, though of course, it has a place within the American tradition, at least from Allston."

26. An excellent review of this critical search in American art from the early days of Cole and Durand can be found in Barbara Novak, "Some American Words: Basic Aesthetic Guidelines, 1825–1870," *The American Art Journal* 1 (Spring 1969): 78–91.

27. George Inness, "A Painter on Painting," *Harper's New Monthly Magazine* 55 (1878): 458.

28. Arthur Hill, a student of Inness's, recalled how his teacher "talked on structural forms, dimensions, distances, spaces, masses and lines. . . . One might have thought he was an architect laying out a large structure" ("Early Recollections of George Inness and George Waldo Hill," *New Salmagundi Papers* [New York, 1922], p. 114).

29. From Paul Valéry, "About Corot" (1932), reprinted in *Degas, Manet, Morisot* (New York, 1960), p. 137ff.

30. Inness, "A Painter on Painting," p. 459. Several of the winter scenes executed by Inness in Montclair, New Jersey, in the early eighties compare favorably with the somewhat more bleak, raw depictions of this season by Rousseau (for example, LeRoy Ireland, *The Paintings of George Inness* [Austin, 1964], cat. nos. 1034, 1108, 1259; and Rousseau's *Le Givre*).

31. Cf. also, Ireland, *Paintings of George Inness*, cat. nos. 1214, 1215, 1218, 1267, 1281.

32. Frederic F. Sherman, *Landscape and Figure Painters of America* (New York, 1917), p. 9.

Chapter 6

1. E. S. [Edward Strahan?], "The International Exhibition," *The Nation* 23 (June 25, 1876): 347–348.

2. Such doubt was crystallized in the following year with the founding of the rebellious Society of American Artists, but apparently was not shared by the steadier patrons of the Hudson River painters. Many of these supporters helped control the selection of the jury for the show. (See Mildred B. Matthews, "The Painters of the Hudson River School in the Philadelphia Centennial Exhibition of 1876," *Art in America* 34 [July 1946]: 143–160.) As reported by John V. Sears, a major reason for the lack of current offerings by Americans in Europe, as well as by many of the illustrious French painters, was less a matter of aesthetical bias and more a simple problem of logistics. The United States government had offered to transport works from Europe on a sailing vessel, "one of the dullest . . . in the navy" according to Sears. As a result, many established painters from abroad refused to submit entries. Their fears were justified; at the time of Sears's review the ship had yet to arrive in America. ("Art in Philadelphia," *The Aldine* 7 [1876–77]: 199).

3. *Appleton's Journal* 13 (January 30, 1875): 148.

4. From the inauguration editorial in *American Art Review* 1 (January 1880): 1.

5. Information from Frank Mott, *A History of American Magazines* 2 (Cambridge, Mass., 1938), pp. 180–191. During the same period, the number of periodicals (not including newspapers) rose from 700 to a high of 2,400 in 1880.

6. "Present Tendencies in American Art," *Harper's Magazine* 58 (December 1878): 481–496. Earlier notice of the impressionists had been taken by Henry James in a brief review of the Durand–Ruel show in Paris in 1876. Without mentioning any of the artists by name, James found their work "curious" and dubbed them the "Irreconcilables" (*New York Tribune*, May 13, 1876).

7. Inness's so-called letter on impressionism (1884), printed in John W. McCoubrey, ed., *American Art, 1700–1960* (Englewood Cliffs, N.J., 1965), pp. 121–122, refers to an "art editor" who had miscast him as an impressionist in a review of the Durand–Ruel show held in 1883 at the Mechanics Building in Boston.

8. See George Inness, "A Painter on Painting," *Harper's New Monthly Magazine* 56 (December 1877–May 1878): 456–461; and "Mr. Inness on Art Matters," *Art Journal*, n.s. 5 (1879): 374–377. In 1875, Inness had delivered an address, "The Logic of the Real Aesthetically Considered," at the Boston Art Club. No record of this talk (noted in the *Boston Transcript*, April 8, 1875) or of the book about his theories that he was preparing at this time is available today.

9. "George Inness," *Century Magazine*, n.s. 2 (May 1882): 57–64.

10. *Ibid.*, p. 60.

11. In New York City alone, companies such as Philip Levy's on Cortlandt Street or B. Mayer's on Beekman Street turned out over 100 paintings a day. These were hawked on corners, sold through galleries, or sent throughout the country on consignment. See Clarence Cook, "Art Degraded to a Trade," *New York Daily Tribune*, March 16, 1878.

12. "Younger Painters of America," *Scribner's Monthly* 20 (January 1880): 326. Brownell, who did not make his first trip to France until the following year, soon made two important contributions to America's growing list of publications on French art and manners: *French Traits* (New York, 1884) and the still useful *French Art* (New York, 1892).

13. For similar sentiments, see Samuel G. W. Benjamin, "W. M. Hunt's Influence on Painting," *American Architect and Building News* 7 (February 14, 1880): 60.

14. Notice of the influx of Boston art in New York was made in this interesting observation from "The Arts," *Appleton's Journal* 13 (May 15, 1875): 632: "We are glad to observe that the Boston artists are getting much better known in New York than was formerly the case. The standard of thought on artistic matters had been quite different in the two places. . . . It has seemed to us that there is perhaps less of business feeling among the Boston painters than here. . . . They are content to make with less attention to established and conventional values. . . ." Hunt, Couture, and the Barbizon painters were not the only benefactors of Boston's progressive attitudes. Frank Duveneck, for example, gained his first foothold in America after a show in the Boston Art Club in 1875. This success in Boston occurred after his "broad and brown" Munich style had been rejected in his native Cincinnati. See "Art," *Atlantic Monthly* 35 (January 1875): 117–121; and *Boston Transcript*, July 27, 1875.

15. Richard Whiteing, "The American Student at the Beaux-Arts," *Century Magazine*, n.s. 1 (November 1881–April 1882): 268.

16. *The Angelus* became the *cause célèbre* in a new policy of protectionism by the French after notice was taken of the alarming number of French works going to America. As a result, the auction at the American Art Galleries resulted in the unusual spectacle of a Frenchman (H. Chauchard) outbidding several Americans for this painting.

17. From an undated article from *Figaro* excerpted in the *Boston Sunday Herald*, May 15, 1881. Information on sales in the preceding sentences are from the records of the Vose Galleries.

18. Information on the Capen–Warren sale is from "Art in New York," *Boston Post*, March 2, 1889. The real drawing power in such sales came from the paintings of Frenchmen like Breton, Meissonier, and Gèrôme than from those of the Barbizon men, even Millet. (The top price at the Morgan sale was $45,000 for Breton's *Communicants*.) By the same token, prices at the Capen–Warren sale were generally lower due to absence of paintings by these same men. For an itemized summary of highlights of the New York market from 1860 to 1882, see B. J. Lessing, *A History of New York City* (New York, 1884), pp. 841–843.

19. From an undated clipping from the *Boston Journal* in the files of the Vose Galleries.

20. Ironically, Robinson's candid appraisal of the marketplace was restated some fifty years later by Millet's grandson, Jean Charles, who was jailed along with a house painter from Fontainebleau for forging Corots, Millets, Pissaros, etc. In admitting his crime, Jean Charles's only defense was that his work was for export only to American and British "experts" who "buy pictures with pedigrees but have not the slightest notion whether they are genuine or not. All you have to do is ask a fabulous price" (*Washington Post*, February 28, 1935).

Chapter 7

1. From a survey of the *19th Century Reader's Guide to Periodical Literature* and *Poole's Guides to Periodic Literature*.

2. M. LaGrange, "Le Salon de 1864," *Gazette des Beaux-Arts* 1 (July 1864): 5.

3. *The Crayon* 7 (December 1860): 353.

4. *The Horse Fair* was lavishly praised at the Salon of 1853 and soon went on tour throughout western Europe and finally was exhibited in America in 1857. During the next thirty years, it was owned consecutively by three Americans. It was donated to the Metropolitan Museum of Art by Cornelius Vanderbilt who had paid $53,000 for it, a record price for a work by any French artist living at that time. (Margareta M. Salinger and Charles Sterling, *French Paintings: A Catalogue of the Collection of The Metropolitan Museum* [Greenwich, Conn., 1966] 2:161–164; and Lois Fink, "The Role of France in American Art, 1850–1870" [Ph.D. dissertation, University of Chicago, 1951], p. 301.)

5. The comparison between Potter and Troyon was an important part of an essay on Troyon by a Connecticut painter of cows, William H. Howe, included in *Modern French Masters*, ed. J. Van Dyke (New York, 1896), p. 149. Potter's painting is now in The Hague Art Museum; formerly it hung in the Louvre (1795–1815), where it was copiously copied. The popularity of *The Young Bull* in America was enhanced when a large reproduction of it was included in E. Fromentin, *Old Masters of Belgium and Holland* (Boston, 1882), p. 162.

6. Wiggins's only surviving son, Colonel Grafton Wiggins of Atlanta, Georgia, informs me that about 1890, millionaire Henry Frick asked the Lotos Club to name a price for a large painting by Wiggins entitled *Plow Horse* owned by the club. Frick was refused and his blank check was returned.

7. Information here is from conversations with William H. Gerdts as well as from his *Painting and Sculpture From New Jersey* (Princeton, 1964), p. 153.

8. Emmanuel Swedenborg, Inness's mystical hero, went so far in his *Correspondences* to differentiate between the "natural" appeal of cattle and the "spiritual" appeal of sheep and lambs.

9. The theme of the shepherd tending his flock was also a specialty of Charles Jacques, who, to a greater extent than Millet, reproduced such works in etchings and drypoints. (See Gabriel Weisberg, *The Etching Renaissance in France: 1850–1880,* a catalog of an exhibition held at the Utah Museum of Fine Arts, 1971, nos. 51, 52.)

10. Samuel Isham, *The History of American Painting* (New York, 1933), p. 495.

11. Whitman's diary of 1881, quoted in F. O. Matthiessen, *American Renaissance: Art and Expression in the Age of Emerson and Whitman* (London and New York, 1941), p. 602.

12. See H. Merwin, "Millet and Walt Whitman," *The Atlantic Monthly* 79 (May 1897): 719–720.

13. Reviewing the Brooklyn Art-Union show in 1851, Whitman found the "spirited well-being" of Walter Libbey's *Boy with a Flute* "typical of the character of Americanism" (Matthiessen, *American Renaissance*, pp. 596–597). Whitman at the time was still under the spell of Ruskin's *Modern Painters*, which he reviewed with unbounded enthusiasm in the *Brooklyn Eagle*, July 22, 1847.

14. Several comments from Fuller's letters concerning his European visits are contained in William Dean Howells's "Sketch of His Life," included in Josiah B. Millet, *George Fuller: His Life and Works* (Boston and New York, 1886), p. 30ff. Regarding Millet's peasant subjects, Fuller felt that "in most of his melancholy pictures your sympathies are moved, and you are so sorry for the poor people that you are glad to pay tribute to his genius." He added: "Frère is, as you know, more cheerful."

15. Helen M. Knowlton, *The Art-Life of William Morris Hunt* (Boston, 1899), pp. 115–116.

16. An analysis of Fuller's technique can be found in J. J. Enneking, "Fuller's Methods in Painting," in Knowlton, *Art-Life*, pp. 74–75. Like Inness's methods, Fuller's seem—in Enneking's description at least—to be a mixture of Venetian and Rembrandtesque styles, although Fuller's palette is anything but Venetian.

17. Frank Mather, *Estimates in Art* (New York, 1931), p. 105.

18. Ibid., p. 106.

19. After its purchase by the Art Institute of Chicago in 1894, *The Song of the Lark* was the winner of two contests held to determine the most popular painting in Chicago ("Chicago's Favorite Painting," *Chicago Tribune*, May 16, 1920).

20. P. Burty, *Mâitres et petits mâitres* (Paris 1877), p. 292.

21. J. Breton, *Nos peintures du siecle* (Paris, n.d.) pp. 123ff. In this respect, Breton's thoughts are kinder than Thomas Moran's acidic remarks about Millet's peasants: "He shows us only the ignorant and debased peasant; he suggests nothing noble or high, nothing that is not degraded. His peasants are very little above animals" (George W. Sheldon, *American Painters* [New York, 1824], p. 147).

22. J. Breton, *The Life of an Artist* (New York, 1890), p. 226.

23. For the inevitable comparison to Millet, in this regard, see "American Artists at The Paris Exhibition," *Harper's New Monthly Magazine* 79 (September 1889): 311–312. Additional biographical information on Knight used here was selected from clippings on file in the library of the National Collection of Fine Arts and National Portrait Gallery, Smithsonian Institution, Washington, D.C.

24. Bastien-Lepage's most famous work, his *Joan of Arc* of 1879, featured a peasant girl from his native Damvillers obscured by painstaking detail in a local orchard; this painting was on loan to Boston's Museum of Fine Arts from 1882 to 1889 before being donated to the Metropolitan Museum of Art.

25. M. D. Conway, "Édouard Frère and Sympathetic Art in France," *Harper's New Monthly Magazine* 43 (November 1871): 805–806. Cf. also Edward Wheelwright, "Personal Recollections of Jean-François Millet," *Atlantic Monthly* 38 (September 1876), pp. 261–262.

26. F. Newlin Price, "Horatio Walker, The Elemental," *International Studio* 77 (August 1923): 359–362; Cf. also "Farm Art is Fertile Theme at Women's Sessions," *Washington Star*, June 20, 1936.

27. A variation on the same theme by Walker is his *De Profundis* (reproduced in *International Studio*, November 1916) with pigs instead of oxen, and a large rainbow in the sky.

28. A lengthy analysis of Walker's elaborate technique can be found in "Pictures Painted to Stay," *The Literary Digest* 95 (August 11, 1923): 31–33. By the turn of the century, Walker had been a gold medalist four times, receiving one from a competitive show at the American Art Galleries in 1887 and another from the Chicago Exposition of 1893. He was an active member of eleven artists' societies in New York and Canada (see obituary in *Washington Star*, October 9, 1938).

Chapter 8

1. Clara M. Kirk, *W. D. Howells and Art in His Time* (New Brunswick, N.J., 1965), p. 205.

2. William D. Howells, "A Traveler from Altruria," *Cosmopolitan* 14 (November 1892): 277.

3. Gustave Geffroy, "French Art in Chicago," *Cosmopolitan Art Journal* 16 (January 1894): 371–372; William G. Constable, *Art Collecting in the United States of America* (London and New York, 1964), pp. 74–75; and, Aline B. Saarinen, *The Proud Possessors* (New York, 1958).

4. James Jackson Jarves, *Art-Thoughts* (New York, 1871), pp. 55–56.

5. Sheridan Ford, *Art: A Commodity* (New York, 1888), pp. 36–37, 40. Durand-Greville's findings were expressed in a note to Ford and published in a series of articles for *Gazette des Beaux-Arts* 2 (1887): 65.

6. Ibid., p. 52. Conversely, Ford reserved strong praise for William Morris Hunt for "collecting true art rather than fashion" (p. 51).

7. Ibid., pp. 35–36. Cf. also Samuel Isham, *The History of American Painting* (New York, 1933), p. 360ff.

8. John Rewald, *The History of Impressionism* (New York, 1961), p. 531: "Durand-Ruel was already known in America as the early defender and dealer of the, by then, highly popular Barbizon school. This reputation has led the American public to the very realistic conclusion—a conclusion which the French had failed to

draw—that since he so consistently supported his new friends, their works ought to have some value."

9. Hamlin Garland, *Crumbling Idols*, ed. J. Johnson (Cambridge, Mass., 1960), p. 106.

10. John Rewald, *Impressionism*, p. 610, no. 36.

11. For information on the Old Lyme group see Arthur H. H. Heming, *Miss Florence and the Artists of Old Lyme* (Essex, Conn., 1971); Robin Richman's introduction to *The Art Colony at Old Lyme*, catalog of an exhibition held at the Lyman Allyn Museum, New London, Conn., 1966.

12. As early as 1840, Samuel F. B. Morse told the National Academy in New York that "facsimile sketches in nature" could be provided through the use of the daguerreotype, thereby easing the preparatory burdens of the artists. See Beaumont Newhall, "The Daguerreotype and the Painter," *Magazine of Art* 42 (November 1949): 249. Cf. also Elizabeth Cook, "The Influence of Photography on American Landscape Painting" (Ph.D. dissertation, New York University, 1970), which concentrates on the use of the daguerreotype by Frederic Church, Albert Bierstadt, and Thomas Moran.

13. For a review of the use of photography by the Barbizon artists and the resemblance of Barbizon painting to photography, see Aaron Shoen, "French Art and Science in the Mid Nineteenth Century: Some Points of Contact," *Art Quarterly* 34 (Winter 1971): 434–455. Cf. also Edward Wheelwright, "Personal Recollections of Jean-François Millet," *Atlantic Monthly* 38 (September 1876): 269; "Paris Notes," *The Crayon* 1 (1855): 198. Useful for a survey of the advances of photography, and the consequent dilemma photography posed to American painters, is George Erlich, "Technology and the Artist: A Study of the Interaction of Technological Growth and Nineteenth Century American Pictorial Art" (Ph.D. dissertation, University of Illinois, 1961), pp. 112–153.

14. See, for example, C. Sabbrin, *Science and Philosophy in Art* (Philadelphia, 1886).

15. Peter Emerson, *Naturalistic Photography* (New York, 1899), p. 112. Emerson quotes at great length from several of Millet's letters (pp. 112–117), finding in Millet's art and works valuable instruction for achieving "directness of expression" and power of characterization.

16. Robert L. Herbert, *Barbizon Revisited*, catalog of an exhibition held at the California Palace of the Legion of Honor et al., 1962.

17. Thomas Cole, "Essay on American Scenery," 1835, in *American Art, 1700–1960* (Englewood Cliffs, N.J., 1965), p. 102.

18. Ibid., p. 106.

19. George Inness, "Letters on Impressionism," in Inness, Jr., *Life, Art, and Letters of George Inness* (New York: 1917), p. 170.

20. "Aesthetic Studies of Art," *The Crayon* 7 (September 1860): 270.

21. On Millet as a literary painter for America, see William C. Brownell, *French Art, Classic and Contemporary, Painting and Sculpture* (New York, 1901), p. 48ff. Millet was often quoted as inquiring of aspiring artists: "Qu'avez-vous à dire?" What do you have to say?

22. Charles Baudelaire, "Salon de 1859," in *Curiosités esthétiques* (Paris, 1892), pp. 53ff, 326–327.

23. George Santayana, "Walt Whitman: A Dialogue," *Harvard Monthly* 10 (May 1890): 88.

24. George Inness, "A Painter on Painting," *Harper's New Monthly Magazine* 56 (December 1877–May 1878): 456–461.

25. David C. Huntington, *The Landscapes of Frederic Edwin Church* (New York, 1966), pp. 65–71. The cogency of this particular comparison was first brought to my attention in Dr. Huntington's seminar on American art problems at the University of Michigan in 1970.

26. Inness, "A Painter on Painting," p. 459.

27. D. H. Lawrence, *Studies in Classic American Literature*, 2d ed. (New York, 1964), p. 54.

28. George Santayana, *The Sense of Beauty: Being the Outline of Aesthetic Theory* (1896, reprint ed., New York, 1955), p. 22.

29. Ibid., p. 135.

30. Ibid., p. 136.

31. Several studies, published and unpublished, are available that analyze in greater detail the implications of Santayana's treatise. Especially recommended are Willard Arnett, *Santayana and the Sense of Beauty* (Bloomington, Ind., 1955); and, J. Ashmore, "Santayana's Theories of Art and Aesthetics: An Introductory Study" (Ph.D. dissertation, Columbia University, 1954).

32. John LaFarge, *Higher Life in Art* (New York, 1908), pp. 29–30.

33. Roger Welchans's dissertation, "The Art Theories of Washington Allston and William Morris Hunt," is an excellent review of Hunt's true value as a popularizer as well as his limitations as a theorist. Cf. also, review of Hunt's *Talks* in *Atlantic Monthly* 36 (1875): 249; and, "Culture and Progress—'Talks on Art,'" *Scribner's Magazine* 10 (1875): 787. In the twentieth century, the teachings of John Sloan and Robert Henri owed much to the inspiring eloquence of Hunt's *Talks.* Henri's *The Art Spirit* (Philadelphia, 1923) has much of the flavor and style of Hunt's work, although the former's pleas for independence were conceived in a more purely American vernacular.

34. See Ruth B. Katz, "John LaFarge as Painter and Critic" (Ph.D. dissertation, Radcliffe, 1951), pp. 164–175.

35. John LaFarge, *Considerations on Painting* (New York and London, 1895), pp. 129–130, n. 1.

LENDERS TO THE EXHIBITION

Allen Memorial Art Museum, Oberlin, Ohio

Art Gallery of Hamilton, Ontario, Canada

The Art Institute of Chicago, Illinois

The Brooklyn Museum, New York

Chapellier Galleries, New York, New York

Corcoran Gallery of Art, Washington, D.C.

Detroit Institute of Arts, Michigan

Indianapolis Museum of Art, Indiana

Johnson Gallery of Middlebury College, Vermont

Library of Congress, Washington, D.C.

The Metropolitan Museum of Art, New York, New York

G. William Miller, Massachusetts

Montclair Art Museum, New Jersey

Montreal Museum of Fine Arts, Quebec, Canada

Museum of African Art, Washington, D.C.

Museum of Fine Arts, Boston, Massachusetts

National Gallery of Canada, Ottawa, Ontario

The Newark Museum, New Jersey

Pennsylvania Academy of the Fine Arts, Philadelphia

The Phillips Collection, Washington, D.C.

Reading Public Museum And Art Gallery, Pennsylvania

Robert C. Vose, Jr., Boston, Massachusetts

Wadsworth Atheneum, Hartford, Connecticut

The Walters Art Gallery, Baltimore, Maryland

Worcester Art Museum, Massachusetts

CATALOG OF THE EXHIBITION

Dimensions are in inches; height precedes width

Paintings, with Biographies of Artists

French

JULES BRETON   1827–1906
Born: Courrières (Pas-de-Calais), France
Died: Paris, France

Breton began his studies in 1843 in Ghent, Belgium, at the Royal Academy. While at the Academy he studied with Felix de Vigne, a friend of his father's who was later to become the artist's father-in-law. Three years later, Breton went to Antwerp to study at the Academy of Fine Arts under Gustaaf Wappers, and in 1847 worked in the atelier of Michel Drolling in Paris. He exhibited for the first time at the Paris Salon in 1849 and, the following year, won a third-class medal. Breton's entry in the Salon of 1857 won a second-class medal and was purchased for the Luxembourg Museum. He received first-class medals in 1859 and 1861, and again in 1867, in which year he also won the Cross of the Legion of Honor and the first-class medal at the Universal Exposition in Paris. In addition to these honors, he was made a member of the Institute in 1882 and of the École des Beaux-Arts in 1886. Beside writing his autobiography in 1890, Breton published two volumes of his own verse, the first in 1875 and the second in 1880. He made excursions to Brittany in 1865 and 1873 and visited the south of France on other occasions, but spent most of his life in Courrières.

Breton's forte was painting studiously grouped peasant women at work or in religious processions. He often worked in the Barbizon area and wrote about it in his novel *Savarette* (1898) and in his engaging treatise on art *La Peinture* (1904); however, he was never considered a member of the Barbizon school. Breton and Millet knew each other well and the two artists were in friendly competition after about 1851. Although both men were capable of investing their art with a sense of nobility and serenity, Breton eschewed Millet's fatalism in favor of an academic correctness that made his canvases somewhat more congenial to bourgeoise tastes. Breton's enormously popular *Song of the Lark* (fig. 64) shows a young farm girl who stands somewhere between the weary workers of Millet and the prettified maidens of Bougereau and the American painter, Ridgeway Knight. Breton knew of the ugliness of peasant life but felt, too, that "there are also to be found among the peasantry, women superbly beautiful, with rounded contours and fresh complexions, in contrast with interesting and devout types of stunted ugliness, such as the painters of the middle ages loved to depict."

1. *The Song of the Lark*   1884   fig. 64
oil on canvas, 43½ × 33¾
The Art Institute of Chicago; Henry Field Memorial
   Collection

JEAN-BAPTISTE CAMILLE COROT   1796–1875
Born: Paris, France   Died: Paris, France

The son of well-to-do clothing merchants in Paris, Corot devoted himself full time to painting. He began his studies in 1822 with Michallon and Jean Victor Bertin, and painted in the area around Paris, in Fontainebleau, and along the Channel coast. In 1825 he went to Italy and worked in the environs of Rome and in central Italy for the next three years. Upon returning to Paris in late 1828, Corot established a routine of traveling throughout France, painting out-of-doors during the warm weather and preparing large works indoors for the Salons during the colder months. Although he had sent two pictures from Italy to the Salon of 1827, he did not exhibit regularly there until after 1831, winning his first official recognition in 1833. Corot made a sec-

2

and after his lifetime perhaps comprise his most original contribution, younger French artists, including members of the impressionist group, found greater stimulation in his plein-air paintings than in these studio creations. Despite the Claudesque, old-world distillations that were a hallmark of much of his art, Corot's interest in photography and his frequent studies of musical harmonies in painting betray a thoroughly modern outlook as well. In America, Corot's early champions at mid-century included Seth Vose, William Morris Hunt, and the Philadelphia patron Richard Lucas. Within a decade or so after his death, Corots and pseudo-Corots were included in countless public and private collections in America. Ironically, during this same period and later, the American artists most frequently compared to Corot (Inness, Martin, Murphy, and Tryon) rarely painted outdoors, thus reversing the procedure that ignited the earlier appeal of Corot in France.

2. *The Laurel Gatherers*   1845–1850
oil on canvas, 20 × 14½
Museum of Fine Arts, Boston; bequest of Mrs. Henry
    Lee Higginson, Sr.

3. *The Farmhouse under the Elder Trees, Normandy*
oil on canvas, 18¼ × 22
Corcoran Gallery of Art, Washington, D.C.; bequest of
    William A. Clark

CHARLES-FRANÇOIS DAUBIGNY   1817–1878
Born: Paris, France   Died: Paris, France

Daubigny's family included several other artists. He took his first lessons from his father, Edmonde François Daubigny, a landscape painter and former pupil of Victor Bertin. In 1836 he spent six months in Italy before returning to Paris to work as a restorer at the Louvre and a painter of ornaments. With the help of his friend Meissonier, he began to publish woodcut illustrations in 1838. Although he made his debut at the Salon in 1838 with both etchings and oils, his chief activity for the next decade was as a graphic artist. In 1840 he studied painting under Paul Delaroche for six months. From 1843 he went regularly to Barbizon as well as to Valmondois and Auvers, where he had spent his youth. In 1848 he won a second-class medal at the Salon and in 1850 and 1851 published two albums of etchings. The winner of a first-class medal at the Salon of 1853, he also sold a painting to Louis Napoleon in the same year. A close relationship with Corot began to develop in 1852 and the two traveled to the Dauphiné to paint. After 1857 and until his death, Daubigny often worked from

ond trip to Italy in 1834, staying for about six months. During the next ten years he spent most of each year in the area around Paris, either at his studio in the city or at the family property in Ville d'Avray, although he also traveled extensively in France and returned several times to Chailly and to Barbizon. Corot made the first of several trips to Switzerland in 1842, and in the following year made his third and last trip to Italy. By about 1850 he had attracted a number of young disciples and, from the summer of 1852, frequently traveled and painted with Charles Daubigny. After 1843, except for brief trips to Holland in 1854 and to London in 1862, he seldom journeyed outside of France. He had a studio built in Coubron in 1873, but died two years after its completion.

Corot's long life was marked by constant travel, a prolific output of paintings, drawings, and graphics, and a legendary charity towards struggling artists. Although the misty *souvenirs* so often copied and forged during

his studio-boat "Botin." He painted mainly in the regions around Paris and along the Channel during the final two decades of his life, with the exception of a trip to London in 1866 and another in 1870–1871.

Daubigny's career, with its bewildering chronology and samplings in many styles, is perhaps best summarized in a piece of advice that he gave to Dwight Tryon when the young American student showed him some of his studio drawings: "We all go through more or less of that work. I think you have had enough, and are ready to go to the country." Daubigny went to the country and the lakes often and his "impressions" of

them—part naturalism, part style and motif—made him perhaps the most influential of the Barbizon artists on Monet, Pissarro, and, briefly, Cézanne. The least subjective of the Barbizon group, Daubigny also attracted more adverse criticism in the sketch-finish controversies during the 1860s. By then, however, his reputation with both the older and the younger generation of French artists was too secure to be seriously threatened.

4. *The Willows* 1864
oil on canvas, 17¾ × 32
Corcoran Gallery of Art, Washington, D.C.; bequest of
    William A. Clark

4

5

NARCISSE VIRGILE DIAZ DE LA PEÑA
1808–1876
Born: Bordeaux, France   Died: Menton, France

Son of Spanish political refugees, Diaz was orphaned at about the age of ten and had his leg amputated while still a boy as the result of an untended snake bite. He worked for some time as an apprentice to a decorator in a porcelain factory, where in 1823 he met Jules Dupré. His formal training was completed with a brief stay in the atelier of Souchon, a painter from Lille. Diaz made his debut at the Salon in 1831 and, in the Salon of 1837, the year after his first visit to Barbizon, he exhibited a view of the Forest of Fontainebleau. After 1837 he became a friend and disciple of Rousseau. By 1847 he often met with Corot, Troyon, Jacque, Dupré, and Millet in Fontainebleau, and his winter studio in Paris was a frequent meeting place for fellow painters.

More than any other Barbizon artist, including Corot, Diaz maintained throughout his career a close alliance with the color and mood of the eighteenth-century French tradition, as well as ties with his French-romantic contemporaries, particularly Delacroix and Decamps. *The Courtesans* (cat. no. 5), a relatively early work of about 1835–1840, treats a favorite subject of this charming, personable artist; its graceful, undulating patterns of light and shade reminds one of how much Renoir admired Diaz's paintings. Diaz became a more astute observer of nature's variety and breadth during his fruitful association with Rousseau (beginning in 1837), although his canvases—including many that display a certain mechanical ingenuity—rarely lost their innately decorative sense. Much of Diaz's enormous production has found its way to our shores, many as early as the 1850s. Some American artists at the end of the century discovered Diaz through the work of the Marseille painter Adolphe Monticelli, who was vigorously championed by Robert Vose, Sr., and his Boston gallery.

5. *The Courtesans*   1835–1840
oil on panel, 11½ × 17¾
Museum of Fine Arts, Boston; gift of Edward Jackson Holmes

JULES DUPRÉ   1811–1889
Born: Nantes, France   Died: L'Isle-Adam, France

When only twelve years old Dupré was apprenticed as a decorator, first in his father's porcelain factory in Creil and later at Saint Yrieix in Limousin. In 1823 he met Narcisse Diaz, who worked with him in the factory. His only formal training was a brief period with the Austrian painter Michel Diebolt. He exhibited for the first time at the Paris Salon in 1831, and two years later won a second-class medal that attracted favorable attention from the French press. During a trip to England in 1834, he was especially attracted to the landscapes of John Constable. From 1835 to 1840 he traveled extensively and worked closely with Théodore Rousseau, and counted among his friends Troyon, Daubigny, Millet, and Decamps. He worked mainly in the area around Berry and Limousin, but also in the Forest of Fontainebleau. In 1849 he separated from Rousseau and, after winning the Legion of Honor in 1850, withdrew to L'Isle-Adam, north of Paris. From the late sixties he often spent his summers on the Channel coast. Dupré did not exhibit at the Salon between 1839 and 1852, and had only one major exhibition after 1852, at the Universal Exposition of 1867 in Paris. He came out of self-imposed retirement in 1876 and lived for several years in Paris, but was largely inactive by 1880.

Like Rousseau, his friend and associate for many years, Dupré worked directly from nature at an early age. His autumn scene from the Forest of Fontainebleau, the *Plateau of Bellecroix* of 1830 (Cincinnati Art Museum), demonstrates that at the early age of twenty, Dupré had already a strong sense of composition—impressive enough to cause Rousseau to remark that "it was Dupré who taught me to paint as a unity." The mutual exchanges between Rousseau and Dupré are evident in their affection for pebble-grain brushwork in trees and shrubs, and in the lavish attention both gave to dramatic skies and light effects. *The Hay Wagon* of 1852 (cat. no. 6), a favorite subject for Dupré, of which there are several variants, is an excellent example as well of his early awareness of Constable and the Dutch landscapists. By the time that this painting was executed, however, Dupré was semiretired and a convert to romantic improvisations in landscape painting, the promise of his youthful freshness largely forgotten. Although his dense impastos and painterly verve won Dupré many admirers among American painters, Hunt and Inness among them, his work was generally regarded as little more than a minor echo of that of his more illustrious Barbizon comrades.

6. *The Hay Wagon*   1852
oil on canvas, 16 × 21¼
Wadsworth Atheneum, Hartford, Connecticut; gift of Dr. and Mrs. Charles C. Beach

6

7

CHARLES ÉMILE JACQUE   1813–1894
Born: Paris, France   Died: Paris, France

Jacque received his only formal training at an early age as an apprentice to an engraver of maps. During his six years in the military service from 1830 to 1836, he was stationed for a time in Burgundy and also visited the Lowlands. After his discharge he worked in London, designing woodcuts for an illustrated edition of the works of Shakespeare. Upon his return to Paris in 1838, Jacque continued his career as a graphic artist and contributed engravings to several journals, including caricatures for *Charivari*. He first submitted an etching to the Paris Salon in 1845 and won a third-class medal for graphic arts in the Salon of 1850. In 1849 he moved with Millet to Barbizon, where he also became a close friend of Rousseau. Jacque left Barbizon in 1854 to live near Paris, where he conducted studies in animal husbandry that eventually led to a book entitled *The Poulterer*. In 1861 and 1864 he won medals for his paintings in the Salon. His American pupils included J. F. Cole and, on an informal basis, Thomas Robinson.

The last survivor of the original Barbizon group, Jacque is most frequently compared (to the detriment of his historical position) to Millet and Troyon. Nevertheless, Jacque's specialty, paintings and prints of animals and peasants, was developed before those of either of his better known colleagues—as early as the late 1830s, when his plates for *Picturesque Brittany* stimulated his appetite for scenes of peasant life. An ardent specialist in animal husbandry throughout his career, Jacque's affection for and curiosity about his domestic subjects often resulted in pictures that have a healthy informality about them, with none of the subjective overtones one usually finds implicit in the works of Millet or Rousseau. Jacque deserves special recognition for the role his etchings served in reminding several of his fellow landscapists that this still-new technique was an excellent means for translating their fresh impressions into prints.

7. *Landscape with Sheep*
oil on canvas, 26¼ × 38½
Detroit Institute of Art, Michigan

JEAN-FRANÇOIS MILLET   1814–1875
Born: Grouchy, France   Died: Barbizon, France

The son of Norman peasants, Millet was educated at the village school and by the curé at Gréville. He began his formal instruction in Cherbourg, first with Mouchel

in 1833 and then with Langlois de Chevreville in 1835. A fellowship awarded by the city of Cherbourg in 1837 enabled him to study in Paris with Paul Delaroche and to draw at the Académie Suisse. Millet exhibited at the Salon of 1840, but it was not until the Salon of 1847 that his work drew widespread notice. From 1841 to 1845 he divided his time between Paris, Cherbourg, and Le Havre. The money from a government commission in the winter of 1848–1849 permitted Millet to move to Barbizon with Charles Jacques in June 1849. After 1850 he became close friends with Rousseau, who took up residence near him in Barbizon. Millet remained in the environs of the Fontainebleau village until his death, except for two trips to Cherbourg and another to Vichy. After winning a first-class medal in the Salon of 1864, he received many more honors, including, in 1868, the Legion of Honor. In 1874 the French government commissioned him to decorate the Paris Pantheon, but he died the following year while still making studies for this ambitious undertaking.

The saga of Millet's self-imposed isolation in Barbizon for nearly twenty-five years made him a hermit-saint to many American visitors to his studio—from William Babcock, William Morris Hunt, and Edward Wheelright during the fifties to Wyatt Eaton and Will Low in later years. These and others came to listen and look, and frequently to buy Millet's work. Although few Americans could fully understand the root matter of Millet's art or the symbolic character of his paintings, they easily responded to the essential dignity of his strong images of farm laborers and their families. Despite a certain drabness in brushwork and occasionally in color, Millet's redeeming qualities were many, including his grasp of atmospheric truth, rich pictorial imagination, remarkable facility for relating figures to the earth about them, and talent for draughtmanship that only Daumier among his contemporaries could equal. An agnostic praised for his religiosity, a political diffident revered by French socialists and American democrats, Millet suffered from overzealous press agentry (most of it posthumous) and from a dearth of understanding regarding the whole range and meaning of his art.

8. *The Sower*   1850   fig. 15
oil on canvas, 39¾ × 32½
Museum of Fine Arts, Boston; bequest of Quincy A. Shaw

9. *Farmyard by Moonlight*   1868   fig. 26
pastel on paper, 28 × 34¼
Museum of Fine Arts, Boston; bequest of Quincy A. Shaw

10. *Return of the Flock*
oil on wood, 21 × 28
Pennsylvania Academy of The Fine Arts, Philadelphia

11. Study for *The Angelus*
charcoal on paper, 12½ × 17¾
Walters Art Gallery, Baltimore

PIERRE ÉTIENNE THÉODORE ROUSSEAU
1812–1867
Born: Paris, France   Died: Barbizon, France

Rousseau's parents had a prosperous draper's business in Paris and several of his relatives were artists. At an early age he began painting with his cousin Alexandre Pau de Saint-Martin and, at the age of fourteen, was studying professionally under Rémond. From 1826 to 1829 he made long painting excursions near Paris, including Fontainebleau, and made copies after Claude and the Dutch masters in the Louvre. He worked for a short time with Guillon Lethière before beginning a lengthy stay in the Auvergne in 1830. Upon returning to Paris he won the support of Ary Scheffer and made his debut at the Salon, contributing regularly from 1831 to 1836. During the 1830s Rousseau traveled extensively throughout France and in 1831 went to Normandy, where he met Paul Huet. In 1833 he was in Chailly and in 1836 he made his first visit to Barbizon, where he remained for several months and met Diaz and Caruelle d'Aligny. About 1837 he began to rent on a nearly annual basis a studio in Barbizon and soon settled there. During the forties he painted in the Landes and at L'Isle-Adam with Jules Dupré, a close friend from 1834 to 1847, and journeyed to the Berry region from 1842 to 1843. Unable to gain entry into the Salon from 1836 until 1848, he finally returned there in 1849, winning a first-class medal. Rousseau's friendship with Dupré was severed in 1849, but Millet's arrival in Barbizon the same year marked the beginning of an enduring association between the two artists. After 1849 Rousseau traveled less frequently, although he still maintained winter quarters in Paris as well as his Barbizon studio.

Although not as versatile in terms of subject matter and media as, for example, his close friend Millet, Rousseau, with his prodigious output, runs an extraordinary gamut from intensely dramatic landscapes to straightforward renditions of some of the least spectacular scenery around the environs of Paris and Fontainebleau. Nature's varied elements were for Rousseau, more than for any other Barbizon painter, living heroes in a struggle against man's encroachment and the erosive

processes of time and weather. Rousseau's personal pantheism supported him during long periods of struggle and deprivation, yet would not allow him ever to be completely satisfied with more than a few of his paintings. Many American painters, the most notable among them George Inness and Alexander Wyant, appreciated Rousseau's synthesis of the French and Dutch baroque traditions, and, more important, gained symbolic support from his struggle to convey a vivid sense of the texture and substance of nature. Unfortunately, Rousseau's lavish use of fugitive paint media in his work has left many paintings in poor condition. Unlike Millet's works, the major holdings of which are in American collections, Rousseau's *oeuvre* can be best appreciated in France. Among the few paintings of exceptional quality by the artist in this country must certainly be included the Johnson Gallery's placidly beautiful *Gorge d'Apremont* (cat. no. 13).

12. *A Gray Day*
oil on canvas, 9¼ × 13¾
Robert C. Vose, Jr., Boston

13. *Gorge d'Apremont*
oil on canvas, 24 × 37
Johnson Gallery of Middlebury College, Vermont; gift of Mrs. Louis A. Turner, 1969

CONSTANT TROYON   1810–1865
Born: Sèvres, France   Died: Paris, France

Even after he began to exhibit at the Salon, Troyon worked for many years at the porcelain factory at Sèvres, where his parents were also employed as decorators. He received his formal training from two other painter–decorators, Riocreux and Poupart, while drawing and painting from nature in his spare time. About 1824 he met Diaz for the first time. Troyon exhibited regularly at the Salon from 1833, winning a third-class medal in 1838 and one of the first-class medals in 1846. In 1843 he met Jules Dupré and went with him on a painting trip to the Landes. In the same year, he was introduced to Rousseau and began to frequent sites in and near the Forest of Fontainebleau. During a trip to Holland in 1847, Troyon studied closely the Dutch animal painters. Between 1847 and 1859 he was awarded many official honors, first in Holland and Belgium and then in France, where in 1849 he was nominated to the Legion of Honor. Thereafter, he worked mainly in Normandy, the Touraine, and in the vicinity of Paris, with occasional trips to England and the Lowlands. In his last years he was accompanied by Boudin to the

12

13

15

Normandy coast, where the two artists painted seascapes.

The first Barbizon painter to gain a broad base of critical and popular support both in Europe and America, Troyon helped directly and indirectly to inspire many younger landscapists throughout the second half of the nineteenth century. His calm noncontroversial manner of painting was usually heralded as a fitting complement to the widespread renewal of interest in seventeenth-century Dutch art; indeed, Troyon's trip to Holland in 1847 was by far the most critical period in his own development. With the exception of Millet's rural studies in Barbizon, the works of few artists of Troyon's era could match his own in providing, as Robert Herbert described it, "an intimate dialectic between his animals and their natural environment." His *Pasture in Normandy* of 1852 (fig. 28) is a relatively early work from the period during which Troyon became a confirmed *animalier*. The countless efforts by American artists that this painting pointedly anticipates include those of Thomas Robinson, J. F. Cole, William Howe, Thomas Craig, and Carleton Wiggins.

14. *Pasture in Normandy*   1852   fig. 28
oil on canvas, 15⅛ × 21⅝
The Art Institute of Chicago; Henry Field Memorial Collection

American (including Canadians)

CHARLES APPEL   1857—after 1934
Born: Brooklyn, New York   Died: ?

Appel was a pupil of F. L. Mora and William Merritt Chase at the New York School of Art. He also studied with Frank Dumond at the National Academy of Design. Most of Appel's professional life was spent in East Orange, New Jersey.

At this writing, only a few scattered facts concerning Appel's life and fewer still of his extant paintings have been discovered. From an art-historical viewpoint, *On the Passaic River*, ca. 1914 (cat. no. 15), is a thoroughly outdated work, but its timeless subject matter and more than adequate competence in technique and composition reveal the sympathetic hand of an artist about whom one would like to know more. George Inness's paintings from his Montclair period, which included a few views of the Passaic, may have provided Appel with a special stimulus, as they did for several other turn-of-the-century landscapists in New Jersey.

15. *On the Passaic River*   ca. 1914
oil on canvas, 17 × 24
Montclair Art Museum, New Jersey

16

EDWARD MITCHELL BANNISTER   1828–1901
Born: Saint Andrews, New Brunswick
Died: Providence, Rhode Island

As a young man Bannister probably worked on trading ships that ran from Saint Andrews along the eastern coast of the United States. Apparently by the 1850s he had settled in Boston, where he became a professional photographer. He studied at the Lowell Institute under Dr. William Rimmer, a noted anatomist and sculptor, and became increasingly active in the Boston art world from 1855 through the Civil War period. Bannister moved to Providence in 1870 or 1871 and for thirty years was a well-respected member of that city's artistic community. He was awarded a bronze medal at the Centennial Exposition of 1876 in Philadelphia for his painting *Under the Oaks* (now lost). In 1878 Bannister helped to found the Providence Art Club, which organized a retrospective exhibition of his works shortly after his death in 1901.

Speculation is all we have to amplify the few known facts about Bannister's life. He was possibly a member of that circle of ardent young painters befriended by William Morris Hunt in Boston during the 1860s.

Despite his black heritage (his father was a native of Barbados), Bannister shunned social commentary in his work—unless one chooses to find it implicitly present in the dark, brooding quality of many of his landscapes. In Boston and later in Providence, Bannister was surrounded by imported Barbizon art and undoubtedly found in it not only a complement to his own feelings toward nature but also a stylistic mode that did not threaten to overwhelm his lack of formal training. Not surprisingly, Bannister was at his most exciting in smaller sketches, such as *After the Shower* (cat. no. 16), a vigorously expressive summary that, in the broadest sense of the term, is truly an "impressionist" painting.

16. *After the Shower*
oil on board, 9 × 10
Museum of African Art, Washington, D.C.

17. *Sunset*   1883
oil on canvas, 16 × 24
G. William Miller, Massachusetts

18. *Sunrise*
oil on canvas
Museum of African Art, Washington, D.C.

17

18

20

J. APPLETON BROWN   1844–1902
Born: Newburyport, Massachusetts
Died: New York, New York

John Appleton Brown received some brief early training with a Boston-area portrait painter, B. C. Porter. In 1865 he went to Boston to open his first studio. Two years later he left for Paris to study under Émile Lambinet. After returning to America, he took another studio in Boston, where he remained throughout his career, holding annual exhibitions of his works. During the summer months, he painted from nature in the Newburyport vicinity. Brown exhibited at the Paris Salon of 1875 and in the early 1880s, spent some months in England working with Edwin Abbey and Charles Parsons, with later brief visits to Italy and the Riviera. A medal winner at the World's Columbian Exposition of 1893 in Chicago, Brown was also an associate academician at the National Academy of Design and a member of the Society of American Artists and the New York Water Color Club.

A cheerful, genial soul enormously popular within the art circles of Boston, Brown was a keen student and occasional collector of Barbizon painting. Before the artist turned to a robust, brightly colored style at mid-career, his subtle delicacy of tone and feathery textures elicited from local critics many comparisons with the work of Corot and Daubigny—a kinship that Brown accepted as a form of flattery rather than derision. *Brook in Summer* (cat. no. 20) and *On the Coast of France* (fig. 46) suggest something of the range of Brown's repertoire, which also included nocturnal scenes, flower gardens, and architectural compositions.

19. *On the Coast of France*   1875   fig. 46
oil on canvas, 20½ × 30
Museum of Fine Arts, Boston; bequest of Ernest Wadsworth Longfellow

20. *Brook in Summer*
oil on canvas, 20 × 27
Museum of Fine Arts, Boston; bequest of Arthur Tracy Cabot

JOSEPH FOXCROFT COLE   1837–1892
Born: Jay, Maine   Died: Boston, Massachusetts

After a public-school education in Boston, Cole became an apprentice with Winslow Homer at J. G. Bufford's lithography shop in that city. From 1860 to 1863 he was in France, where he was a pupil under Émile Lambinet and during the winters, studied drawing in government schools. After a sketching trip in Italy, Cole set up a studio in Boston in late 1863 or early 1864. With active support from William Morris Hunt, he had sold enough by 1865 to return to Paris, where he studied under Charles Jacque. Cole exhibited in the Salons of 1866 and 1867 as well as in the Universal Exposition of 1867 in Paris, and spent his summers painting in Normandy and Belgium. In late 1870 he returned to Boston but went back to France in 1872, remaining for five years. During this period he exhibited at the Salons of 1873, 1874, and 1875, and frequently at the London Royal Academy. Cole received a medal at the Centennial Exposition of 1876 in Philadelphia. He was back

in Massachusetts in 1877, living in Winchester at Mystic Lakes where, except for brief trips to California and Europe, he spent the rest of his life.

With the exception of William Morris Hunt, few Americans knew the Barbizon artists more intimately than Cole, who had frequent contacts with Troyon, Corot, Daubigny, and Diaz while studying at Jacque's studio in 1865. Although best known for his views of grazing cattle and sheep, Cole devoted increasing time during the last fifteen years of his life to misty scenes of the marshlands and meadows near Providence and Winchester. Although falling short of the symphonic level of much American tonalism, Cole's paintings, such as *The Abbajona River, Winchester* (cat. no. 21), exhibit an ingratiating, if minor, vein of this late-century phenomenon.

21.   *The Abbajona River, Winchester*   after 1877
oil on canvas, 18¼ × 26
Museum of Fine Arts, Boston; gift of Alexander
   Cochrane

THOMAS BIGELOW CRAIG   1849–1924
Born: Philadelphia, Pennsylvania
Died: Woodland, New York

Thomas Bigelow Craig resided in Philadelphia for the first forty years of his life. Apparently self-taught, Craig exhibited in 1869 at the Pennsylvania Academy of the Fine Arts (where he may have been a student), and at the National Academy of Design in New York in 1879, 1881, and each year from 1884 to 1900. Elected an associate academician in 1897, he was also a member of the Artists' Fund Society and the Salmagundi Club. Craig moved to New York City in 1889 and to Rutherford, New Jersey, in 1899.

An artist of largely regional interest, Craig enjoyed fair commercial success but received little more than disdain from exhibition reviewers in the East. The open shed, grazing cows, quiet stream, and bright summer light in *The Mill Pond, Rutherford* (fig. 60) are staples in most of Craig's landscapes, but in this painting, they are united in an agreeable manner that stamps the work as one of his most successful efforts.

22. *The Mill Pond, Rutherford*   fig. 60
oil on canvas, 20¼ × 30¼
The Newark Museum, New Jersey

(ROBERT) BRUCE CRANE   1857–1937
Born: New York, New York
Died: Bronxville, New York

Son of an ornamental designer, Bruce Crane graduated from a public school in New York City and, between 1875 and 1877, worked in a New York architect's office. In 1879 he began studying under Alexander H. Wyant in New York City, later continuing his studies in Europe. Crane exhibited at the National Academy of Design in 1879 and thereafter contributed regularly to the Academy, which elected him an associate in 1889 and a full academician in 1901. One of the most prolific prizewinners of his generation, Crane received honors including the Webb Prize of 1897 from the Society of American Artists, and medals at the International Exposition of 1904 in Saint Louis, and the National Academy of Design's exhibition of 1912. He belonged to the Lyme Art Association and spent many summers after 1900 at Old Lyme, Connecticut. For the last twenty-three years of his life, he maintained a residence in Bronxville, New York.

Crane was at his best and most typical in simply designed views of the russet and gray fields of late autumn or early winter. He was much admired by J. F. Murphy,

to whom he was frequently compared. After examining a "large gray-hillside" by Crane (quite possibly *December Uplands*, (cat. no. 23) in a Lotos Club exhibition of the Evans Collection, the painter John Francis Murphy called it "the best landscape in the room." Never one to emphasize the unusual in nature, Crane preferred to evoke, as Frederic Sherman noted in 1926, "intimations of mood and emotion that stir one mildly."

23. *December Uplands*   1919
oil on canvas, 30 × 40
National Collection of Fine Arts, Washington, D.C.

24. *Landscape*
oil on canvas, 15 × 23
Reading Public Museum And Art Gallery, Pennsylvania

ELLIOTT DAINGERFIELD   1859–1932
Born: Harpers Ferry, Virginia
Died: New York, New York

Daingerfield grew up in Fayetteville, North Carolina, where his family moved when he was two years old. In 1880 he went to New York, where he studied briefly with Walter Satterlee and exhibited for the first time at the National Academy of Design. During the next four years, he taught in Satterlee's still-life class and studied intermittently at the Art Students League. After moving to the Holbein Studios in 1884, he became good friends with George Inness. Daingerfield first went to Blowing Rock, North Carolina, in 1886 to recuperate from a severe attack of diptheria; thereafter, he divided his time largely between New York and Blowing Rock. He taught composition at the Philadelphia School of Design and the Art Students League in New York City in 1896 and toured Europe in the summer of 1897. In 1902 he was commissioned to paint murals for the Chapel of the Church of St. Mary the Virgin, New York City, and in the same year was elected associate academician of the National Academy of Design and received the Academy's Clark Prize for the best figure composition. In 1911 he completed his still-useful book, *George Inness, The Man and His Art,* and made a painting trip to the Grand Canyon for the Santa Fe Railroad Company Commission.

An artist whose vagaries of style elude classification, Daingerfield's affinity for the Barbizon mood in landscape was the result both of his experiences in the farmlands of North Carolina and the technical advice he received from his friends George Inness and Henry Ward Ranger (both fellow residents at the Holbein Studios). Daingerfield's early efforts in North Carolina

25

earned for him the inevitable title of "The American Millet," but he soon directed his attention to paintings of religious subjects and returned to landscape only to meet occasional commissions or to seek relaxation through a change of subject matter. *Return from the Farm* (cat. no. 26) has been tentatively dated 1915–1920, probably an accurate estimate based on comparisons of similar works from the same period (for example, *Evening Glow* in the North Carolina University Art Museum). *The Return from the Farm* is strikingly similar in its scumbled effects to many earlier autumn scenes by Henry Ward Ranger, and in this respect is more vigorous than Daingerfield's landscapes of the nineties in the Inness mode.

25. *Midnight Moon*
oil on canvas, 30 × 36
The Brooklyn Museum, New York; J. B. Woodward Fund

26. *Return from the Farm*   cover
oil on canvas, 15 × 20½
National Collection of Fine Arts, Washington, D.C.

CHARLES H. DAVIS   1856–1933
Born: Amesbury, Massachusetts
Died: Mystic, Connecticut

Davis left school at the age of fifteen to work in a carriage factory where he remained for five years. His schoolmaster father then sent him to study for three years under Otto Grundman at the School of the Museum of Fine Arts, Boston. Financed by an Amesbury businessman, Davis studied in Paris for two seasons (1880–1881) under Lefebvre and Boulanger at the Académie Julian, making frequent visits to Barbizon and the Fontainebleau region. As the result of his first exhibition in the United States in 1884, Davis realized enough money to allow him to remain in France for nearly ten years. Between 1886 and 1931 he received many awards, including a silver medal at the Universal Exposition of 1889 in Paris. He also exhibited at the famous Armory Show of 1913 in New York. Soon after his return to America in 1890, Davis settled in Mystic, Connecticut, where he lived for the remaining forty years of his life. During these years, he selected

27

most of his subjects from a local rural area cut by the curve of a small river.

Until the early nineties most of Davis's landscapes emphasized the somber and the quiet in nature. One such work, *Deepening Shadows,* was greatly admired by Wyant and Inness; Thomas Clarke, Inness's most vigorous advocate, was also an early supporter of Davis. Animals, figures, and buildings rarely occupy an important place in Davis's paintings which, after about 1895, usually emphasized broad, blue skies, cumulus clouds, and brighter colors than those in the earlier works. *Edge of the Forest, Twilight* (cat. no. 27) is undoubtedly an earlier work by Davis and looks enough like the Apremont region near Fontainebleau to have been a souvenir from one of Davis's Barbizon visits. Although not a convincing painting throughout, this particular effort offers an early example of Davis's special affinity for "sky painting."

27. *Edge of the Forest, Twilight*
oil on canvas, 19¾ × 27
National Collection of Fine Arts, Washington, D.C.;
    anonymous lender

HENRY GOLDEN DEARTH   1864–1918
Born: Bristol, Rhode Island
Died: New York, New York

Dearth received brief early instruction from Horace Johnson, a portrait painter from Connecticut. Later, he studied in Paris for about four years at the École des Beaux-Arts and in the atelier of Aimé Morot. Dearth returned to America in 1887 and opened a studio in New York City in the following year. He first exhibited at the National Academy of Design in 1888 and was elected an academician in 1906. Dearth's numerous awards include the Webb Prize at the Society of American Artists in 1893; a bronze medal at the International Exposition of 1900 in Paris; and silver medals at the Pan-American Exposition of 1901 in Buffalo, and at an exhibition in Buenos Aires in 1907. During the last two decades of his life, Dearth spent his winters in New York and summers in Normandy, and a few months of each year in his studio at Montreuil-sur-Mer by the English Channel. Although little known today, Dearth was honored after his death by a memorial exhibition that traveled to nineteen of the most important museums

and galleries in America.

According to Charles Buchanan, Dearth's early work showed him to be "more or less repainting Barbizon." However, the melancholy mood and sonorous colors of his *An Old Church at Montreuil* (cat. no. 28) more closely reflect a technical and temperamental kinship with Homer Martin's late work. (The particular subject of this painting was also a favorite of Martin's.) Like Martin, Dearth had a small but loyal following among American collectors, many of whom were attracted by his gifts as a tediously deliberate technician. Buchanan's rather hyperbolic obituary on Dearth described his landscapes as "inexpressively exquisite" and Dearth himself as "a supreme gentleman of aesthetics." Whether such lofty praise was meant to apply to the atypically spontaneous *Sand Dunes, Wastelands* (cat. no. 29) as well as to the more studied landscapes is difficult to tell. At any rate, Dearth changed his mode of expression drastically from about 1900 until his death, devoting himself almost entirely to works featuring Oriental objects and elegantly dressed women painted in bright, broken colors.

28. *An Old Church at Montreuil*
oil on canvas, 19¾ × 27
National Collection of Fine Arts, Washington, D.C.;
    gift of William T. Evans

29. *Sand Dunes, Wastelands*
oil on canvas, 16 × 30
Reading Public Museum And Art Gallery, Pennsylvania

LOUIS PAUL DESSAR   1867–1952
Born: Indianapolis, Indiana
Died: Preston, Connecticut

Dessar was six years old when his family moved to New York City. He attended the College of the City of New York from 1881 until the fall of 1883, at which time he entered the National Academy of Design to study under Lemuel Wilmarth and John Q. A. Ward until 1886. During these three years, he maintained a studio in New York, painting in the summers from 1884 to 1886 at his parents' home in Nyack, New York. In the fall of 1886 he went to Paris, where he entered the Académie Julian. There, he studied under Bouguereau and Robert-Fleury for three years, taking additional classes at the École des Beaux-Arts in 1889 and 1890. During the summers between 1887 and 1891, he sketched in London and on the Island of Jersey, and in Brittany, Madrid, Toledo, in the Forest of Fontainebleau, Brolle, and Étaples. Dessar returned briefly to New York in 1891 to marry and was back in France by the fall to begin an eight-month stay at Giverny. He built a home at Étaples in 1892, returning to New York during the winters of 1894 to 1897 to paint portraits. In 1900, with encouragement from his close friend Henry Ward Ranger, Dessar bought a farm on Becket Hill near Lyme, Connecticut, where he lived for the remainder of his long life.

Dessar's early training in France was a wise beginning in the 1880s for an aspiring portrait painter; ironically, it provided the principal stimulus for his shift to landscape painting. According to William McCormick, Dessar was inspired to make this change after viewing several Barbizon landscapes in the drawing room of one of his wealthy sitters. Dessar's specialty from about 1897 on was dimly lit views of farmyards and pastures populated only by farm workers with oxen or small flocks of sheep, guided in their movements by little more than a glint of moonlight or a fading sun. Dessar's farmers are only small-scale allusions to Millet's peasants and eschew any hint of social commentary. *A Load of Brush* (cat. no. 30) is somewhat exceptional here, not only because of the size and the strong, insistent silhouette of its subjects, but also because of the faceless anonymity of the rather wooden farmer, frozen in dark shadow with his docile beasts. *Return to the Fold* (cat. no. 31) is, on the other hand, a more representative example of Dessar's deceptively meticulous studies of evening light.

30. *A Load of Brush*
oil on canvas, 28 × 35½
National Collection of Fine Arts, Washington, D.C.; gift of John Gellatly

31. *Return to the Fold*   fig. 71
oil on canvas, 15 × 18⅛
National Collection of Fine Arts, Washington, D.C.; gift of William T. Evans

CHARLES WARREN EATON   1857–1937
Born: Albany, New York
Died: Glen Ridge, New Jersey

Eaton studied at the National Academy of Design and the Art Students League in New York. For most of his professional life, he maintained both a studio in New York City and a summer studio in Colebrook, Connecticut. His landscapes won many prizes, including the Proctor Prize in 1902 and the Shaw Prize in 1903, both at the Salmagundi Club in New York; in 1904, a silver medal at the Louisiana Purchase Exposition in Saint Louis; the Inness Gold Medal at the National Academy of Design; and a gold medal at the Paris Salon of 1906. Eaton's paintings of Glacier Park, Washington, were shown at the Rochester Gallery in 1922, and a memorial exhibition of his work was shown by the Montclair Museum in 1938.

A recluse and lifelong bachelor, Eaton derived most of his best known landscapes from Glacier Park, the canals of Bruges, or the Berkshire pine forests near his summer studio in Connecticut. Simple designs based on a few elemental forms severely limited in color and tone keynote most of Eaton's landscapes. His *Strip of Pines* of 1908 (cat. no. 32) shows one of his favorite compositions, repeated several times with slight changes. (An earlier version of 1904 is in the collection of The Brooklyn Museum.)

32. *Strip of Pines*   1908
oil on canvas, 30 × 36
Montclair Art Museum, New Jersey;
    gift of William T. Evans, 1915

WYATT EATON   1849–1896
Born: Philipsburg (Quebec), Canada
Died: Newport, Rhode Island

When he was eighteen years old, Wyatt Eaton came to New York City, where he studied at the National Academy of Design and under Joseph Oriel Eaton (no relation). In 1872 he left for Europe, first spending a few weeks in London (where he became acquainted with Whistler) before continuing on to France. For the next four years, his time was divided between Barbizon, where he became a close friend of Millet and his family, and the studio of Gérôme at the Ecole des Beaux-Arts in Paris. Eaton exhibited in Paris at the Salons of 1874 and 1876, as well as at the Universal Exposition of 1878. Upon his return to the United States in 1876, he taught drawing at the Cooper Union School in New York City and was active in the formation of the Society of American Artists, serving as the group's first secretary and later as its president. He revisited France in 1883 and remained in Barbizon until he returned to New York in 1886. The portraits that he executed during a trip to Canada in 1892 and 1893 were so successful that other important commissions followed, and he spent the remainder of his rather short life chiefly in Canada.

While studying in the very popular atelier of Gérôme

32

at the École des Beaux-Arts, Eaton was "overwhelmed" at a local exhibition by the sight of Millet's *Woman with a Lamp*. His subsequent trip to Barbizon to seek out the Frenchman in his hamlet only served to increase Eaton's hero worship. This visit he later described with insight and humor in a lengthy article published in *Century Magazine* (1889). Eaton's *The Harvest Field* of 1884 (cat. no. 33) was painted shortly before his success as a portrait painter induced him to devote himself almost completely to that specialty. The clear, rounded forms, firm outlines, and deliberate posing of the mother and child in *The Harvest Field* hint at a possible compromise on the Canadian's part between the soft, austere naturalism of Millet and the more academic techniques taught in Gérôme's studio.

33. *The Harvest Field*   1884
oil on canvas, 35½ × 46⅛
Montreal Museum of Fine Arts; gift of R. B. Angus, 1889

JOHN JOSEPH ENNEKING   1841–1916
Born: Minster, Ohio
Died: Hyde Park, Massachusetts

J. J. Enneking lived on a farm until the death of his parents in 1856, at which time he was taken by an aunt

and uncle to Cincinnati. He attended Mount St. Mary's College in Cincinnati from 1858 until the outbreak of the Civil War impelled him into joining the Union forces. He received several battle wounds during his military service. In 1868 he moved to Boston, where he studied industrial drawing and lithography. Enneking went abroad in 1872, traveling through England, Holland, Austria, and Italy before stopping for six months in Munich to study with Adolph-Henrich Lier. He then spent three months in Venice before going to Paris, where he was a pupil for about three years at Léon Bonnat's studio. He also studied for a short time under Charles Daubigny and became an acquaintance of Millet and Corot. After returning to Boston in 1876, Enneking opened a studio in Hyde Park, Massachusetts, but revisited Europe in 1878 for another year, sketching and studying in Paris and Holland. After this trip, he settled in Boston for the rest of his life. Enneking won medals at the Massachusetts Charitable Mechanic Association of 1878 in Boston; the Pan-American Exposition of 1901 in Buffalo; and the Panama–Pacific International Exposition of 1915 in San Francisco.

While a student of Bonnat's in Paris, Enneking was a frequent visitor to Daubigny's studio, where the aging Barbizon painter corrected the young American's latest

efforts. Enneking's *Pond in Winter Twilight* of 1876 (cat. no. 34), with its plaintive, twilight mood, suggests something of Daubigny's guidance, although only the mood and not the technique was retained by Enneking in his later years. The smaller corners of nature—trout brooks and dense forest interiors—painted against broken patches of November twilight, were to become his most frequent vehicles for expression. Enneking's gradual change is usually ascribed to the influence of George Fuller, who, during the 1880s occupied a studio in Boston with Enneking.

34. *Pond in Winter Twilight*   1876
oil on canvas, 10 × 16
Robert C. Vose, Jr., Boston

GEORGE FULLER   1822–1884
Born: Deerfield, Massachusetts
Died: Deerfield, Massachusetts

George Fuller was brought up on a farm in Deerfield, Massachusetts, and periodically returned to it throughout his life. In 1841 he was an itinerant portraitist with his half brother, Augustus, in northern New York. During the winter of 1841–1842, he studied in Albany, New York, with sculptor Henry Kirke Brown. During the following two winters, he studied at the Boston Artists' Association and shared a studio with sculptor Thomas Ball. Fuller took classes at the National Academy of Design in 1847 after moving to New York City, which—except for one year in Philadelphia and three

34

winters in the South—was to be his home for the next twelve years. After assuming management of the Deerfield farm in 1859 upon the death of his father, Fuller spent five months touring Europe in 1860 to study the old masters and to sketch. For the next fifteen years, he devoted himself largely to farming, but in the spring of 1876, economic necessity and the "discovery" of a new style and technique brought Fuller back to Boston again, and he exhibited there to considerable acclaim during the remaining eight years of his life.

Fuller's trip abroad in 1860 included a study of a wide spectrum of the old and new in European painting; Millet, the Pre-Raphaelites, Corot, and Rembrandt were among the artists given special attention. The lengthy sojourn on his Deerfield farm that followed this trip allowed Fuller's discoveries to mellow in his mind until he had slowly developed a mode of vision that was peculiarly his own. Eastern America's growing taste for the sweet, sad look of America's tone poets undoubtedly contributed to the somewhat exaggerated acclaim accorded Fuller during his final years. The anonymous maiden of *The Afterglow* (cat. no. 37) and the unassuming youngster in *Dandelion Girl* (fig. 62), typical subjects of Fuller's late style, dwell more within an aura than a real space and are bathed in a dim but highly varnished glow. The mood evoked is one that, in James Flexner's words, "luxuriates in not being forced to accept from the senses any data that does not serve

its immediate imaginative ends." Not surprisingly Fuller was a great favorite of the New England *literati* and his wistful sense of nostalgia was often compared to that of Corot, an artist with whom he had little else in common.

35. *Dandelion Girl*   1877   fig. 62
oil on canvas, 50 × 40¼
Museum of Fine Arts, Boston;
    gift of Dr. and Mrs. George Faulkner,
    through the Trustees of The Faulkner Hospital

36. *The Tomato Patch*   ca. 1878   fig. 63
oil on canvas, 20¼ × 30
Detroit Institute of Arts, Michigan

37. *The Afterglow*   ca. 1880
oil on canvas, 22 × 27
The Phillips Collection, Washington, D.C.;
    bequest of Mrs. A. V. Tack

WINCKWORTH ALLAN GAY   1821–1910
Born: West Hingham, Massachusetts
Died: West Hingham, Massachusetts

At the age of seventeen, Gay began to study drawing under Robert W. Weir at West Point. In 1847 he went to Paris to continue his studies under Constant Troyon.

He visited Italy, Switzerland, and Holland before returning to the United States in 1850. After his return he opened a studio in Boston, which he occupied until 1874 when he went abroad to spend the winter in Egypt. In 1877 Gay held an exhibition in Boston of over one hundred of his pictures to finance a five-year trip abroad. He spent almost three years in Japan, passing one winter each in China and in India, before continuing west to Paris, where he remained for two years. Soon after arriving back in Boston, he held another large exhibition. In 1894 Gay retired to his hometown of West Hingham, Massachusetts, where he remained for the last few years of his long life.

Gay was a member of a family long prominent in eastern Massachusetts and was apparently free to plan his career much as he pleased. Although the first American to study with a Barbison artist and one of the first to visit the town itself, Gay does not indicate in the bulk of his mature work that he was overwhelmed by the art of the men from Fontainebleau. Nevertheless, his modest landscapes, exhibited during the fifties at the Boston Athenaeum with paintings by Hunt, Millet, Diaz, and others, served to suggest to that city contemporary developments in French landscape painting.

38. *A Farm House* ca. 1868
oil on canvas, 15¾ × 25½
Museum of Fine Arts, Boston;
  bequest of Mrs. Edward Wheelwright

39. *The Waggoner*
oil on canvas,
Museum of Fine Arts, Boston

ROBERT SWAIN GIFFORD 1840–1905
Born: Island of Naushon, Massachusetts
Died: New York, New York

Robert Swain Gifford received his first instruction in drawing during the late 1850s from Albert van Beest and William Bradford at New Bedford, Massachusetts. Later, Walton Richetson, a New Bedford sculptor, shared his studio with Gifford. In 1864 Gifford opened a studio in Boston, but in 1866 settled in New York City. One year later, he was elected an associate of the National Academy of Design and was made a full academician in 1878. In 1869 he sketched in Washington, Oregon, and California, and in 1870 made an extensive trip abroad, visiting England, France, Spain, Italy, Morocco, and Egypt. Four years later, he made a similar journey that included Corsica, Algeria, and parts of North Africa seldom visited by tourists. About

ten years later, he returned for a third visit to the Middle East. After this, Gifford divided his time between his New York studio and his summer home at Nonquitt, Massachusetts, with the exception of a three-month voyage to Alaska in 1899 with a scientific party led by E. H. Harriman. Beginning in 1877 and for nearly thirty years thereafter, he taught art classes at the Cooper Union School in New York. Gifford won medals at the Centennial Exposition of 1876 in Philadelphia, at the Universal Exposition of 1889 in Paris, at the Pan-American Exposition of 1901 in Buffalo, and at the Charleston Exposition of 1902. One of the earliest Americans to take up the technique of etching, Gifford helped to establish the New York Etching Club in 1877.

Born on a small New England island under the most difficult circumstances (seven of his ten siblings died in childhood), Gifford's early paintings, which featured dramatic seascapes with storm-tossed boats, reflected his natural respect for this subject as well as his lessons with the Dutch painter van Beest. During his second trip abroad in 1874, Gifford visited the art museum in Marseille, whose "fine collection of modern French paintings" may have reinforced his admiration for the Barbizon artists he had first seen in Boston several years before. Within a few years after his return, Gifford's style was largely purged of his previously overblown romanticism, which was replaced by stark, simpler compositions, wide spacious vistas, and, most typically, a

38

39

cold, somber mood drawn from the barren dunes and rugged cedars of the New England coast. The Metropolitan Museum's *Near the Coast* (cat. no. 40), variants of which can be found in several other Gifford paintings and etchings, was awarded a $2,500 prize in the first Prize Fund Exhibition held at the American Art Gallery in 1885. In May of 1974, seventy years after his death, Gifford was given a full retrospective exhibition by the New Bedford Whaling Museum.

40. *Near the Coast* ca. 1885
oil on canvas, 32⅛ × 51¼
The Metropolitan Museum of Art, New York;
 gift of an Association of Gentlemen, 1885

EUGENE HIGGINS 1874–1958
Born: Kansas City, Missouri
Died: New York, New York

After the death of his mother in 1878, Eugene Higgins lived with his father, an Irish stonecutter and builder, in a Saint Louis boardinghouse. After attending public school and a commercial college in Saint Louis, he studied art in Paris at the Académie Julian (1897–1898) and at the École des Beaux-Arts (1899–1904) under Gérôme. During his seven years in France, he copied in the Louvre and made visits to Spain, Holland, and Italy. Upon his return to the United States in 1904, he traveled briefly before establishing his studio in New York, where he remained except for summers spent in Old Lyme, Connecticut. He showed two paintings and one drawing in the Armory Show of 1913 in New York City. Higgins was elected an academician at the National Academy of Design in 1928. In 1957, the year before he died, the Library of Congress purchased 240 of his etchings.

Higgins's role in this exhibition is essentially epilogic, but no less pertinent for that reason. His first impulse to paint allegedly came at the age of twelve when he read an inspiring article on Millet. Although Rembrandt would eventually displace Millet as Higgins's true idol, the subjects that were to occupy the Missourian's art for

41

most of his long life were direct descendants of the beleaguered peasants of mid-nineteenth-century France. Essentially a figure painter, Higgins drew, painted, and etched the unfortunate: flood victims, refugees, dirt farmers, and the shipwrecked. *The Black Cloud* (cat. no. 42), which was awarded the Altman Prize at the National Academy of Design in 1931, in a very real sense is a rear view of Millet's famous *Les Errants* (Denver Art Museum), both works memorializing the plight of homeless wanderers victimized by financial depressions, drought, and the flight from fields to cities. *Nomads* (cat. no. 41) depicts a similar subject at a somewhat safer distance and in spirit is closer to the work of Robert Loftin Newman and Albert Pinkham Ryder.

41. *Nomads*
oil on canvas, 8½ × 12
The Phillips Collection, Washington, D.C.

42. *The Black Cloud*
oil on canvas, 30 × 40
National Collection of Fine Arts, Washington, D.C.;
    bequest of Henry Ward Ranger through the National
    Academy of Design

ARTHUR HOEBER   1854–1919
Born: New York, New York
Died: Nutley, New Jersey

Hoeber was a student of J. Carroll Beckwith at the Art

Students League in New York City before leaving for a six-year stay in Paris where he studied with Gérôme at the École des Beaux-Arts and with Gustave Courtois. He made his debut at the Paris Salon in 1883 with the painting *Sur la grande route*. Two years later, also at the Paris Salon, he showed *The Daily Bread*. From the late eighties until his death, Hoeber was a fairly regular exhibitor at the National Academy of Design, the Society of American Artists, and the American Water Color Society. Hoeber was a free-lance writer on the arts and an art critic for the *New York Times*. He contributed in 1896 a eulogy on Narcisse Diaz for John Van Dyke's *Modern French Masters* and later finished his *The Barbizon Painters: Being the Story of the Men of Thirty*, which was published in 1912.

Because so few of Hoeber's paintings are readily accessible today, it is impossible to make any conclusive statement about his art. His subjects included figure groups, landscapes, and genre scenes and at least a few of them deserve more than passing interest. Favorite subjects for several of Hoeber's landscapes were the marshes and tidewater streams near Nutley, New Jersey, where Hoeber was a member of a small artists' colony near the turn of the century. *Salt Marshes of Northern New Jersey* (cat. no. 43) is nearly an abstraction in a Whistlerian mode; its broad, spacious planes defining a damp, vacant stretch of uninhabitable land. In this respect, the design and spirit of Hoeber's paintings are very much in concert with those of his American contemporaries Homer Martin, William Lathrop, and J. F. Murphy.

43. *Salt Marshes of Northern New Jersey*
oil on canvas, 20 × 24
Reading Public Museum And Art Gallery, Pennsylvania

WINSLOW HOMER   1836–1910
Born: Boston, Massachusetts
Died: Prout's Neck, Maine

Winslow Homer began his art career in 1854 or 1855 as an apprentice to J. H. Bufford, a lithographer in Boston. He left two years later to begin free-lance illustration. In 1859 Homer moved to New York, which remained his winter home until the 1880s, and studied for a brief time at the National Academy of Design and with Frederic Rondel. Between 1862 and 1865 he made illustrations of Civil War scenes for *Harper's Weekly* and turned seriously to landscape painting after the war's close. Homer was elected an associate of the National Academy of Design in 1864 and in the following year a full academician. His first trip abroad came

44

in 1866 and 1867, with ten months spent in France. During the summers of 1868 through 1881, Homer made several trips to the White Mountains, the Adirondacks, and Gloucester, Massachusetts. In 1881 he went to England, staying near Tynemouth, and returned to America late in 1882. The following summer, he settled in Prout's Neck on the coast of Maine, his home thenceforth. After 1884, Homer made hunting and fishing trips in the summers to the Adirondacks or Quebec with his brother and spent part of several winters in Nassau, Bermuda, or Florida.

No examination of the Barbizon mood in American painting can avoid recognition of Homer's singular contribution, despite the fact that his highly selective and independent course of study had only the most oblique connection with the art of the men from Fontainebleau. That Homer numbered among his few friends several admirers of Barbizon art; that he had ample opportunity to study Barbizon painting in Boston, New York, and Paris; that his favorite subjects included American workers on the farm or in seacoast villages, are all facts, but these facts do not adequately explain the peculiar appeal of Homer's special brand of realism. Nevertheless, during the years between his 1867 visit to Paris and his departure for Tynemouth in 1881, Homer executed several small studies of rural life in New England or Normandy that demonstrate a new sense of finesse in his handling of paint and diffused light, as well as an aura of circumspection usually missing in the artist's earlier work. His *Two Girls with Sunbonnets in Field* (fig. 38) from about 1877 is a remarkable achievement in this regard, a work comparable to the portraits of peasant youngsters by Millet that are so often enshrouded in the soft glow of twilight. The earlier *Girl with a Pitchfork* (cat. no. 44), which was probably painted from a Normandy sketch, is a prototype for the heroic fisherwoman in many Homers executed much later at Tynemouth and Prout's Neck.

44. *Girl with a Pitchfork*   1867
oil on canvas, 20 × 10½
The Phillips Collection, Washington, D.C.

WILLIAM HENRY HOWE   1846–1929
Born: Ravenna, Ohio
Died: Bronxville, New York

During his youth, Howe engaged in mercantile activities in Grand Rapids, Michigan, and later in Saint Louis, where he also studied elementary drawing. Soon after (in 1880), he went abroad to continue his studies, first for two years at the Royal Academy in Düsseldorf and then in Paris under Felix de Vuillefroy and Otto de Thoren, an Austrian painter of cattle. During these twelve years in Europe, he made many sketching trips to Normandy and Holland and exhibited at the Paris Salons from 1883 to 1893. Upon his return to America in 1893, he set up a studio in New York City, but soon moved to Bronxville, New York, to help found a small artists' colony there. After 1902 he spent his summers in Old Lyme, Connecticut. Howe won gold medals at the Universal Exposition of 1889 in Paris, the Pennsylvania Academy of the Fine Arts in 1890, and the Crystal Palace Exposition of 1890. He was elected an academician of the National Academy of Design in 1897 and was decorated by the French government with the Cross of the Legion of Honor in 1898.

Although an early admirer of both the Dutch painter Émile Van Marcké and the Austrian painter de Thoren, Howe's true source of inspiration seems to have derived from the better known examples of landscapes with cattle by Constant Troyon. For John Van Dyke's anthology *Modern French Masters* (1896), Howe contributed a lengthy eulogy on the French *animalier*. Howe departs from his European prototypes, however, in his predilection for large bovine portraits instead of scenes where animal and land coexist in harmony. Often close to life size, works such as Howe's *Monarch of the Farm* (cat. no. 45) represented a level of late-nineteenth-century taste that very nearly brought the barn stall into the American living room.

45. *Monarch of the Farm*   1891
oil on canvas, 35½ × 48¼
National Collection of Fine Arts, Washington, D.C.;
    gift of Mrs. William H. Howe

46. *My Day at Home*   1906
oil on canvas, 24 × 30
National Collection of Fine Arts, Washington, D.C.;
    gift of William T. Evans

46

WILLIAM MORRIS HUNT   1824–1879
Born: Brattleboro, Vermont
Died: Appledore, Isles of Shoals, New Hampshire

Hunt was the son of a Vermont congressman. He learned to draw at an early age, his first teacher being an Italian artist named Gambadella. After leaving Harvard College in his third year, Hunt was taken in 1844 by his widowed mother and her other four children to the south of France. After travel in the Middle East, they stopped in Rome where William did some drawing in the studio of American sculptor, Henry Kirke Brown.

In 1845, he entered the Düsseldorf Academy, but left the next year for Paris where he became a pupil of Thomas Couture from 1846 to 1852. The sight of Millet's *The Sower* at the Salon of 1851 in Paris inspired Hunt to spend most of the next two years with Millet at Barbizon. Hunt returned to the United States in 1854 and two years later moved to Newport, Rhode Island, where he painted and took a few pupils. In

47

50

1862, he settled permanently in Boston where the demand for his portraits grew as did the size and popularity of his classes. His last trip to Europe was made in 1867. The great Boston fire of 1872 destroyed Hunt's Summer Street studio and with it his collection of French paintings. He traveled to Mexico in 1875 and in the same year was commissioned to paint two murals for the new State Capital at Albany, New York. Shortly after their completion (and rapid demise due to faulty installation), Hunt drowned off the coast of New Hampshire.

The aversion of many Easterners to French art was regarded by Hunt to be an "unpardonable conceit" and to balance the record, he encouraged and supported a bevy of younger American artists as well as numerous patrons and collectors in the Boston area. The lessons wrought from his training with Couture and Millet added to his ready wit and compelling presence gave Hunt more than enough equipment to articulate the aesthetic concerns of these men as well as those of several other French artists, especially from among the Barbizon group. Hunt preached a gospel of directness, simplicity, harmony of effect, and a willingness to accept the relative beauty of even the most common subjects. Although one of New England's finest portraitists for over twenty years, Hunt made no secret of his difficulties in painting convincing landscapes, finding natural light and the constant changes it effects a particularly vexing problem. As a result, even his most charming landscapes (which are usually more indebted to Corot or Daubigny than to Millet) give the appearance of a shorthand method grafted on to a studio design—usually one derived from the many charcoal sketches, which Hunt was especially fond of executing.

47. *By the River*   ca. 1850–1855
oil on panel, 10¾ × 17¼
Museum of Fine Arts, Boston;
    gift of Mrs. Edwin C. Cushman

48. *French Peasant Woman with Pig*   1850–1855
    fig. 16
oil on panel, 17¼ × 11
Museum of Fine Arts, Boston;
    gift of the Isaac Fenno Collection

49. *Sheep Shearing at Barbizon* (AFTER MILLET)
    ca. 1852   fig. 17
oil on panel, 10 × 15½
Museum of Fine Arts, Boston;
    bequest of Mrs. Edward Wheelwright

50. *The Belated Kid*   1857
oil on canvas, 54 × 38½

Museum of Fine Arts, Boston;
  bequest of Elizabeth Howes

51. *Reflections of a River Bank*
oil on canvas, 23½ × 33
Robert C. Vose, Jr., Boston

GEORGE INNESS   1825–1894
Born: near Newburgh, New York
Died: Bridge-of-Allan, Scotland

George Inness was educated in Newark, New Jersey, after his family moved to a farm in the area in 1830. In 1841 he worked for one year as an apprentice for Sherman and Smith, a firm of map engravers in New York City. He began to exhibit in 1844 at the National Academy of Design and showed there regularly for fifty years; however, he was not made a member until 1868. In 1845 he exhibited at the American Art-Union for the first time and for about one month studied painting with Regis Gignoux in New York City before opening his own studio there in 1846. In 1847 he made his first trip abroad, visiting briefly in England and Italy. Partially subsidized by his patron Ogden Haggerty, Inness returned to Italy again, remaining from 1850 to 1852. He journeyed to Paris in 1854, returning to his New York City studio in 1855. Inness retained this studio after he established residence in Medfield, Massachusetts, a suburb of Boston, in 1859. In the early 1860s Inness painted in the Adirondacks, the Catskills, the Berkshires, and in North Conway, New Hampshire. In 1864 he moved to Eagleswood, New Jersey, where he accepted a few students and in 1867 moved again to Brooklyn, New York. During the seventies, Inness continued to travel and to change residence frequently, living and working in Italy from 1870 to 1872, in France from 1873 to 1874, in Boston in 1875, and in New York from 1876 to 1878, before establishing residence in Montclair, New Jersey, in 1878. In the years that followed, Inness visited Mexico City, Cuba, Florida, and the Yosemite Valley and other parts of California. An epileptic and an incessant traveler, Inness died while on yet another tour of Europe.

Although Inness was nearly an exact contemporary of many of the major figures of the Hudson River school,

54

including Frederic Church and Jasper Cropsey, his motives and especially his methods were never fully in tune with his peers. Inness's infatuation with old-master devices lasted less than a decade. Beginning about 1855, Barbizon art and his own rather frenetic search for a more exciting coalition of artistic form and natural fact gradually led him to a style of painting that has earned him a reputation as America's most important landscapist of the second half of the nineteenth century. In an era when a growing majority of American artists declared their support of the subjective over the objective in art, Inness, with his grasp of summary form, resonant color, and exquisitely delicate compositions offered a standard on which his bevy of younger admirers—Alexander Wyant, J. F. Murphy, Carleton Wiggins, and William Keith to mention a few—were able to model their own approach to nature and art. During the last decade of his life, when Inness was at the height of his fame and his powers, the irresistably "modern" look of his haunting landscapes led many critics and artists to see in Inness America's logical follower of the

French impressionists. To counter their spurious reasoning, Inness reminded these interpreters that despite the fact that "we are all subject to impressions" his art was irrevocably based on a "universal principle of truth."

52. *Christmas Eve*   1866   fig. 33
oil on canvas, 22 × 30
Montclair Art Museum, New Jersey; museum purchase,
   Lang Acquisition Fund, 1948

53. *The Rising Storm*   ca. 1879   fig. 52
oil on canvas, 30 × 45
Museum of Fine Arts, Boston; gift of George Higginson

54. *The Brook, Montclair*   1882
oil on canvas, 20 × 30
Reading Public Museum and Art Gallery, Pennsylvania

55. *Sundown*   1894   fig. 48
oil on canvas, 43 × 68½
National Collection of Fine Arts, Washington, D.C.;
   gift of William T. Evans

56

GEORGE INNESS, JR.   1854–1926
Born: Paris, France   Died: Cragsmoor, New York

Although born in Paris, George Inness, Jr., spent his childhood moving with his family from the area around Boston, Massachusetts, to the environs of New York City, and finally to Eagleswood, New Jersey. He was a pupil of his father's in Rome between 1870 and 1872, and studied for a time with Léon Bonnat in Paris, where his family resided in 1873 and 1874. In 1875 he returned to America with his family, living with them in Boston until their move in 1876 to New York City. There he shared a studio with his father until 1878, the year that he and his family moved to Montclair, New Jersey. He first exhibited at the National Academy of Design in 1877 and was elected an associate in 1893 and a member in 1899. Following the death of his father in 1894, the younger Inness went to Paris, where he had a studio from 1895 to 1899. Exhibiting annually at the Paris Salon during those years, he won a gold medal in 1898 and was elected an officer of the Académie des Beaux-Arts in 1902. Upon his return to the United States in 1900, he established studios at Cragsmoor, New York, and at Tarpon Springs, Florida. His awards include a silver medal at the Pan-American

Exposition of 1902 and, during the same year, the gold medal of the American Art Society. He was the author of *Life, Art, and Letters of George Inness* (1917) and of a privately printed volume, *Random Thoughts*, composed of anecdotes, stories, and essays.

The shadow of his famous father was a difficult one for the younger Inness to escape. To his credit, he made a valiant effort in that direction. One of his first ploys was to devote his art to paintings dominated by figures or animals, a province usually avoided by the elder Inness. According to the son, he decided to "liberate" himself through a series of religious subjects after his father died in 1894, at which time he had a vision during which father and son conversed about the latter's future. The most conspicuous result of this meeting was a series of eight large canvases, begun in 1918 and finished in 1922, that depicted in allegorical form such themes as *Promise, Realization,* and *Fulfillment.* These paintings reside today in the Church of The Good Shepherd in Tarpon Springs, Florida.

56. *Landscape and Cattle*   1879
oil on canvas, 12 × 18
Montclair Art Museum, New Jersey

JOSEPH JEFFERSON IV 1829–1905
Born: Philadelphia, Pennsylvania
Died: Palm Beach, Florida

Joseph Jefferson, the fourth and most famous of the family of actors with that name, made his stage debut at the age of four in Washington, D.C., and continued to perform for over seventy years, making his last appearance in 1904. By 1856 he had saved enough money for a trip to Europe to study the theater there. He returned to New York later that same year. After the death of his wife in 1861, Jefferson set out for Australia, where he remained until 1865. From Australia he went to London to act in a new version of "Rip Van Winkle" (which was to become his best known characterization). He returned to the United States and after 1889 confined his annual tours of the country to the autumn and spring. His summers were spent at Buzzards Bay, Massachusetts, near his friend Grover Cleveland, with his plantation in Louisiana or his home in Palm Beach, Florida, serving as winter quarters. Jefferson spent a great deal of his leisure time painting, and exhibited at the Pennsylvania Academy of the Fine Arts in 1868, the National Academy of Design in New York in 1890, and a one-man show in Washington, D.C., in 1899.

Jefferson's autobiography clearly reveals his long-term admiration both of the Barbizon painters and the nineteenth-century Dutch landscapists. He was an eager collector of both schools, but in his own painting found the Barbizon influence to be a mixed blessing. "The error of our American artists consists in too much sterile imitation of the foreign schools. . . . I have myself found much trouble avoiding this, for now and then suggestions of Corot and Daubigny kept unconsciously intruding themselves from pure admiration of their work." As a landscapist, Jefferson never considered himself to be more than a talented amateur, but his fame as an actor managed to achieve for his art a measure of renown denied to more serious painters.

57. *The Old Mill by the Sea* 1895
oil on canvas, 13¾ × 21½
Allen Memorial Art Museum, Oberlin, Ohio

DAVID JOHNSON 1827–1908
Born: New York, New York
Died: Walden, New York

David Johnson was born in New York City, where he spent most of his life, with numerous sketching trips into New England and upstate New York. Although he first exhibited at the National Academy of Design and the American Art-Union in 1849, his only formal training was a few lessons in 1852 from Jasper F. Cropsey. Although a recluse during the final decades of his life, Johnson was active in the New York art scene during the fifties and sixties. He was one of the founders of the Artists' Fund Society in 1859 and was elected an academician of the National Academy of Design in 1861. A medal winner both at the Centennial Exposition of 1876 in Philadelphia and the Massachusetts Charitable Mechanic Association of 1878 in Boston, Johnson also exhibited at the Salon of 1877 in Paris.

When Johnson's *Housatonic River* was shown at the Paris Salon in 1877, it was enthusiastically received by the French press, perhaps because of his studious imitation of Théodore Rousseau. *Bayside, New Rochelle, New York* of 1886 (cat. no. 58) certainly conveys something of Johnson's earnest assimilation of Rousseau's style, especially in the graceful tree that shades the lonely fisherman in the foreground. The rest of the painting, however, betrays the habits of a tired hand and tends to render suspect Johnson's oft-cited title of "The American Rousseau."

58. *Bayside, New Rochelle, New York* 1886
oil on canvas, 19½ × 24
The Metropolitan Museum of Art, New York; bequest of Maria DeWitt Jesup, 1915

JOHN BERNARD JOHNSTON 1847–1886
Born: Boston, Massachusetts
Died: Boston, Massachusetts

Johnston apparently stayed in Boston for his entire life. During the early 1870s, he was a pupil of, and assistant to, William Morris Hunt, helping his mentor to prepare the huge mural for the Albany legislature.

Very few facts about Johnston's rather brief life have been recorded. In Boston he undoubtedly knew Hunt's friends Thomas Robinson and J. F. Cole, as well as the fine collection of Barbizon art acquired by Hunt (a collection largely destroyed by a fire in Hunt's studio in November 1872). Although five of Johnston's works currently reside in the Boston Museum of Fine Arts, only a scattered few have come to our attention from other sources. That the artist is worthy of something more than complete neglect is especially evidenced by the tender sentiment and richly coordinated brushstrokes of Johnston's *New-Born Calf* (cat. no. 59), a work that compares most favorably with similar attempts in this genre by his Boston colleagues.

59. *New-Born Calf*
oil on canvas, 18⅛ × 22
Museum of Fine Arts, Boston; gift of Artists of Boston

57

59

HUGH BOLTON JONES 1848–1927
Born: Baltimore, Maryland
Died: New York, New York

Jones began his art studies at the Maryland Institute and was later a pupil of Horace Robbins. He first exhibited in 1874 at the National Academy of Design and was a regular contributor to their annual shows for the rest of his career. Beginning in 1876, Jones traveled and painted in Europe for four years. Although the majority of his activity centered on the artists' colony at Pont Aven in Brittany, he also sketched in Spain, England, Italy, and Morocco. While abroad, he exhibited in London, at the Paris Salon of 1878, and the Universal Exposition in Paris of the same year. Upon his return in 1880, Jones shared a studio with his younger brother, Francis, in New York. He became a member of the Society of American Artists in 1881 and was elected an academician at the National Academy of Design in 1883.

A prolific painter represented in several major public collections in the eastern United States, Jones concentrated his finest efforts before the turn of the century on a series of landscapes reflecting the flat meadows of New Jersey and New England. His experiments with the palette and broken color of the impressionists during the final decades of his life did little to rescue his fading reputation.

60. *Autumn*
oil on canvas, 10½ × 14
The Metropolitan Museum of Art, New York; bequest of Thomas B. Salter, 1907

WILLIAM KEITH 1839–1911
Born: Old Meldrum, Aberdeenshire, Scotland
Died: Berkeley, California

Keith emigrated to New York City with his family in 1850. He first went to San Francisco in 1859 as a wood engraver on assignment for Harper Publications. Returning again in the early sixties, he worked as an engraver, forming a partnership with Durbin Van Vleck in 1865 before opening a studio as a painter around 1866. A sale of his paintings in 1869 enabled him to study informally in Düsseldorf, and to visit Dresden and Paris between 1870 and 1871. After traveling and sketching in Maine, he set up a studio in Boston for a while before returning to California in 1872. A strong friendship developed between Keith and the Scottish-born naturalist John Muir after their meeting in 1872 in the Yosemite Valley. Throughout the seventies the

60

two made frequent treks into the remote mountainous areas of the West. Keith spent almost three years—from 1883 to 1885—studying in Munich and traveling in the south of Europe. Shortly after his return to San Francisco, he built a permanent residence in Berkeley, California. Keith made a sketching trip to Alaska in 1886 and an extensive western trip with Muir in 1887, and went abroad in 1893 and again in 1899. In 1891, he enthusiastically hosted George Inness for six weeks in his San Francisco studio. The great San Francisco fire of 1906 destroyed Keith's studio and hundreds of his paintings.

During his long and productive career in California, Keith was alternately lauded as an established figure of national stature or dismissed with faint praise as a follower of George Inness and the Barbizon school. Although best known for his California landscapes, Keith's pastoral mood in his later work—reflected in sunlit meadows, great groves of oak trees, and twilight skies—seemed to convey a kind of old-world poetry that too

often lacked the breadth and excitement of the Pacific Coast vistas. Inness declared to Keith that the more spectacular scenery in the area was impossible to paint, but Keith's artistic ideals, so close to those of Inness during the 1890s (both were students of Swedenborgianism at the time), were never irrevocably joined to the details of a specific site. Keith's technique was to apply paint directly and rapidly in the initial stages, and then follow with a series of glazes—the increasingly mellowing effect of which bears witness to the instructions that Inness imparted to Keith during his San Francisco visit. Keith did not take pupils, but his followers were legion and combined to give a flavor distinctively Barbizon to many Pacific Coast collections during the early decades of the twentieth century.

61. *Landscape*
oil on canvas, 22 × 27
The Metropolitan Museum of Art, New York; gift of
    Allison V. Armour, 1926

62

WILLIAM LANGSON LATHROP   1859–1938
Born: Warren, Illinois
Died: Montauk Point, Long Island, New York

Lathrop was a doctor's son, raised on a farm on the shores of Lake Erie. His attitude toward nature was, like George Fuller's perhaps, conditioned by "the sadness of his long struggle to survive on his farm." After finishing high school in 1874, Lathrop went to New York City to study art briefly before entering the United States Naval Academy. Failing at the latter, as well as in his attempt to start an artistic carreer in New York City, he returned to teach school and tend farm in Illinois. In the early 1880s Lathrop finally secured steady employment as a graphic artist with Charles Parsons at *Harper's,* where his "gift for simplification" was especially appreciated. In 1886 Lathrop went abroad to France, Holland, and England, visiting the more provincial regions and avoiding the larger cities. Lathrop's major break came when one of his small watercolors won the Evans Prize at the New York Water Color Club in the late 1890s. His first public exhibition soon followed and, while he was represented by the Macbeth Galleries, Lathrop won the Webb Prize at the Society of American Artists exhibition in 1899.

In New York City, Lathrop roomed with John Twachtman in a Twelfth Street tenement in which Albert Pinkham Ryder was a neighbor. During the summer, he lived with J. A. Weir in Branchville, New York. By the early years of the twentieth century, Lathrop had moved to New Hope, Pennsylvania, where he established an art colony that included Edward Redfield, Charles Rosen, William Ramsey, and several others. Lathrop also taught classes in his New Hope studio.

"Passion and Patience" was Lathrop's formula for success. His work is almost always marked by very simple compositions—usually little more than earth, sky, and a few trees, not unlike similar arrangements by such contemporaries as Ben Foster and Charles Davis; however, unlike the work of several of his friends (Daniel Garber, Redfield, and Foster), Lathrop's strong, elemental poetry is closer to that of Corot or Daubigny than it is to the more complex color schemes of the American impressionists. *The Muskrat Hunter* (cat. no. 62) is filled with damp, empty, gray space evoking a mood that was a special trademark for many of Lathrop's paintings.

62. *The Muskrat Hunter*
oil on canvas, 30 × 40

Reading Public Museum and Art Gallery, Pennsylvania

63. *The Three Trees*
oil on canvas, 25 × 32
National Collection of Fine Arts, Washington, D.C.;
    gift of William T. Evans

HOMER DODGE MARTIN   1836–1897
Born: Albany, New York
Died: Saint Paul, Minnesota

Except for a few weeks of art instruction in the studio
of James MacDougal Hart in Albany, Homer Martin
was a self-taught painter. By the late fifties he had his
first studio, located in the old museum building in Albany. He first exhibited at the National Academy of
Design in 1857, being elected an associate in 1868, and
an academician in 1875. Martin left Albany during the
winter of 1862–1863 to paint for some months in the
New York City studio of James Smillie before moving
to the Tenth Street Studio Building in which he worked
until 1881. During these years he made frequent sketching trips to the Adirondacks, the Catskills, the Berkshires, and the White Mountains. In 1876, on his first
trip abroad to France, Holland, and England, he met

Whistler, with whom he struck up a friendship that
developed further during Martin's second sojourn to
Europe between 1881 and 1886. A major portion of this
trip was spent in Villerville and Honfleur, France. He
returned to New York in 1887. In the summer of 1892,
Martin visited England and France again for several
months. In the hope that rest and clean air might im-
prove his rapidly failing eyesight, he moved to Saint
Paul, Minnesota, in 1893.

The pace of Martin's development as a landscapist
was a painfully slow and measured one. Usually em-
ploying only pencil drawings for on-the-spot observations, Martin developed a noted reliance on memory,
which served to deprive his art of the vigorous attraction imparted by firsthand observations. As a result,
Martin's best known works concentrate on remembered
moods rather than indigenous details. Not surprisingly,
his most frequent subjects during the last two decades
of his career—the sand dunes of Lake Ontario, Newport, or Normandy, for example—were those that helped
to impart a sense of simple, almost casual design. To
the degree that Martin's personal poetics could have
been effectively influenced by his contemporaries, fairly
important roles were played by his friends John LaFarge
and Whistler (especially the former) and by the French-

64

men Camille Corot and Eugène Boudin. LaFarge's quest for the picture "that seems to have done itself" aptly describes the nearly artless anonimity of many of Martin's late landscapes.

64. *Sand Dunes, Lake Ontario*
oil on canvas, 36 × 60⅞
The Metropolitan Museum of Art, New York; gift of George A. Hearn, 1906

65. *The Mussel Gatherers*   1886   fig. 43
oil on canvas, 29⅛ × 46½
Corcoran Gallery of Art, Washington, D.C.; bequest of Mrs. Mabel Stevens Smithers

66. *Wild Coast, Newport*
oil on canvas, 14½ × 23¼
National Collection of Fine Arts, Washington, D.C.

ROBERT CRANNELL MINOR 1839–1904
Born: New York, New York
Died: Waterford, Connecticut

After a brief and unsuccessful attempt to work with his father as a coal dealer, Minor began studying painting in New York under Alfred C. Howland, a teacher who knew several of the Barbizon artists firsthand. In the mid-sixties, Minor went to Europe to continue his training, remaining for almost ten years. After some experimentation in Paris, he joined the artists' colony at Barbizon, where he was a disciple of Narcisse Diaz. He subsequently studied at the Antwerp Academy in Belgium under Joseph van Luppen. Minor traveled extensively in Germany and Italy, and spent two years painting landscapes in the south of England. He exhibited at the Paris Salon of 1872 and at the Royal Academy and the Grosvenor Gallery in London before returning to the United States in the mid-seventies. Back in New York City, Minor opened a studio on Washington Square. He spent many seasons painting in northern New York, especially at Keene Valley in the Adirondacks, before he settled in Waterford, Connecticut, not far from New Haven. Elected an associate of the National Academy of Design in 1888, Minor was made a full academician in 1897.

According to Eugen Neuhaus, Minor lived in Barbizon for three years although, like many facts surrounding Minor's career, this information is difficult to verify. Minor's most frequent subjects were interior forest scenes treated in a manner first developed by Rousseau and Diaz in the 1840s. *October* (cat. no. 68) is probably a view of the Fontainebleau forest, a likelihood enhanced by comparison with a similar work now in the Yale University collection, the title of which refers specifically to that site. Although primarily a painter of small bucolic "cabinet pieces," Minor amply demonstrated in *A Hillside Pasture* (cat. no. 67) that he could also handle larger, more ambitious canvases. Nevertheless, despite several comparisons in his lifetime to George Inness, there is little evidence to indicate that Minor was able or willing—as Inness was—to develop a mode of expression sufficiently apart from the Barbizon manner to define a style peculiarly his own.

67. *A Hillside Pasture*
oil on canvas, 31½ × 23
National Collection of Fine Arts, Washington, D.C.; gift of William T. Evans

68. *October*
oil on canvas, 12 × 16
National Collection of Fine Arts, Washington, D.C.; bequest of Martha L. Loomis

67

MARY NIMMO MORAN   1842–1899
Born: Statavon, Scotland
Died: East Hampton, New York

Mary Moran came to the United States during childhood and did not become interested in art until her marriage in 1862 to the soon-to-be-famous painter, Thomas Moran. Originally a landscape painter, she was far better known after 1880 as a landscape etcher, having been elected in 1879 to the New York Etching Club and, in 1881, to the Painters-Etchers Society of London as the only woman among its sixty-five original members. Mrs. Moran's paintings and etchings were exhibited sporadically at the National Academy of Design, The Society of American Artists, and, from 1869 to 1899, at the Pennsylvania Academy of the Fine Arts.

Mary Moran first took up painting to be a better companion for her husband on his many sketching trips. Little is known about her paintings, an activity she indulged in only infrequently after she was induced by her husband to try etching in 1879. She painted and etched directly from nature, a habit readily apparent in the small *View of Newark from the Meadows* (cat. no. 69) of about 1880. This study of the Jersey meadows fronting the thriving metropolis of Newark presents a curiously ambivalent attitude towards the city, which is bathed in a glorious light but seems to be both threat and promise amidst the untrammeled nature that surrounds it. One is more readily reminded in this painting of the river views of Daubigny and Rousseau (whose paintings were copied in prints by Thomas Moran) than of the landscapes that Martin Johnson Heade painted of this same area decades before.

68

69. *View of Newark from the Meadows*   ca. 1880
oil on canvas, 8 × 16
The Newark Museum, New Jersey

69

JOHN FRANCIS MURPHY   1853–1921
Born: Oswego, New York
Died: New York, New York

At the age of seventeen, Murphy left Oswego, New York, and found a job in Chicago as a painter of advertising billboards. He soon returned to the East, spending several years near Orange, New Jersey, where he taught a group of students during the summer. In 1875 he opened a studio in New York City and the following year exhibited for the first time at the National Academy of Design, to which he was thereafter an annual contributor. His election to the Salmagundi Club in 1878 was the beginning of nearly fifty years of close association with that group. After being awarded the second Hallgarten Prize at the National Academy in 1885, he was elected a full academician two years later. In 1887 he built a studio in the Catskills at Arkville, New York, where he spent his summers and autumns. His winter studio was in the Chelsea district of New York. Murphy's numerous awards include a medal at the World's Columbian Exposition of 1893 in Chicago; the Evans Prize of 1894 at the American Water Color Society; a silver medal at the Pan-American Exposition of 1901 in Buffalo; a gold medal at the Charleston Exposition in 1902; and a silver medal at the Panama–Pacific International Exposition in San Francisco in 1915.

An affable, even-tempered man who made friends easily, Murphy nevertheless spent most of his professional life in seclusion and was one of the first important painters after Thomas Cole to actually reside in the Catskills. Although no one can praise Murphy for being a multifaceted landscapist, his innumerable versions of barren, wasted fields and farms have about them a dry, plaintively lyrical quality that continues to endear him to viewers who do not demand more drama or color in their art. Contemporary taste tends to favor Murphy's small, warmly colored paintings from the late 1880s and 1890s, although in his lifetime Murphy received a greater acclaim for a lengthy series of Indian summer landscapes, such as his *The Sprout Lot* (cat. no. 72), which usually date from the early years of the twentieth century and were painted in thin browns and grays over a studiously prepared ground. Although both chided and praised for his superficial resemblance to Corot, Murphy can best be appreciated and understood when his work is compared to that of other likeminded American painters, particularly Bruce Crane, Henry Ranger, and to a lesser degree, George Inness and Alexander Wyant.

70.   *Path to the Village*   1882   frontispiece
oil on canvas, 21 × 32
National Collection of Fine Arts, Washington, D.C.;
    gift of William T. Evans

71.   *Under Gray Skies*   1893
watercolor and pastel, 14 × 18½
Indianapolis Museum of Art; gift of Mrs. E. H. Adriance

72.   *The Sprout Lot*   1915
oil on canvas, 26¾ × 40
National Collection of Fine Arts, Washington, D.C.;
    gift of John Gellatly

71

72

shown at the Museum of Fine Arts, Boston. Newman made his last trips abroad in 1908 and again in 1909.

An artist who has been periodically "rediscovered" since his death, most recently in a large retrospective mounted by the National Collection of Fine Arts in October 1973, Newman is far too elusive a figure to warrant inclusion in the rolls of Americans most directly indebted to the Barbizon artists. However, vestiges of Barbizon art that Newman understood well enough to assimilate into his own peculiarly radiant style can be found in several of his paintings. The Worcester *Girl and Baby* (cat. no. 73) with its soft, willowy lines, glowing colors, and firm, maternal embrace demonstrates how poignantly Newman could evoke the memory of Millet without prostituting his own hauntingly evocative sense of drama.

73. *Girl and Baby*
oil on canvas, 10⅟₁₆ × 7¾₁₆
Worcester Art Museum, Massachusetts; gift from The
    Estate of Mr. and Mrs. Edward A. Tattersall

HENRY RANKIN POORE   1859–1940
Born: Newark, New Jersey
Died: Orange, New Jersey

Son of a prominent clergyman, Henry Rankin Poore spent most of his youth in California (1869–1876). He studied at the National Academy in New York for a year, then at the Pennsylvania Academy of the Fine Arts until 1880, when he entered the University of Pennsylvania. Poore and Peter Moran toured New Mexico in the summer of 1882, preparing an article on the Pueblo Indians for the United States government. Poore returned in 1890 on a similar mission. After graduation from the university in 1883, Poore studied for two years in Paris under Lumenais and Bouguereau, making an extensive tour of Europe before returning to the United States. During 1891 and 1892 he went to France and England, coming back to begin a long teaching career at the Pennsylvania Academy. The first of his several textbooks on art was published in 1903. After 1906 he spent his summers painting in the artists' colony at Old Lyme, Connecticut.

A prize-winning illustrator for *Scribner's* as well as a conservative writer on art matters, Poore painted a series of New England winter landscapes in 1910 from a portable studio mounted on runners and pulled by four oxen. His *Passing Teamsters* (cat. no. 74), probably a result of such an excursion, is a bleak scene keynoted by mounds of wet snow and the barely discernible appearance of what may be a funeral cortege groping

ROBERT LOFTIN NEWMAN   1827–1912
Born: Richmond, Virginia
Died: New York, New York

Robert Loftin Newman lived in the Richmond area until 1838, when his mother remarried and moved to Clarksville, Tennessee. On his first trip abroad in 1850, he studied for about five months with Thomas Couture in Paris before returning to Clarksville. On a second trip to Paris in 1854, William Morris Hunt introduced him to J. F. Millet and to Barbizon, where he spent several months. After his return to this country, Newman remained in Clarksville until the Civil War. After his discharge from the Confederate Army, it would seem that he settled in New York. In 1882 he made a third trip abroad, spending part of his time at Barbizon. Upon his return to New York, he roomed between 1882 and 1892 with Wyatt Eaton. The only exhibition of his work during his lifetime was held at Knoedler Galleries in 1894, with over half of the works included also being

its way through the woods. Superficially related to the tone poems of Tryon and Twachtman, Poore's *Passing Teamsters* departs from their greater sense of the abstract by including a thoroughly Barbizon note in the dogged teamsters.

74. *Passing Teamsters*
oil on canvas, 14 × 20
Montclair Art Museum, New Jersey

MILNE RAMSEY   1846–1915
Born: Philadelphia, Pennsylvania
Died: Philadelphia, Pennsylvania

Brought up in Philadelphia, Ramsey served for nine months in the Pennsylvania Militia during the Civil War before enrolling about 1863 in the Pennsylvania Academy of the Fine Arts. He exhibited there regularly from 1865 through 1892. In 1867 he had established his own studio in Philadelphia, but in the later sixties moved to Paris, where he continued his studies with Léon Bonnat for five years. In Paris he shared a studio with Edwin Blashfield on the Boulevard de Clichy from the mid-seventies until 1880, at which time he acquired his own studio on the Rue Tourlaque. Ramsey exhibited at most of the Paris Salons between 1869 and 1881. While abroad, he made trips to Switzerland, Austria, and Italy, and spent his summers after the outbreak of the Franco-Prussian War with the artists' colony at Pont Aven in Brittany. During these years he maintained connections with Philadelphia and New York, making periodic return visits and exhibiting at the National Academy of Design as well as at the Pennsylvania Academy. Ramsey returned to Philadelphia about 1882, and opened a studio where he gave private classes. In 1893 he moved to New York City, but by the late

75

1890s, had moved to Lawrence Park in Bronxville, New York. He divided his time between this new home and Atlantic City until he gave up both to return permanently to Philadelphia in the early 1900s.

Ramsey's early reputation was based on costume figure pieces, but after his return to Philadelphia from France in 1882, he devoted most of his time and energy to meticulously arranged still lifes composed from assorted bottles, jars, and bric-a-brac in his studio. Throughout this transition and for the rest of his career, Ramsey frequently turned to landscape painting as a needed diversion, painting many of his best sketches on the tops of cigar boxes. Undoubtedly well versed in the pictorial techniques of both Barbizon and contemporary Dutch landscapists, Ramsey painted oil and watercolor views of New Jersey marshlands or, perhaps, a remembered region in Normandy, Brittany, or Holland that usually depict flat, vacant stretches of ponds and grasslands. *Pastoral Landscape* of 1897 (cat. no. 75) is a simple, quite pleasurable view painted with a light, unassuming touch reminiscent of Daubigny's and that in some of Jules Dupré's sunnier views.

75. *Pastoral Landscape*   1897
oil on canvas, 12 × 16
Chapellier Galleries, New York

HENRY WARD RANGER   1858–1916
Born: Syracuse, New York
Died: New York, New York

Son of a commercial photographer, Henry Ward Ranger attended Syracuse University between 1873 and 1875. He opened a studio in New York about 1884 and then traveled extensively abroad, making lengthy visits to museums in England and on the Continent. His travels included a trip with Horatio Walker to Holland, where he spent two or three years. Beginning in 1899, he began spending his summers sketching in the vicinity of Old Lyme, Connecticut. He set up a country studio at Noank, Connecticut, where he spent six or seven months of the year, spending the late autumn and early winter in New York City, and mid-January to early spring in Puerto Rico or Jamaica. Around 1900, Ranger helped

establish an artists' colony at Old Lyme and in 1901 was elected an associate of the National Academy of Design. He was made a full academician in 1906. Ranger's many honors and awards included a bronze medal at the International Exposition of 1900 in Paris and a silver medal at the American Art Society in 1907 in Philadelphia. According to the terms of his will, Ranger bequeathed his entire residuary estate to the National Academy of Design for the purchase of paintings by living American artists, such work to be distributed or accessioned by the National Collection of Fine Arts.

A sound business man, congenial raconteur, and clever experimenter with pigments, Ranger deserves special credit for giving the original impetus to the "American Barbizon" colony in Old Lyme. His specialty was forest interiors in which one is led in quiet stages back into the woods or down a winding stream. He lavished great attention on the bark of large, partially lit trees, their autumn leaves rendered in thick dabs of paint over damp varnish. An assiduous student of Barbizon and nineteenth-century Dutch art during all of his formative years, Ranger maintained a deanship among American landscapists of his era. This did not produce a bevy of promising followers, however, although the stamp of his meditative approach to nature can be found in the landscapes of several of his contemporaries, including Elliott Daingerfield and Hugh Bolton Jones.

76. *Connecticut Woods*   1899   fig. 70
oil on canvas, 28 × 36
National Collection of Fine Arts, Washington, D.C.

77. *Bradbury's Mill Pond, No. 2*   1903
oil on canvas, 26 × 36
National Collection of Fine Arts, Washington, D.C.

THOMAS H. ROBINSON   1835–1888
Born: Pictou, Nova Scotia
Died: Providence, Rhode Island

When he was eight years old, Robinson's family moved to Providence. There he worked for three years designing and cutting wood blocks for calico printing. His only formal art instruction was at a local school for mechanical drawing, plus a few weeks at Cummins Art School in New York. Robinson made his first trip abroad at the age of nineteen and spent most of the next three years in Paris where he received some instruction from August Bonheur and copied in Parisian galleries. He also made excursions to London, the Rhine, Switzerland, Rome, and Venice. After a brief return to Providence, he soon made two more trips abroad, coming under the influence of Gustave Courbet during the first. Following his third Parisian visit, Robinson took a studio in Boston where he spent the rest of his life painting and making frequent trips to Providence and Paris as a purchasing agent for Seth Vose. He exhibited at the Centennial Exposition of 1876 in Philadelphia. About 1878 Robinson bought a farm near Algiers, where he spent four winters doing Moroccan studies.

Robinson was very much an integral part of the Providence–Boston art scene for nearly three decades, although his abilities as a promoter and agent for French art far outweigh his contributions with the brush. The subjects for most of his paintings came from a small menagerie of farm animals that he kept in the backyard of his Providence studio. *Oxen Ploughing* (fig. 29), with its large scale and stark landscape, conveys a sense of presence usually avoided by Robinson in his more intimate studies of animal anatomy.

78. *Oxen Ploughing*   fig. 29
oil on canvas, 30 × 50
Museum of Fine Arts, Boston; gift by contribution

GEORGE HENRY SMILLIE   1840–1921
Born: New York, New York
Died: Bronxville, New York

At the age of twenty Smillie received his first art lessons from his father, James Smillie, an eminent steel engraver. Shortly thereafter, he studied landscape painting briefly with James MacDougal Hart. In 1862 he opened a studio in New York City and exhibited for the first time at the National Academy of Design, where he was elected an associate in 1864. Smillie spent most of his professional life in New York, but sketched for several summers in the White Mountains and in the Adirondacks. In 1871, he sketched in the Rockies and the Yosemite Valley, and in 1874 in Florida. In 1881 he married Nellie Sheldon Jacobs, formerly a pupil of his older brother, James D. Smillie, with whom the couple subsequently shared a studio in New York. In 1885 George Smillie and his wife made an extended tour of Europe. He was elected an academician of the National Academy of Design in 1882 and served as recording secretary from 1892 to 1902. He was also an early member, and later an officer, of the American Water Color Society.

A member of one of the most active and influential families in the art circles of New York City, George Smillie was acquainted at an early age with his father's many engraved translations from such American landscapists as Thomas Cole, Asher Durand, and Jasper Cropsey. Quite naturally then, he was able to embrace a wide range of landscape subjects, from quiet New England meadows to bold mountain passages and rocky coastlines. His most popular subject matter, however, was to be found in the interior and along the shores of Long Island. Although paintings like the *Long Island Farm* (cat. no. 80) are distinctively Barbizon in their sympathetic rural mood, they can be more readily traced to similar efforts in this vein by Smillie's teacher, James Hart.

79. *Autumn on the Massachusetts Coast*   1888
oil on canvas, 25½ × 50½
Corcoran Gallery of Art, Washington, D.C.; gift of Ralph Cross Johnson

80. *Long Island Farm*
oil on canvas, 19 × 33
Corcoran Gallery of Art, Washington, D.C.

DWIGHT WILLIAM TRYON   1849–1925
Born: Hartford, Connecticut
Died: South Dartmouth, Massachusetts

While working in Hartford from 1864 to 1871 as a bookkeeper-clerk, Dwight Tryon taught himself ornamental calligraphy and studied the history of art. He opened a studio in 1873 in Hartford. During the next three years, he made sketching trips in the White Mountains and at Mount Desert, Maine, and Block Island. In 1876 he went to Paris and studied with Jacquesson de la Chevreuse and at the École des Beaux-Arts; he also worked briefly with Daubigny, Harpignies, and Guillemet. His summers from 1877 to 1881 were spent in Brittany, Venice, and Dordrecht, and, with Abbott Thayer, on the island of Guernsey. In 1881 he re-

turned to New York, opening a studio in the Rembrandt Building. From 1885 to 1923 he was professor of art at Smith College, Northampton, Massachusetts. He occupied these summers with painting, sailing, and fishing on the Massachusetts seacoast. Tryon's fruitful relationship with collector Charles L. Freer began in 1889. He was elected associate of the National Academy of Design in 1891. Tryon resigned from the Smith College faculty in 1923 and stopped painting in the following year due to illness. Upon his death, Tryon's considerable fortune was bequeathed to the art gallery at Smith College, which bore his name. Despite a large retrospective of Tryon's work at the University of Connecticut in 1971, the two largest holdings of his work—at Smith College and the Freer Gallery, Washington, D.C. —are usually kept in storage.

Tryon's best known work dates from about 1890 until his death. Nelson White aptly described a typical Tryon from this period as a "long narrow picture representing a line of rather straight trees with the delicate foliage of early spring set against a dawn or evening sky or perhaps a bit of New England pasture with stone walls, or an outcropping of glacial granite boulders with bronzed oaks or golden-leaved birches under a mid November sky." Tryon's tender poetics were very much of a piece with turn-of-the-century American tonalism, which attached special meaning to evocative vagueness and disdained the concrete in nature. About 1890, Tryon began a lengthy series of studies in pastel, a medium whose attractions (and limitations) closely parallel his delicate handling of oil paints.

81. *Moonrise at Sunset*   1890
oil on wood, 24 × 29⅛
The Metropolitan Museum of Art, New York; gift of George A. Hearn, 1910

82. *Midsummer Moonrise*   1892
oil on wood, 19 × 25¾
National Collection of Fine Arts, Washington, D.C.; gift of the IBM Corporation

83. *Moonlight*
oil on wood, 13¾ × 21¹³⁄₁₆
The Metropolitan Museum of Art, New York; gift of George A. Hearn, 1906

HORATIO WALKER 1858–1938
Born: Listowel (Ontario), Canada
Died: Ile d'Orléans (Quebec), Canada

Horatio Walker spent his early youth in Canada before his family moved to Rochester, New York. He received instruction from both R. F. Gagen and miniaturist John A. Fraser while working from 1873 to 1876 in a photographic studio in Toronto. He returned to the United States and visited several cities before establishing a studio in New York in 1878. During the summer of 1880, he sketched in rural Quebec. In 1882 he made the first of his periodic trips to Europe, painting in Spain, Holland, and France with Henry Ranger. In later years, he also visited Africa, Russia, and the Near East. After his marriage in 1883, he spent summers on Ile d'Orléans in Quebec and winters in his studio in New York. By 1893 he was an academician at the National Academy of Design and a winner of four gold medals at major exhibitions, including the World's Columbian Exposition in Chicago.

Habitually referred to as "The American Millet," Walker studied farm life wherever he could find it. His paintings, like Millet's to some extent, could vacillate between such sentimentalized genre as his best known work *Ave Maria* (fig. 68) and rugged, rather fatalistic scenes of French-Canadian farmers working in the dim light and rugged soil of the Far North. Having been raised among the hardy inhabitants of the Ile d'Orléans, Walker came by his subject matter more naturally than most of his Barbizon-school predecessors and their American counterparts.

84. *Ave Maria*   1906   fig. 69
oil on canvas, 46 × 34
Art Gallery of Hamilton, Ontario; gift of the Women's
   Committee, 1963

85. *Sheepyard, Moonlight*   1906
oil on canvas, 18 × 24
National Collection of Fine Arts, Washington, D.C.

86. *The Harrower, Morning*
oil on canvas, 24 × 35¾
The Metropolitan Museum of Art, New York; gift of
   George A. Hearn in Memory of Arthur Hoppock
   Hearn, 1911

HOMER RANSFORD WATSON 1855–1936
Born: Doon (Ontario), Canada
Died: Doon (Ontario), Canada

Homer Watson spent most of his life in the rural pioneer area where he was born. He left school in 1866 after the accidental death of a brother, his father having died in 1861. While working in a photographic studio in Toronto in 1874 and 1875, he copied paintings in the Toronto Normal School. On a visit to New York in 1876–1877, he met George Inness, examined Hudson River school paintings, and painted in the Adirondacks. He returned to Doon in 1877 to work as an illustrator. Watson was elected a member of the Royal Canadian Academy in 1882 and in the same year met Oscar Wilde, who later introduced him to Whistler. On a two-year trip abroad in 1887 and 1889, he visited England and Scotland, and studied works by several masters. Between 1891 and 1910 he revisited London on five different occasions, and sketched with Horatio Walker on the Ile d'Orléans in 1896. He resided in Doon while working on paintings of World War I between 1914 and 1918. In 1929 he traveled extensively in western Canada.

Watson was, like his countryman Horatio Walker, an excellent example of the nineteenth-century landscapist who overcame a lack of formal training by venturing forth to look closely at the work of more accomplished artists, only to return for additional sustenance to his native environment. Like many of the Barbizon artists with whom he was frequently compared, Watson was enormously impressed with the landscapes of John Constable, which he had been able to examine in depth during his first visit to England in the early 1880s. *Flood Gate* (cat. no. 87), probably Watson's most famous work with its heavy impasto and dramatic lighting, is an intriguingly rugged variant of many of Constable's favorite themes.

87. *Flood Gate*   1900
oil on canvas, 32½ × 46¾
National Gallery of Canada, Ottawa

SARAH DE ST. PRIX WYMAN WHITMAN
1842–1904
Born: Baltimore, Maryland
Died: Boston, Massachusetts

Sarah Whitman was one of William Morris Hunt's pupils in Boston. She went abroad in 1879 to study in France with Thomas Couture, Hunt's former master, at his home at Villiers-le-Bel, but upon Couture's death returned to Boston the same year. In 1901 she received a bronze medal at the Pan-American Exposition in Buffalo. A member of the Society of American Artists, she was also an honorary member of the Copley Society

of Boston. For many years, Mrs. Whitman was on the governing committee of the School of Fine Arts, Boston. Several of her paintings are in the collection of the Museum of Fine Arts, Boston, to which she bequeathed a residuary estate of about $125,000.

One of the most competent of Hunt's many women students, Sarah Whitman was probably best known for her paintings of flowers, although she was also an accomplished portraitist and landscape painter. Her *Hayrick* (cat. no. 88) is one of the most interesting of her mostly unexceptional excursions into landscape painting.

88. *The Hayrick*
oil on canvas, 20⅛ × 30
Worcester Art Museum, Massachusetts;
   gift of Mrs. John L. Gardner

86

87

88

90

CARLETON WIGGINS   1848–1932
Born: Turners (later Harriman), New York
Died: Old Lyme, Connecticut

After completing his public school education in Brooklyn, Carleton Wiggins worked as a law clerk in New York City from 1863 to 1865. After 1865 he studied painting with Johann Hermann Carmiencke in Brooklyn, drawing at the National Academy of Design, and later painting landscapes with George Inness in Eagleswood, New Jersey. He first exhibited at the National Academy in 1870, although he was not elected an academician until 1906. In 1881 he went to Europe to paint from nature and to study art in the public galleries: he also exhibited that year in the Paris Salon. For many years Wiggins maintained a studio in New York, but spent his summers after 1902 in Old Lyme, Connecticut, where he moved permanently in 1915. He was active in many leading art organizations, including the Lyme Art Association, the American Water Color Society, the Lotos Club, and the Salmagundi Club (of which he was president in 1911 and 1912). One of his two sons,

Guy Wiggins, was also a well-known landscape painter.

In 1894, the same year that his illustrious teacher George Inness died, Wiggins won a gold medal at the Paris Salon, and for a dozen years or so thereafter, his blissful scenes of cattle and sheep brought top prices from American collectors. At their best, Wiggins's paintings reflect, as one critic wrote, "health, self content, and dignity." Works such as *Evening after a Shower* (fig. 59) and *The Red Oak* (cat. no. 90) display his indebtedness to the softly colored moods of Inness's mature landscapes. Unfortunately, Wiggins's willingness to turn out scores of vapid contributions for the art trade serves to confront us as often with his unevenness as with his ability.

89.   *Evening after a Shower*   fig. 59
oil on canvas, 20¾ × 33¾
National Collection of Fine Arts, Washington, D.C.;
    gift of William T. Evans

90.   *The Red Oak*
oil on canvas, 25 × 29½
The Newark Museum, New Jersey

ALEXANDER HELWIG WYANT   1836–1892
Born: Evans Creek, Ohio
Died: New York, New York

Raised in Defiance, Ohio, Alexander H. Wyant worked during his teens as a sign painter in nearby Port Washington. In 1857 he was impressed with some paintings by George Inness at an exhibition in Cincinnati and soon left for New York to meet Inness. After returning to Cincinnati, Wyant secured the support of Nicholas Longworth and went to study in New York in 1860. After an interlude of two years in Cincinnati, he moved back to New York City in 1863. He exhibited for the first time at the National Academy of Design in 1864 and was elected an associate there in 1868 and an academician in 1869. Wyant went abroad in 1865, studying for a few months with the Norwegian painter Hans Fredrik Gude at Karlsruhe, and making brief stops in England and Ireland before settling again in New York. From 1867 he exhibited his watercolors almost annually and was instrumental in the founding of the American Water Color Society in 1878. A partial stroke while on a government expedition to Arizona and New Mexico in 1873 led to paralysis of his right arm. Between 1864 and 1880 he worked in his studio in New York City, teaching himself to paint with his left hand. After his marriage in 1880, he began to spend most of his time in Keene Valley, New York. He moved

in 1889 to Arkville, New York (in the Catskills), occasionally revisiting his New York City studio.

Wyant's signature style was developed slowly and not without several false starts along the way. Special contributions came from his initial contact with Inness shortly after that artist's sojourn in France; the startling revelations disclosed to Wyant by his study of Constable and Rousseau; and his stroke in 1873, which accelerated the artist's movement away from the sort of detailed examination of natural facts that one finds, for example, in his well-known *Mohawk Valley* (fig. 39). After 1866 Wyant gradually shifted toward a more fluid handling of paint, with increasing reliance on a palette emphasizing shades of white, gray, and the earth colors. In his later years Wyant's solitary, introspective mood came to blend more closely than ever with his landscapes, especially those from the Arkville area, where a kindred spirit, J. F. Murphy, also worked.

91.   *A Gray Day*   1891
oil on canvas, 16¼ × 22
Museum of Fine Arts, Boston;
    bequest of George H. Webster

92.   *Autumn at Arkville*
oil on canvas, 20 × 28
National Collection of Fine Arts, Washington, D.C.;
    gift of William T. Evans

Checklist of Prints in the Exhibition

French

93. Jean-Baptiste Camille Corot   1796–1875
Souvenir d'Italie   1855
cliche-verre
10¾ × 13⁹⁄₁₆
Library of Congress, Washington, D.C.

94. Charles-François Daubigny   1817–1878
Le Grand Parc à Moutons   1862
cliche-verre
7¼ × 13¾
Library of Congress, Washington, D.C.

95. Charles-François Daubigny   1817–1878
L'Arbre aux Corbeaux   1867
etching
8½ × 11¾
Library of Congress, Washington, D.C.

96. Charles Émile Jacque   1813–1894
La Bergère
etching
15¼ × 20⅞
Library of Congress, Washington, D.C.

97. Charles Émile Jacque   1813–1894
L'Orage
etching
10¼ × 15³⁄₁₆
Library of Congress, Washington, D.C.

98. Jean-François Millet   1814–1875
La Grande Bergère   1862
etching

12⅝ × 9¼
Library of Congress, Washington, D.C.

99. Jean-François Millet   1814–1875
The Potato Diggers
lithograph
9⅜ × 12½
Library of Congress, Washington, D.C.

100. Pierre Étienne Theodore Rousseau   1812–1867
Le Cerisier de la Plante à Biau
cliche-verre
8⁹⁄₁₆ × 10⅞
Library of Congress, Washington, D.C.

American

101. J. Foxcroft Cole   1837–1892
A Village Street in France
etching
9¼ × 11
Library of Congress, Washington, D.C.

102. R. Swain Gifford   1840–1905
The Path to the Shore   1879
etching
4⅜ × 7¹⁵⁄₁₆
National Collection of Fine Arts, Washington, D.C.

103. Eliza Greatorex   1820–1897
Dakota   1884
etching
8¹⁄₁₆ × 12
Library of Congress, Washington, D.C.

The National Collection of Fine Arts wishes to acknowledge the generous assistance of the Department of Prints and Drawings, Library of Congress, in the preparation of this part of the exhibition.

104. Charles Frederick William Mielatz
      1864 Germany–1919 USA
Untitled (*Landscape with Windmill*)   1884
etching
6¹¹⁄₁₆ × 10⅜
National Collection of Fine Arts, Washington, D.C.

105. Mary Nimmo Moran   1842 Scotland–
      1899 USA
Salt Water Ponds   1884
etching
9¾ × 11⁵⁄₁₆
National Collection of Fine Arts, Washington, D.C.;
      transfer from National Museum of History and Tech-
      nology, Division of Graphic Arts

106. Peter Moran   1841 England–1914 USA
Untitled (*A New England Orchard*)   ca. 1880–1890

etching on paper mounted on paperboard
11¹⁵⁄₁₆ × 17¹⁵⁄₁₆
National Collection of Fine Arts, Washington, D.C.;
      transfer from National Museum of History and Tech-
      nology, Division of Graphic Arts

107. Stephen Parrish   1846–1938
Mills at Mispek
etching
8¾ × 11½
Library of Congress, Washington, D.C.

108. Charles Platt   1861–1933
Bass River, Cape Cod   1889
drypoint
8¾ × 16⅞
Library of Congress, Washington, D.C.

SELECTED BIBLIOGRAPHY

Compiled by Peter Bermingham, assisted by Amelia Banister

General Sources

Books

Arnett, Willard E. *Santayana and the Sense of Beauty.* Bloomington: Indiana University Press, 1955.

Barker, Virgil. *American Painting: History and Interpretation.* New York: Macmillan Co., 1950.

Beecher, Henry Ward. *Star Papers; or, Experiences of Art and Nature.* Boston: Phillips, Sampson & Co.; New York: J. C. Derby, 1855.

Benjamin, Samuel G. W. *Art in America: A Critical and Historical Sketch.* New York: Harper & Bros., 1880.

————. *Contemporary Art in America.* New York: Harper & Bros., 1877.

Bizardel, Yvon. *American Painters in Paris.* Translated by Richard Howard. New York: Macmillan Co., 1960.

Boas, George, ed. *Courbet and the Naturalist Movement; Essays Read at the Baltimore Museum of Art, May 16, 17, 18, 1938.* Baltimore: The Johns Hopkins Press, 1938.

Boime, Albert. *The Academy and French Painting in the Nineteenth Century.* London: Phaidon, 1971.

Bonnemère, Eugène. *Histoire des Paysans depuis la fin du Moyen Age jusqu'à nos Jours.* 2 vols. Paris: F. Chamerot, 1856.

Born, Wolfgang. *American Landscape Painting; An Interpretation.* New Haven: Yale University Press, 1948.

Brimo, René. *L'évolution du gôut au États-Unis d'après l'histoire des collectiones.* Paris: J. Fortune, 1938.

Brooks, Van Wyck. *New England: Indian Summer, 1865–1915.* New York: E. P. Dutton & Co., 1940.

Brownell, William C. *French Art, Classic and Contemporary, Painting and Sculpture.* Rev. ed. New York: Charles Scribner's Sons, 1901.

Caffin, Charles H. *American Masters of Painting; Being a Brief Appreciation of Some American Painters.* Garden City, N.Y.: Doubleday, Page & Co., 1913.

Canaday, John E. *Mainstreams of Modern Art.* New York: Holt, Rinehart & Winston, 1959.

Canat, René. *Du sentiment de la solitude morale.* Paris: Librairie Hachette, 1904.

Carpenter, Edward. *Angel's Wings.* London: Swan Sonneschein & Co., 1898.

Champney, Benjamin. *Sixty Years' Memories of Art and Artists.* Woburn, Mass.: Wallace & Andrews, 1900.

Cheney, Edna D. *Gleanings in the Field of Art.* Boston: Lee & Shephard Co., 1881.

Clark, Eliot. *History of the National Academy of Design, 1825–1953.* New York: Columbia University Press, 1954.

Clark, Kenneth. *Landscape Into Art.* London: J. Murray, 1949.

Clark, T. C. *The Absolute Bourgeoise: Artists and Politics in France, 1848–1851.* Greenwich: New York Graphic Society, 1973.

Constable, G. William. *Art Collecting in the United*

General Sources: Citations for Books, Exhibition Catalogs, and Manuscripts are arranged alphabetically; citations for Periodicals and Newspapers are arranged chronologically. **Artists:** Surnames are arranged alphabetically and citations for each artist are arranged chronologically.

States of America; An Outline of a History. London and New York: Nelson Publishing Co., 1964.

Cook, Clarence. *Art and Artists of Our Time*. New York: Selmar Hess, 1888.

Cortissoz, Royal. *John LaFarge: A Memoir and a Study*. Boston and New York: Houghton Mifflin Co., 1911.

————. *The Painter's Craft*. New York and London: Charles Scribner's Sons, 1930.

Couture, Thomas. *Conversations on Art Methods*. New York: G. P. Putnam's Sons, 1879.

Dictionary of American Biography. 11 vols. New York: Charles Scribner's Sons, 1936–1964.

Dorbec, Prosper. *L'Art du Paysage en France*. Paris: H. Laurens, 1925.

Downes, William Howe. *Masters in American Art*. New York: Houghton Mifflin Co., 1908.

Flexner, James Thomas. *That Wilder Image: The Paintings of America's Native School from Thomas Cole to Winslow Homer*. Boston: Little, Brown & Co., 1962.

Garraty, John A., ed. *The Transformation of American Society 1870–1890*. Columbia: University of South Carolina Press, 1968.

Gerdts, William H. *Painting and Sculpture From New Jersey*. New Jersey Historical Series, vol. 21. Princeton: D. Van Nostrand Co., 1964.

Gowans, Alan. *The Restless Art; A History of Painters and Painting, 1760–1960*. Philadelphia: J. B. Lippincott Co., 1966.

Groce, George C., and David H. Wallace. *The New-York Historical Society's Dictionary of Artists in America, 1564–1860*. New Haven: Yale University Press, 1957.

Harris, Neil. *The Artist in American Society; The Formative Years, 1790–1860*. New York: G. Braziller, 1966.

Hartmann, Sadakichi. *A History of American Art*. 2 vols. Boston: L. C. Page, 1902.

Hoeber, Arthur. *The Barbizon Painters: Being the Story of the Men of Thirty*. New York: Frederick A. Stokes Co., 1915.

Huntington, David C. *The Landscape of Frederic Edwin Church; A Vision of an American Era*. New York: G. Braziller, 1966.

The Index of Twentieth Century Artists. 5 vols. New York: College Art Assoc., 1936.

Isham, Samuel. *The History of American Painting*. 2d ed. with supplement by R. Cortissoz. Originally published in 1905. New York: Macmillan Co., 1933.

James, Henry. *Autobiography*. Edited by F. W. Dupee. New York and London: Criterion Books, 1956.

————. *The Painter's Eye*. Edited by J. L. Sweeney. London: Rupert-Hart-Davis, 1956.

Jarves, James Jackson. *The Art-Idea*. Edited by B. Rowland, Jr. 2d ed. Cambridge: Harvard University Press, Belknap Press, 1960.

Jones, Howard M. *America and French Culture, 1750–1843*. Chapel Hill: University of North Carolina Press, 1927.

Kavolis, Vytautas. *Artistic Expression—A Sociological Analysis*. Ithaca, N.Y.: Cornell University Press, 1968.

Kirk, Clara M. *W. D. Howells and Art in His Time*. New Brunswick, N.J.: Rutgers University Press, 1965.

Knowlton, Helen M. *Hints for Pupils in Drawing and Painting*. Boston: Houghton, Osgood & Co., 1879.

LaFarge, John. *Considerations On Painting*. New York and London: Macmillan Co., 1895.

————. *The Higher Life in Art*. New York: McClure Co., 1908.

Lessing, B. J. *A History of New York City*. New York: George E. Perine, 1884.

Low, Will H. *A Chronicle of Friendships, 1873–1900*. New York: Charles Scribner's Sons, 1908.

————. *A Painter's Progress*. New York: Charles Scribner's Sons, 1910.

Marx, Leo. *The Machine in the Garden: Technology and the Pastoral Ideal in America*. New York: Oxford University Press, 1964.

Mather, Frank J., Jr.; Charles R. Morey; and William J. Henderson. *The American Spirit in Art*. The Pageant of America, vol. 12. New Haven: Yale University Press, 1927.

Matthiessen, F. O. *American Rennaissance: Art and Expression in the Age of Emerson and Whitman*. London and New York: Oxford University Press, 1941.

McCoubrey, John W., ed. *American Art, 1700–1960*. Sources and Documents in the History of American Art. Englewood Cliffs, N.J.: Prentice Hall, Inc., 1965.

Michel, Émile. *La Forêt de Fontainebleau dans la Nature . . . et dans l'Art.* Paris: H. Laurens, 1901.

Miller, Lillian B. *Patrons and Patriotism; the Encouragement of the Fine Arts in the United States, 1790–1860.* Chicago: University of Chicago Press, 1966.

Montgomery, Walter, ed. *American Art and American Art Collections.* 2 vols. Boston: E. W. Walker & Co., 1889.

Mott, Frank L. *A History of American Magazines.* 4 vols. Cambridge: Harvard University Press, 1938.

Mumford, Lewis. *The Brown Decades; A Study of the Arts in America, 1865–1895.* 2d rev. ed. New York: Dover Publications, 1955.

Museum of Fine Arts, Boston. *American Paintings in the Museum of Fine Arts, Boston.* 2 vols. Boston: Museum of Fine Arts, 1969.

Neuhaus, Eugen. *The History and Ideals of American Art.* Stanford: Stanford University Press, 1931.

Novak, Barbara. *American Painting in the Nineteenth Century; Realism, Idealism and the American Experience.* New York: Praeger, 1969.

Reitlinger, Gerald. *The Economics of Taste.* 3 vols. London: Barrie & Rockliff, 1961.

Reverdy, Anne. *L'école de Barbizon; évolution du prix des tableaux.* Paris: Moutlon, 1973.

Rewald, John. *The History of Impressionism.* Rev. ed. New York: The Museum of Modern Art, 1961.

Saarinen, Aline B. *The Proud Possessors; The Lives, Times, and Tastes of Some Adventurous American Art Collectors.* New York: Random House, 1958.

Santayana, George. *The Sense of Beauty: Being the Outlines of Aesthetic Theory.* New York: Charles Scribner's Sons, 1896.

Scheyer, Ernest. *The Circle of Henry Adams: Art and Artists.* Detroit: Wayne State University Press, 1970.

Sheldon, George W. *American Painters.* New York: D. Appleton & Co., 1879.

———. *Hours With Art and Artists.* New York: D. Appleton & Co., 1882.

———. *Recent Ideals of American Art.* 3 vols. New York and London: D. Appleton & Co., 1888.

Sherman, Frederic F. *Landscape and Figure Painters of America.* New York: Privately printed, 1917.

Shinn, Earl [Strahan, Edward], ed. *The Art Treasures of America.* 3 vols. Philadelphia: G. Barrie, 1880.

Simmons, Edward. *From Seven to Seventy: Memoirs of a Painter and a Yankee.* New York and London: Harper & Bros., 1922.

Sloane, Joseph C. *French Painting Between the Past and the Present.* Princeton: Princeton University Press, 1951.

Smith, Charles S. *Barbizon Days: Millet-Corot-Rousseau-Barye.* New York: A. Wessels Co., 1903.

Stein, Roger L. *John Ruskin and Aesthetic Thought in America, 1840–1900.* Cambridge: Harvard University Press, 1967.

Sterling, Charles and Margaretta M. Salinger. *French Paintings: A Catalogue of the Collection of the Metropolitan Museum of Art.* Vol. 2. Greenwich: New York Graphic Society, 1966.

Stranahan, C. H. *A History of French Painting From Its Earliest to its Latest Practice; Including an Account of the French Academy of Painting, Its Salons, Schools of Instruction and Regulations.* New York: Charles Scribner's Sons, 1888.

Swan, Mabel. *The Athenaeum Gallery, 1827–1873.* Introduction by Charles Knowles Bolton. Boston: The Merrymount Press, 1940.

Tuckerman, Henry T. *Book of the Artists: American Artist Life, Comprising Biographical and Critical Sketches of American Artists, Preceded by an Historical Account of the Rise and Progress of Art in America.* 2d ed. Originally published in 1867. New York: J. F. Carr, 1967.

Van Dyck, John C. *American Painting and Its Tradition, as Represented by Inness, Wyant, Martin, Homer, LaFarge, Whistler, Chase, Alexander, Sargent.* New York: Charles Scribner's Sons, 1919.

———, ed. *Modern French Masters: A Series of Biographical and Critical Reviews by American Artists.* New York: The Century Co., 1896.

Winner, Viola H. *Henry James and the Visual Arts.* Charlottesville: University of Virginia Press, 1970.

Winsor, Justin, ed. *The Memorial History of Boston.* Vol. 4. Boston: Ticknor & Co., 1881.

Exhibition Catalogs

A. Goupil Gallery. *Catalogue of the Annual Exhibition in New York of the works of The French School of Art.* New York, 1860.

Boston Athenaeum. Annual Exhibition Catalogues, 1850 to 1873 in the Fine Arts library of the Boston Athenaeum. Boston, Massachusetts.

California Palace of the Legion of Honor et al. *Barbizon Revisited* by Robert L. Herbert. San Francisco: Clarke & Way, Inc., 1962.

California Palace of the Legion of Honor. *The Color of Mood, American Tonalism, 1880–1910* by Wanda H. Corn. San Francisco, 1972.

Coe Kerr Gallery, Inc. *Alfred Cornelius Howland, 1838–1909* by William H. Gerdts. New York, 1971.

The Lyman Allyn Museum. *The Art Colony at Old Lyme 1900–1935.* Edited by Jane Hayward and William Ashby McCloy. Introduction by Robin Richman. New London, Conn., 1966.

The National Academy of Design. *The Belmont Collection at the Rooms of the National Academy of Design— 1857.* New York, 1857.

The Paine Art Center and Arboretum. *The Barbizon Heritage.* Oshkosh, Wis., 1970.

R. C. & N. M. Vose Galleries. *French Masters of 1830* by Robert Vose.

Shore Galleries. *Mark Fischer, 1841–1923; American Impressionist* by M. L. D'Otrange Mastai. Boston, 1969.

University of Maryland Art Gallery. *American Pupils of Thomas Couture* by Marchal E. Landgren. College Park, 1970.

————. *Thomas Couture: Paintings and Drawings in American Collections* by Jane Van Nimmen and Alain de Leiris. College Park, 1970.

Utah Museum of Fine Arts. *The Etching Renaissance in France: 1850–1880* by Gabriel Weisberg. Salt Lake City, 1971.

Manuscripts

Bermingham, Peter. "Barbizon Art in America: The Role of the French Barbizon School in the Development of American Landscape Painting, 1850 to 1900." Ph.D. dissertation, University of Michigan, 1972.

Erlich, George. "The International Exposition: An Index to American Art of the Nineteenth Century." Master's thesis, University of Illinois, 1951.

————. "Technology and the Artist: A Study of the Interaction of Technological Growth and Nineteenth Century Pictorial Art." Ph.D. dissertation, University of Illinois, 1961.

Fink, Lois. "The Role of France in American Art, 1850–1870." Ph.D. dissertation, University of Chicago, 1969.

Gordon, Jean. "The Fine Arts in Boston, 1815–1879." Ph.D. dissertation, University of Wisconsin, 1965.

Jacacci Papers. "Art Collections in New York City." Archives of American Art, Smithsonian Institution, Washington, D.C.

Katz, Ruth B. "John LaFarge as Painter and Critic." Ph.D. dissertation, Radcliffe, 1951.

"The Memoirs of Seth Morton Vose and Robert Vose." Vose Galleries, Boston, Massachusetts.

Simoni, John P. "Art Critics and Criticism in Nineteenth Century America." Ph.D. dissertation, Ohio State University, 1952.

Weiss, Ila J. S. "Sanford Robinson Gifford (1829–1880)." Ph.D. dissertation, New York University, 1968.

Newspapers

"Art Matters." *New York Tribune,* May 1, 1852.

Cook, Clarence C. "Art Items." *New York Daily Tribune,* June 16, 1860.

————. "National Academy of Design; The Thirty-Ninth Exhibition, I." *New York Daily Tribune,* April 23, 1864.

————. "National Academy of Design; The Thirty-Ninth Exhibition, V." *New York Daily Tribune,* May 21, 1864.

————. "National Academy of Design; The Fortieth Annual Exhibition, IV." *New York Daily Tribune,* June 9, 1865.

————. "National Academy of Design; The Fortieth Annual Exhibition, VI." *New York Daily Tribune,* July 3, 1865.

———. "The Yale Fine-Arts School." *New York Daily Tribune*, August 2, 1867.

"Fine Arts. The Belmont Gallery." *New York Daily Tribune*, April 21, 1870.

Cook, Clarence C. "A New Art Departure." *New York Tribune*, March 9, 1878.

———. "Art Degraded to a Trade." *New York Tribune*, March 16, 1878.

"The Harper Collection of Paintings." *New York Daily Tribune*, March 4, 1880.

"Art in New York." *Boston Post*, March 2, 1889.

"The Listener." *Boston Transcript*, June 17, 1908.

"Corot Came to U.S. by Grace of Seth Vose." *Boston Evening Transcript*, November 17, 1934.

Periodicals

"The International Art-Union." *Bulletin of the American Art-Union* 2 (November 1849): 10–15.

"Memoranda of the Mode of Working by Several French Artists." *Bulletin of the American Art-Union* 2 (November 1849): 19–20.

"Boston Athenaeum Review." *The Crayon* 1 (1855): 24.

Stillman, William. "Duty in Art." *The Crayon* 1 (1855): 49.

Cranch, Christopher P. "French Landscape." *The Crayon* 1 (1855): 184.

"Paris Notes." *The Crayon* 1 (1855): 198.

"Originality." *The Crayon* 1 (1855): 261.

"The Belmont Collection." *The Crayon* 5 (January 1858): 23.

Cook, Clarence C. "The Cry From the Studios." *Galaxy* 3 (1867): 440.

Conway, M. D. "Eduoard Frère and Sympathetic Art in France." *Harper's New Monthly Magazine* 43 (November 1871): 802–805.

"The Arts." *Appleton's Journal* 13 (May 15, 1875): 632.

"An Unfinished Discussion on Finish." *Art Journal*, n.s. 5 (1879): 317.

Benjamin, Samuel G. W. "Present Tendencies of Ameri-can Art." *Harper's Magazine* 58 (December 1878–May 1879): 481–496.

———. "W. M. Hunt's Influence on Painting." *American Architect and Building News* 7 (1880): 60.

———. "National Academy of Design, Fifty-Fifth Exhibition." *American Art Review* 1 (1880): 306–313.

———. "The Pennsylvania Academy of the Fine Arts; Fifty-First Annual Exhibition." *American Art Review* 1 (1880): 397–401.

———. "National Academy of Design: Fifty-Sixth Exhibition." *American Art Review* 2 (1881): 21–29.

———. "Society of American Artists." *American Art Journal* 2 (1881): 71–77.

Whiteing, Richard. "The American Art Student at the Beaux-Arts." *Century Magazine*, n.s. 1 (November 1881–April 1882): 259–272.

"Americans in Europe." *Magazine of Art* 7 (January 1883): 1–7.

Van Dyke, John C. "Artistic Nature." *Studio* 2 (November 17, 1883): 219–221.

Cook, Clarence C. "The Durand–Ruel Collection of Paintings at the National Academy of Design." *The Studio*, n.s. 3 (1887): 2.

Durand-Gréville, Edmund. "La Peinture aux Etats-unis." *Gazette des beaux-arts* 36 (1887): 65.

Downes, William Howe. "Boston Painters and Paintings." *Atlantic Monthly* 64 (July–December 1888): 388.

"The Effects of the Art Tariff." *Critic*, n.s. 10 (July 21, 1888): 33.

Cook, Clarence C. "Art in Providence." *The Studio* 6 (1891): 201–202.

"An American Expert." *Collector* (January 1, 1891): 1.

De Kay, Charles [Henry Eckford]. "A Turning Point in the Arts." *Cosmopolitan Magazine* 15 (1893): 265–279.

Geffroy, Gustave. "French Art in Chicago." *Cosmopolitan Art Journal* 16 (January 1894): 371–372.

Daingerfield, Elliott. "Nature Versus Art." *Scribner's Magazine* 49 (1911): 253–256.

Whitaker, George W. "Reminiscences of Providence Artists." *Providence Magazine* 26 (February 1914): 3–6.

"The Arthur J. Secor Gift." *Toledo Museum Bulletin* 41 (April 1922).

Jones, Howard M. "The Influence of European Ideas in 19th Century America." *American Literature* 7 (November 1935): 241–273.

Baur, John I., ed., "The Autobiography of Worthington Whittredge." *Brooklyn Museum Journal* 1 (1942): 6–66.

Draper, Benjamin P. "American Indians, Barbizon Style: The Collaborative Paintings by Millet and Bodmer." *Antiques* 44 (September 1943): 108–110.

Huth, Hans. "Impressionism Comes to America." *Gazette des beaux-arts*, American edition, (April 1946): 225–252.

Matthews, Mildred B. "The Painters of the Hudson River School in the Philadelphia Centennial Exhibition of 1876." *Art in America* 34 (July 1946): 143–160.

Newhall, Beaumont. "The Daguerreotype and the Painter." *Magazine of Art* 42 (November 1949): 249–261.

Katz, Ruth B. "John LaFarge, Art Critic." *Art Bulletin* 33 (June 1951): 105–118.

Goldman, Bernard. "Realist Iconography: Intent and Criticism." *Journal of Aesthetics and Art Criticism* 18 (December 1959): 183–192.

"A Great Day for Robert Vose." *Brown Alumni Monthly* 61 (April 1961): 1–2.

Lanes, Jerold. "Kensett at the Whitney." *Art Forum* 7 (December 1968): 51–53.

Novak, Barbara. "Some American Words: Basic Aesthetic Guidelines, 1825–1870." *American Art Journal* 1 (Spring 1969): 78–91.

Maddox, Jerald C. "Creative Photography 1869–1969." *Quarterly Journal of the Library of Congress* 28 (January 1971): 2–27.

Shoen, Aaron. "French Art and Science in the Mid Nineteenth Century: Some Points of Contact." *Art Quarterly* 34 (Winter 1971): 434–455.

Fink, Lois. "American Artists in France." *American Art Journal* 5 (November 1973): 32–49.

French

BRETON

Smith, Garnet. "Jules Breton, Painter of Peasants." *Magazine of Art* 16 (1893): 409–416.

"Breton." *Masters in Art* 8 (October 1907): 381–420.

COROT

Robaut, Alfred, and Étienne Moreau-Nélaton. *L'oeuvre de Corot*. 4 vols. Paris: H. Laurens, 1905.

Moreau-Nélaton, Étienne. *Corot Raconté par Lui-Même*. 2 vols. Paris: H. Laurens, 1924.

Fells, H. Granville. "Corots in America." *Connoisseur* 94 (June 1934): 283–288.

Bazin, Germain. *Corot*. Paris: P. Tisné, 1942.

DAUBIGNY

Tryon, Dwight. "Charles Daubigny." In *Modern French Masters*. Edited by John Van Dyke, 1896.

Dorbec, Prosper. *L'Art du paysage en France*. Paris: H. Laurens, 1925.

Moreau-Nélaton, Étienne. *Daubigny Raconté par Lui-même*. Paris: H. Laurens, 1925.

Gregg, Richard N. *Charles Francis Daubigny*. Oshkosh, Wis.: Paine Art Center and Arboretum, 1964.

Lanes, Jerrold. "Daubigny Revisited." *Burlington Magazine* 106 (October 1964): 456–462.

DIAZ

Silvestre, Théophile. *Histoire des Artistes Vivants*. Paris, 1856.

Clarétie, Jules. *Diaz*. Catalog of a retrospective exhibition held at the École des Beaux-Arts, Paris, 1877.

Silvestre, Théophile. *Les Artistes Français*. Paris, 1878.

LaFarge, John. *The Higher Life in Art*. New York: McClure Co., 1908.

DUPRÉ

Clarétie, Jules. *Peintres et Sculpteurs Contemporains*. Paris: Librairie des bibliophiles, 1873.

―――. *M. Jules Dupré, 1811–1875*. Les Hommes du Jour. Paris, Librairie Illustrée, 1879.

Hustin, Arthur. "Jules Dupré." *l'Art* 47 (1889): 155–164.

JACQUE

Clarétie, Jules. *Peintres et Sculpteurs Contemporains*. 2d ed. Paris: Librairie des bibliophiles, 1884.

Guiffrey, J. *L'Oeuvre* [graphic work only] *de Charles Jacque*. Paris, 1866; *Supplement*. Paris, 1884.

Wickenden, Robert J. "Charles Jacque." *Print-Collector's Quarterly* 2 (February 1912): 77–101.

MILLET

Manuscript copies of articles on paintings by Jean-François Millet prepared for Quincy Adams Shaw. William Morris Hunt Memorial Library, Museum of Fine Arts, Boston, n.d.

Wheelwright, Edward. "Personal Recollections of Jean-François Millet." *Atlantic Monthly* 38 (September 1876): 257–276.

Sensier, Alfred. *Jean-François Millet: Peasant and*

Painter. Translated by Helena de Kay. Boston: J. R. Osgood & Co., 1881.

————. *La Vie et l'Oeuvre de Jean-François Millet.* Edited by Paul Mantz. Paris: A. Quantin, 1881.

Guiffrey, J. "Jean-François Millet jugé par les Américains." *Revue de l'art français ancien et moderne* 3 (June 1887): 189–191.

Eaton, Wyatt, "Recollections of Jean-François Millet." *Century Magazine* 38 (May 1889): 90–104.

Merwin, H. C. "Millet and Whitman." *Atlantic Monthly* 79 (May 1897): 719–720.

Moreau-Nélaton, Étienne. *Millet Raconté par Lui-même.* 3 vols. Paris: H. Laurens, 1921.

Draper, Benjamin P. "American Indians, Barbizon Style: The Collaborative Paintings by Millet and Bodmer." *Antiques* 44 (September 1943): 108–110.

Herbert, Robert L. "Millet Reconsidered." *Museum Studies,* no. 1, The Art Institute of Chicago (1966): 29–65.

ROUSSEAU

Sensier, Alfred. *Souvenirs sur Th. Rousseau.* Paris, 1872.

————. *Études et Croquis de Th. Rousseau, Reproduits et Publies par Armand-Durand.* Paris: Armand-Durand, 1873.

Dorbec, Prosper. *Théodore Rousseau.* Paris: H. Laurens, 1910.

TROYON

Dumesnil, Henri. *Troyon, Souvenirs Intimes.* Paris: H. Laurens, 1888.

Hustin, Arthur. *Constant Troyon.* Paris: Librairie de l'art, 1893.

American (including Canadians)

APPEL

Fielding, Mantle. *Dictionary of American Painters, Sculptors, and Engravers.* Addendum by James Carr. 2d ed. New York: James F. Carr, 1965.

BANNISTER

Edward Mitchell Bannister, 1828–1901: Providence Artist. Essay by Daniel Robbins. Catalog of an exhibition organized by the Rhode Island School of Design for the Frederick Douglass Institute, Washington, D.C., 1966.

Ott, J. K. *The Barbizon School in Providence; Edward Mitchell Bannister, 1828–1901.* Catalog of an exhibition held at Olney Baptist Church, Providence, August 1965.

BROWN

Downes, William Hose. "John Appleton Brown, Landscapist." *American Magazine of Art* 14 (August 1923): 436–439.

Museum of Fine Arts, Boston. *American Paintings in the Museum of Fine Arts.* Boston. 2 vols. Boston: Museum of Fine Arts, 1969.

COLE

Vinton, Frederick. *Memorial Exhibition of Joseph Foxcroft Cole (1837–1892).* Catalog of an exhibition held at the Museum of Fine Arts, Boston, 1893.

Jarvis, James Jackson. *The Art-Idea.* Edited by B. Rowland, Jr. 2d rev. ed. Cambridge: Harvard University Press, The Belknap Press, 1960.

CRAIG

Obituary. *New York Times,* September 2, 1924.

Gerdts, William H. *Painting and Sculpture From New Jersey.* New Jersey Historical Series, vol. 21. Princeton: D. Van Nostrand Co., 1964.

CRANE

"The Landscape of Bruce Crane." *Art in America* 14 (August 1926): 211–215.

Obituary. *New York Herald Tribune,* October 30, 1937.

DAINGERFIELD

Kasanov, Nina. "American Landscapes of the Nineteenth Century in the North Carolina Museum of Art." *North Carolina Museum of Art Bulletin* 8 (June 1969): 3–15.

Hobbs, Robert. *Elliott Daingerfield: Retrospective Exhibition.* Catalog of an exhibition held at The Mint Museum of Art, Charlotte, North Carolina, 1971.

DAVIS

Fraser, W. Lewis. "Charles H. Davis." *Century* 48 (1894): 219.

"Charles H. Davis—Landscapist. *International Studio* 75 (June 1922): 177–183.

DEARTH

Obituary. *New York Times*, March 28, 1918.

Buchanan, Charles L. "Henry Golden Dearth." *International Studio* 64 (June 1918): cxvi–cxviii.

Carey, E. L. "The Painting of Henry Golden Dearth." *American Magazine of Art* 10 (April 1919): 196–201.

DESSAR

McCormick, William B. "Louis Dessar, Tonalist." *International Studio* 79 (July 1924): 295–297.

Washington, D.C. Archives of American Art, Smithsonian Institution. De-Witt McClellan Lockman interview with Louis Dessar, Sherwood Studio, 1927. Microfilm.

Obituary. *New York Times*, February 16, 1952.

EATON, Charles W.

Obituary. *New York Times*, September 12, 1937.

Montclair Art Museum. *Memorial Exhibition of Paintings by Charles Warren Eaton (1856–1937)*. Catalog of an exhibition held at the Montclair Art Museum, N.J., 1938.

EATON, Wyatt

Hellman, George S. "Wyatt Eaton." *The Art World* 3 (December 1917): 204–209.

Sherman, Frederic F. "Figure Pieces by Wyatt Eaton." *Art in America* 7 (June 1919): 171–178.

ENNEKING

Davol, Ralph. "The Work of John J. Enneking." *American Magazine of Art* 8 (June 1917): 320–323.

Closson, William Baxter. "The Art of John J. Enneking." *International Studio* 76 (October 1922): 3–6.

Pierce, Patricia J., and Rolf H. Kristiansen. *John Joseph Enneking: American Impressionist Painter*. North Abington, Mass.: Pierce Galleries, 1972.

FULLER

Millet, Josiah B., ed. *George Fuller, His Life and Works*. Boston and New York: Houghton Mifflin Co., 1886.

Caffin, C. H. "Some American Figure Painters." *The Critic* 44 (1904): 221–230.

Downes, William Howe. "George Fuller's Pictures." *International Studio* 75 (July 1922): 265–273.

Flexner, James T. *Nineteenth-Century American Painting*. New York: G. P. Putnam's Sons, 1970.

GAY

Obituary. *Boston Transcript*, February 24, 1910.

Isham, Samuel. *The History of American Painting*. 2d ed. with supplement by R. Cortissoz. Originally published in 1905. New York: Macmillan Co., 1933.

Dictionary of American Biography. Vol. 4. New York: Charles Scribner's Sons, 1936–1964.

GIFFORD

Koehler, Sylvester R. "R. Swain Gifford, N.A." *American Art Review* 1 (1880): 417–422.

Gaw, Cooper. "Robert Swain Gifford, Landscape-Painter." *Brush and Pencil* 15 (April 1905): 201–211.

American Art Galleries. *Illustrated Catalogue of Oil Paintings and Water Colors of the Late R. Swain Gifford, N.A.* Catalog of an exhibition held at the American Art Galleries, New York, 1906.

Hall, Elton W. *R. Swain Gifford, 1840–1905*. Catalog of an exhibition held at the New Bedford Whaling Museum, Mass., 1906.

HOEBER

Gerdts, William H. *Painting and Sculpture From New Jersey*. New Jersey Historical Series, vol. 21. Princeton: D. Van Nostrand Co., 1964.

HOMER

Downes, William Howe. *The Life and Works of Winslow Homer*. Introduction by John W. Beatty. Boston and New York: Houghton Mifflin Co., 1911.

Goodrich, Lloyd. *Winslow Homer*. New York: Macmillan Co., 1945.

Gardner, Albert T. E. *Winslow Homer, American*

Artist: His World and His Work. New York: Bramhall House, 1961.

HOWE

"William Henry Howe: A Chief of Cattle Painters." *Art World* 3 (October 1917): 4–6.

Dictionary of American Biography. Vol. 5. New York: Charles Scribner's Sons, 1936–1964.

Hayward, Jane, and William Ashby McCloy, eds. *The Art Colony at Old Lyme, 1900–1935.* Introduction by Robin Richman. Catalog of an exhibition held at the Lyman Allyn Museum, New London, Conn., 1966.

HUNT

Hunt, William M. *W. M. Hunt's Talks on Art.* Series 1. Compiled by H. M. Knowlton. Boston: H. O. Houghton & Co., 1875.

Benjamin, Samuel G. W. "W. M. Hunt's Influence on Painting." *American Architect and Building News* 7 (February 14, 1880): 60.

Millet, F. D. "Mr. Hunt's Teaching." *Atlantic Monthly* 46 (August 1880): 191.

Angell, Henry C. *Records of William M. Hunt.* Boston: J. R. Osgood & Co., 1881.

Knowlton, Helen M. *The Art–Life of William Morris Hunt.* Boston: Little, Brown & Co., 1899.

Shannon, Martha A. S. *Boston Days of William Morris Hunt.* Boston: Marshall Jones Co., 1923.

Danes, Gibson. "A Biographical and Critical Study of William Morris Hunt, 1824–1879." Ph.D. dissertation, Yale University, 1949.

———. "William Morris Hunt and His Newport Circle." *Magazine of Art* 48 (April 1950): 144–150.

Welchans, Roger A. "The Art Theories of Washington Allston and William Morris Hunt." Ph.D. dissertation, Case Western Reserve University, 1970.

INNESS

Inness, George. "A Painter on Painting." *Harper's New Monthly Magazine* 56 (December 1877–May 1878): 456–461.

Eckford, Henry [E]. "Mr. Inness on Art Matters." *Art Journal*, n.s. 5 (1879): 374–377.

Daingerfield, Elliott. *George Inness: The Man and His Art.* New York: Privately printed, 1911.

Inness, George, Jr. *Life, Art, and Letters of George Inness.* Introduction by Elliott Daingerfield. New York: The Century Co., 1917.

McCausland, Elizabeth. *George Inness: An American Landscape Painter, 1825–1894.* Catalog of an exhibition held at the Walter Vincent Smith Art Gallery, Springfield, Mass., 1946.

Ireland, LeRoy. *The Paintings of George Inness.* Austin: University of Texas Press, 1964.

Montclair Art Museum. *George Inness of Montclair: An Exhibition of Paintings Chiefly From the Artist's Montclair Period: 1878–1894.* Catalog of an exhibition held at the Montclair Art Museum, N.J., 1964.

Cikovsky, Nicolai, Jr. "The Life and Work of George Inness." Ph.D. dissertation, Harvard University, 1965.

———. "George Inness and the Hudson River School: the Lackawanna Valley." *American Art Journal* 2 (Fall 1970): 36–57.

———. *George Inness.* New York: Praeger, 1971.

INNESS, JR.

Ries, Estelle H. "The Mantle of Genius." *American Magazine of Art* 3 (March 18, 1905): 7.

Inness, George, Jr. *Life, Art, and Letters of George Inness.* Introduction by Elliott Daingerfield. New York: The Century Co., 1917.

JEFFERSON

Jefferson, Joseph. *The Autobiography of Joseph Jefferson.* New York: The Century Co., 1890.

MacDonough, Glen. "Joseph Jefferson, The Painter." *Monthly Illustrator* 5 (September 1895): 267–272.

Wilson, Francis. *Joseph Jefferson; Reminiscences of a Fellow Player.* New York: Charles Scribner's Sons, 1906.

JOHNSON

Obituary. *American Art Annual* 7 (1909–1910).

Clement, Clara E., and Laurence Hutton. *Artists of the Nineteenth Century and Their Works.* 3d ed. Saint Louis: North Point, Inc. 1969.

JOHNSTON

Knowlton, Helen M. *The Art-Life of William Morris*

Hunt. Boston: Little, Brown & Co., 1899.

Museum of Fine Arts, Boston. *American Paintings in the Museum of Fine Arts, Boston.* 2 vols. Boston: Museum of Fine Arts, 1969.

JONES

"American Painters—H. Bolton Jones." *Art Journal* 6 (February 1880): 53–54.

Dictionary of American Biography. Vol. 5. New York: Charles Scribner's Sons, 1936–1964.

KEITH

Atkins, Henry. "William Keith, Landscape Painter of California." *International Studio* 33 (November 1907): 36–42.

Neuhaus, Eugen. *William Keith: The Man and the Artist.* Berkeley: University of California Press, 1938.

Cornelius, Brother Fidelius. *Keith, Old Master of California.* New York: G. P. Putnam's Sons, 1942.

LATHROP

Price, F. Newlin. "The Art of William Lathrop." *International Studio* 78 (November 1923): 132–138.

Neuhaus, Eugen. *The History and Ideals of American Art.* Stanford: Stanford University Press, 1931.

Obituary. *Art Digest* 13 (October 1, 1938): 23.

MARTIN

"American Painters—Homer D. Martin." *Art Journal,* n.s., 6 (November 1880): 321–323.

Martin, Elizabeth G. *Homer Martin: A Reminiscence.* New York: William Macbeth, 1904.

Mather, Frank J. *Homer Martin: A Poet in Landscape.* New York: Privately printed, 1912.

Carroll, Dana H. *Fifty-Eight Paintings by Homer D. Martin.* New York: Privately printed by Frederic Fairchild Sherman, 1913.

Mandel, Patricia C. F. "Homer D. Martin: American Landscape Painter (1836–1897)." Ph.D. dissertation, New York University, 1973.

———. "The Stories Behind Three Important Late Homer D. Martin Paintings." *Archives of American Art Journal* 13 (1973): 2–8.

MINOR

Isham, Samuel. *The History of American Painting.* 2d ed. with supplement by R. Cortissoz. Originally published in 1905. New York: Macmillan Co., 1933.

Dictionary of American Biography. Vol. 6. New York: Charles Scribner's Sons, 1936–1964.

MORAN

Everett, Morris T. "The Etchings of Mary Nimmo Moran." *Brush and Pencil* 8 (April 1901): 3–16.

Wilkins, Thurman. *Thomas Moran, Artist of the Mountains.* Norman: University of Oklahoma Press, 1966.

Huber, Christine J. *The Pennsylvania Academy and Its Women: 1850 to 1920.* Catalog of an exhibition held at the Pennsylvania Academy of the Fine Arts, Philadelphia, 1973.

MURPHY

Lawrence, Harold T. "J. Francis Murphy." *Brush and Pencil* 10 (July 1902): 205–218.

Buchanan, Charles. "Justice for J. Francis Murphy." *American Art News* 20 (December 1921): 6.

Clark, Eliot J. *J. Francis Murphy.* New York: Privately printed by Frederic Fairchild Sherman, 1926.

American Art Association, Inc. *Paintings and Drawings by J. Francis Murphy.* Catalog of an auction held by the American Art Association, Inc., New York, November 26, 1926.

NEWMAN

Sherman, Frederic F. "Robert Loftin Newman: An American Colorist." *Art in America* 4 (April 1916): 177–184.

Landgren, Marchal E. "Robert L. Newman." *American Magazine of Art* 28 (March 1935): 134–140.

———. *Robert Loftin Newman, 1827–1912.* Introduction by Joshua C. Taylor. Catalog of an exhibition held at the National Collection of Fine Arts, Smithsonian Institution, Washington, D.C., and the Tennessee Fine Arts Center, Cheekwood, Nashville. 1974.

POORE

Coburn, Frederick W. "Henry Rankin Poore." *International Studio* 37 (March 1909): 20–24.

Obituary. Art Digest 14 (September 1940): 12.

RAMSEY

Gerdts, William H. and Russell Burke. *American Still-Life Painting*. New York: Praeger, 1971.

Chapellier Galleries. *The Art of Milne Ramsey*. Essay by William Gerdts. Catalog of an exhibition held at the Chapellier Galleries, New York, 1974.

RANGER

Bell, R. H. *Art Talks With Ranger*. New York and London: G. P. Putnam's Sons, 1914.

Obituary. *American Magazine of Art* 9 (January 1917): 118–119.

Daingerfield, Elliott. "Henry Ward Ranger, Painter." *The Century* 97 (November 1918): 82–89.

Dictionary of American Biography. Vol. 8. New York: Charles Scribner's Sons, 1936–1964.

ROBINSON

Allen, Edward. *Thomas Robinson: A Memoir*. Providence: Privately printed, 1888.

Fink, Lois. "American Artists in France." *American Art Journal* 5 (November 1973): 32–49.

SMILLIE

Isham, Samuel. *The History of American Painting*. 2d ed. with supplement by R. Cortissoz. Originally published in 1905. New York: Macmillan Co., 1933.

Dictionary of American Biography. Vol. 8. New York: Charles Scribner's Sons, 1936–1964.

TRYON

White, Henry C. *The Life and Art of Dwight William Tryon*. Boston and New York: Houghton Mifflin Co., 1930.

University of Connecticut Museum of Art. *Dwight W. Tryon: A Retrospective Exhibition*. Essay by Nelson C. White. Catalog of an exhibition held at the University of Connecticut Museum of Art, Storrs, 1971.

WALKER

Price, F. Newlin. "Horatio Walker, The Elemental." *International Studio* 77 (August 1923): 359–362.

"Farm Art is Fertile Theme at Women's Sessions." *Washington Star*, June 20, 1936.

Obituary. *Washington Star*, October 9, 1938.

WATSON

Hubbard, R. H. *The Development of Canadian Art*. Ottawa: National Gallery of Canada, 1963.

Harper, J. Russell. *Early Painters and Engravers in Canada*. Toronto: University of Toronto Press, 1970.

WHITMAN

Obituary. *American Art Journal* 5 (1905–1906).

University of Maryland Art Gallery. *American Pupils of Thomas Couture*. Essay and catalog by Marchal E. Landgren. Catalog of an exhibition held at the University of Maryland Art Gallery, College Park, 1970.

WIGGINS

Wiggins, Grafton. "Carleton Wiggins, 1848–1932." Manuscript in the possession of the author, n.d.

Obituary. *Art Digest* 6 (July 1932): 14.

Gerdts, William H. *Paintings and Sculpture From New Jersey*. New Jersey Historical Series, vol. 21. Princeton: D. Van Nostrand Co., 1964.

WYANT

Gage, Eleanor R. "Alexander H. Wyant: A Pioneer of American Landscape Painting." *Arts and Decoration* 2 (August 1912): 349–351.

Clark, Eliot. *Alexander Wyant*. New York: Privately printed, 1916.

Brewster, Eugene V. "Wyant, The Nature Painter." *Arts and Decoration* 10 (February 1919): 197.

Clark, Eliot. *Sixty Paintings by Alexander H. Wyant*. New York: Privately printed by Frederic Fairchild Sherman, 1920.

Utah Museum of Fine Arts. *Alexander Helwig Wyant, 1836–1892*. Essay and chronology by Robert C. Olpin. Catalog of an exhibition held at the University of Utah Museum of Fine Arts, Salt Lake City, 1968.

Olpin, Robert C. "Alexander H. Wyant, 1836–1892; American Landscape Painter: An Investigation of His Life and Fame and a Critical Analysis of His Work With a Catalogue Raisonné." Ph.D. dissertation, Boston University, 1971.

Staff for the Exhibition

DIRECTOR OF EXHIBITION
Peter Bermingham, Curator of Education

INSTALLATION DESIGNER
Val E. Lewton

ASSISTANTS
Amelia Banister
Helene Czarniecki
Margaret Roberts

DEPARTMENT OF PRINTS AND DRAWINGS
Janet Flint, Curator
Charles Booth

OFFICE OF EXHIBITION AND DESIGN
David B. Keeler, Chief
Oliver Anderson
Carole Ann Broadus
Frank Caldwell
John Fleming
Ralph Logan
James Maynor
George Nairn
Gervis Perkins
Georgine Reed
Antonia Ropa

OFFICE OF THE REGISTRAR
W. Robert Johnston, Registrar
Andrea Brown
Burgess Coleman, Jr.
Joshua Ewing
Deborah Jensen
Martha Russell

CONSERVATION LABORATORY
Thomas Carter, Conservator
Susan Brooke
Cleo Mullins

OFFICE OF PUBLIC AFFAIRS
Margery Byers, Chief

OFFICE OF PUBLICATION
Carroll S. Clark, Editor
Kathleen Preciado

PHOTOGRAPHIC CREDITS

All color illustrations are by Eugene L. Mantie. These illustrations are through the courtesy of the following:

Allen Memorial Art Museum, cat. no. 57; Art Gallery of Hamilton, Lloyd Bloom: fig. no. 69, cat. no. 84; The Art Institute of Chicago, fig. nos. 28, 40, 51, 54, 63, 64; The Brooklyn Museum, fig. no. 41, cat. no. 25; The California Palace of the Legion of Honor, fig. no. 18; Chapellier Galleries, Walter Russell: cat. no. 75; Cincinnati Art Museum, fig. no. 11; Cooper-Hewitt Museum of Decorative Arts & Design, fig. no. 38; Corcoran Gallery of Art, fig. nos. 43, 49, 73, cat. nos. 3, 4, 65, 79, 80; Detroit Institute of Arts, fig. no. 62, cat. nos. 7, 36; Frick Art Reference Library, fig. nos. 31, 42; George Walter Vincent Smith Art Gallery, fig. no. 22; Indianapolis Museum of Art, cat. no. 71; Johnson Gallery, Atwata Photographers: cat. no. 13; Kennedy Galleries, fig. no. 23; The Louvre, fig. nos. 2, 50, 53; Lyme Historical Society—Florence Griswold Association, fig. no. 58; Mauritshuis (The Hague), fig. no. 57; The Metropolitan Museum of Art, fig. nos. 34, 39, 45, 68, cat. nos. 40, 58, 60, 61, 64, 81, 83, 86; G. William Miller, cat. no. 17; Montclair Art Museum, cat. no. 15, Lillian Bristol: fig. no. 33, Virginia Weckel: cat. nos. 32, 74, Jean Lange: cat. no. 56; Montreal Museum of Fine Arts, cat. no. 33; Museum of African Art, cat. nos. 16, 18; Museum of Art, Carnegie Institute, fig. no. 47; Museum of Fine Arts, Boston, fig. nos. 3, 4, 5, 9, 10, 12–17, 24, 26, 27, 29, 35, 46, 51, 52, 62, 63, 66, cat. nos. 2, 5, 20, 21, 38, 39, 47, 50, 59, 91; National Gallery of Art, fig. no. 19; National Gallery of Canada, cat. no. 87; The New Britain Museum of American Art, E. Irving Blomstramm: fig. no. 20; The Newark Museum, cat. no. 69, Armen Photographers: fig. no. 60, Jake Eickenbush: cat. no. 90; The New-York Historical Society, fig. nos. 21, 36; Paine Art Center, fig. no. 6; The Pennsylvania Academy of the Fine Arts, fig. nos. 66, 67, The Phillips Studio: cat. no. 10; The Phillips Collection, cat. nos. 37, 41, 44; Reading Public Museum and Art Gallery, cat. nos. 24, 29, 43, 54, 62; Toledo Museum of Art, fig. nos. 37, 64, 65; Ville de Fontainebleau Collection, fig. no. 7; Vose Galleries of Boston, Inc., fig. no. 30, John D. Schiff: fig. no. 32; Robert C. Vose, cat. nos. 12, 34, Herbert V. Vose: cat. no. 51; Wadsworth Atheneum, E. Irving Blomstramm: cat. no. 6; Wallace Collection, fig. no. 8; Walters Art Gallery, fig. no. 61, cat. no. 11; Worcester Art Museum, cat. nos. 73, 88.

FREDERIC EDWIN CHURCH. Foreword by David W. Scott. Preface by Richard P. Wunder. 85 pages; 23 b&w illustrations; 3 color plates. 1966. $4.45.

GEORGE CALEB BINGHAM: 1811–1879. Introduction by David W. Scott. Essay by E. Maurice Bloch. 99 pages; 36 b&w illustrations. 1967. 75¢.

JASPER F. CROPSEY: 1823–1900. Foreword by Joshua C. Taylor. Essay by William S. Talbot. 114 pages; 92 b&w illustrations; 4 color plates. 1970. $2.50.

NATIONAL PARKS AND THE AMERICAN LANDSCAPE. Foreword by Joshua C. Taylor. Essay by William H. Truettner and Robin Bolton-Smith. 141 pages; 117 b&w illustrations; 3 color plates. 1972. $3.25.

LILLY MARTIN SPENCER (1822–1902): THE JOYS OF SENTIMENT. Introduction by Joshua C. Taylor. Essay and annotated list of known works by Robin Bolton-Smith and William H. Truettner. 256 pages; 133 b&w illustrations; 5 color plates. 1973. $6.25.

ROBERT LOFTIN NEWMAN (1827–1912). Introduction by Joshua C. Taylor. Essay and annotated list of known works by Marchal E. Landgren. 192 pages; 268 b&w illustrations; 3 color plates. 1973. $5.45.

These publications are available from the National Collection of Fine Arts Museum Shop and can be ordered by mail. To order, please make your check or money order payable to "Smithsonian Shop" and include mailing and handling charge (35¢ for books from $1 to $5; 50¢ for books $6 and up). Mail to: Museum Shop, National Collection of Fine Arts, Smithsonian Institution, Washington, D.C. 20560. All books are sent fourth-class rate unless otherwise specified; therefore, please allow at least four weeks for delivery.